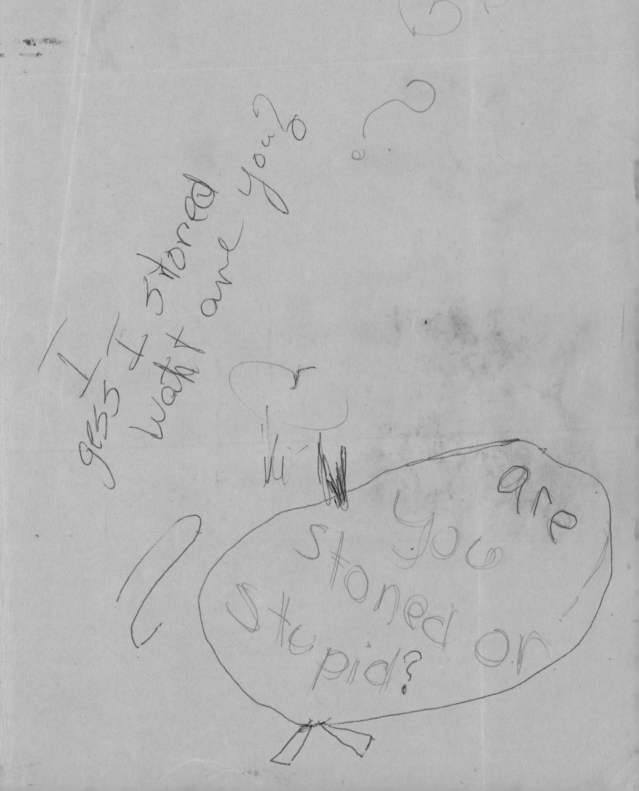

McGRAW-HILL'S
OUR NATION, OUR WORLD

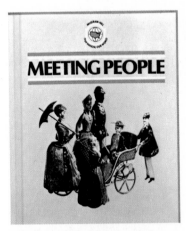

MEETING PEOPLE

School, Self, Families,
Neighborhood, and
Our Country

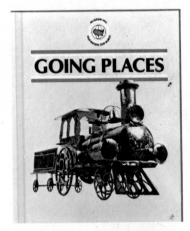

GOING PLACES

People in Groups, Filling
Needs in Communities
and on Farms

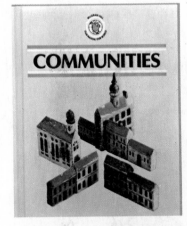

COMMUNITIES

Geography and History of
Cities in the United
States, Canada, and Mexico

EARTH'S REGIONS

Geography and Ways of
Living on Five Continents,
Studying the 50 States

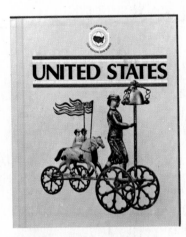

UNITED STATES

Chronological History
of the United States,
North America Today

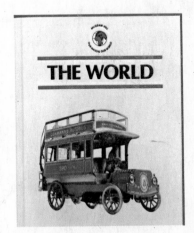

THE WORLD

World History, Ancient
Civilizations, Important
Nations Today

1

CONSULTANTS

BONNIE AMASON
A.M. Davis Elementary School
Richmond, Virginia

DR. L. JO ANNE BUGGEY
Educational Consultant
Minneapolis, Minnesota

MILDRED CROWELL
Jamestown Academy
Williamsburg, Virginia

CORA DVERSDALL
Parkview Elementary School
Oklahoma City, Oklahoma

DON FELICE
Falling Creek Middle School
Richmond, Virginia

JUDY A. FISHER
Dennis Elementary School
Oklahoma City, Oklahoma

CAROLYN FITZGERALD
Powhatan Middle School
Powhatan, Virginia

SANDY HANNINGTON
Central Elementary School
Yukon, Oklahoma

CAROLYN HERBST
Eli Whitney Vocational High School
Brooklyn, New York

DR. RONALD J. HERMANSEN
Staff Assistant, Social Studies
Granite School District
Salt Lake City, Utah

DR. LEONORE HOFFMANN
City University of New York
Former Director, Federal Projects
Modern Language Association

SISTER M. JEANNETTE, I.H.M.
Archdiocese of Philadelphia
Philadelphia, Pennsylvania

ELAINE S. JONES
Woodinville, Washington

SISTER SHARON KERRIGAN
Diocese of Joliet
Joliet, Illinois

HERELYNN KIDD
Shedeck Elementary School
Yukon, Oklahoma

MARY S. McDADE
St. Joseph's School
Petersburg, Virginia

JEAN McGRADY
Western Oaks Elementary School
Bethany, Oklahoma

SISTER GLENN ANNE McPHEE
Archdiocese of Los Angeles
Los Angeles, California

ELAINE MAGNUSON
Canyon Creek Elementary School
Bothell, Washington

SHERRILL MILLER
Seattle, Washington

FRED PEFFER
Central Elementary School
Yukon, Oklahoma

SUZANNE PHELPS
Traub Elementary School
Midwest City, Oklahoma

BETSY PIERCE
Hamilton-Holmes Elementary School
King William, Virginia

SUSIE REYNOLDS
Overholser Elementary School
Bethany, Oklahoma

JOANNE ROBERTSON
Redmond, Washington

SISTER ANN SCHAFER
St. Luke's School
Seattle, Washington

KENNETH SUNDIN
Hollywood Hill Elementary School
Woodinville, Washington

JANE THOMAS
Robious Middle School
Midlothian, Virginia

NORA WASHINGTON
Byrd Primary School
Hadensville, Virginia

RONALD GRIGSBY KIRCHEM
Editorial Consultant and Contributing Writer

Editor in Chief: Leonard Martelli
Senior Editor: Alma Graham
Editing and Styling: Linda Richmond, Caroline Levine
Photo Editing Supervision: Rosemary O'Connell
Production Supervision: Salvador Gonzales, Judith Tisdale

Assistant Editors: James Allan Bartz, Ronald J. Bogus
Photo Editor: Alan Forman
Design by: Function Thru Form Inc.
Cover Design by: Blaise Zito Associates
Cover Photography by: Bill Holland
Photo Credit: From the Collection of The
Perelman Antique Toy Museum

UNITED STATES

BY George Vuicich, Leonard Martelli, Alma Graham, Cleo Cherryholmes, Gary Manson

WEBSTER DIVISION, McGRAW-HILL BOOK COMPANY

New York   St. Louis   San Francisco   Auckland   Bogotá   Düsseldorf
Johannesburg   London   Madrid   Mexico   Montreal   New Delhi
Panama   Paris   São Paulo   Singapore   Sydney   Tokyo   Toronto

3

LIST OF MAPS AND CHARTS

FUN FACTS AND STRANGE FACTS

TIME LINES

WHERE WE ARE IN TIME AND PLACE

ISBN 0-07-039945-X

1985 printing

Copyright © 1983 by McGraw-Hill, Inc. All Rights Reserved. Printed in the United States of America. Except as permitted under the Copyright Act of 1976, no part of this publication may be reproduced or distributed in any form or by any means, or stored in a data base or retrieval system, without the prior written permission of the publisher.

6 7 8 9 10 KGP KGP 91 90 89 88 87 86 85

CONTENTS

1777   1795

1818

1861

1912   1959

7

MAPPING NORTH AMERICA

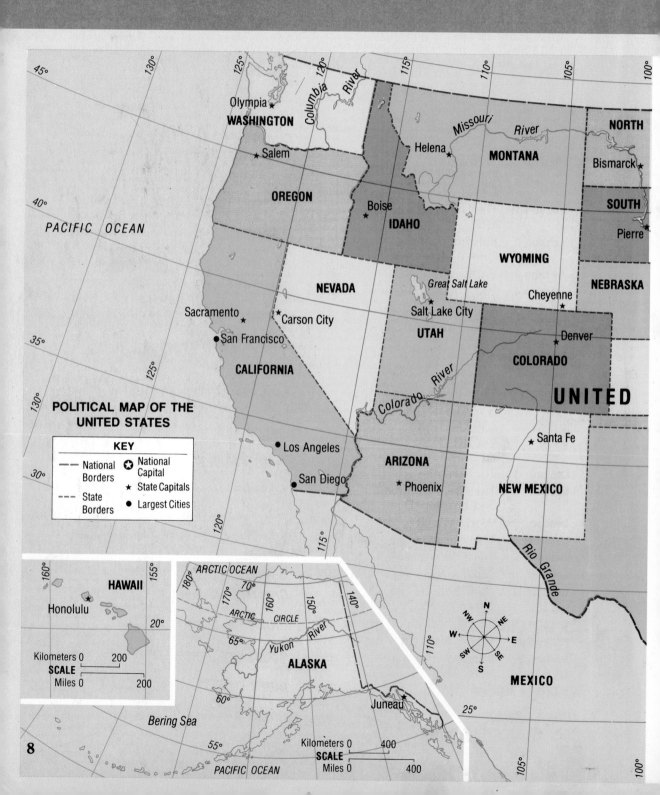

POLITICAL MAP OF THE UNITED STATES

KEY

—— National Borders	⊛ National Capital
	★ State Capitals
- - - State Borders	● Largest Cities

WASHINGTON
Olympia ★
Salem ★

OREGON

Columbia River

Helena ★
MONTANA

Missouri River

NORTH

Bismarck ★

SOUTH

Pierre ★

Boise ★
IDAHO

PACIFIC OCEAN

WYOMING

NEBRASKA

Great Salt Lake
Cheyenne ★

NEVADA

Salt Lake City ★
UTAH

Denver ●

Sacramento ★   ★ Carson City

● San Francisco

COLORADO

CALIFORNIA

Colorado River

UNITED

Santa Fe ★

● Los Angeles

ARIZONA

● San Diego

★ Phoenix

NEW MEXICO

Rio Grande

HAWAII

Honolulu ★

20°

Kilometers 0   200
SCALE
Miles 0   200

ARCTIC OCEAN

ARCTIC CIRCLE

Yukon River

ALASKA

60°

Juneau ★

Bering Sea

N
NW   NE
W   E
SW   SE
S

MEXICO

Kilometers 0   400
SCALE
Miles 0   400

PACIFIC OCEAN

CANADA

DAKOTA

Lake Superior

MINNESOTA

MICHIGAN

WISCONSIN

Lake Huron

Lake Ontario

MAINE

Augusta

VERMONT

Montpelier ★

NEW HAMPSHIRE

Concord

Boston

MASSACHUSETTS

Providence

RHODE ISLAND

St. Lawrence River

DAKOTA

St. Paul ★

Mississippi River

Madison ★

Lake Michigan

Detroit

Lansing

Lake Erie

Niagara Falls

NEW YORK

Albany

Hartford

CONNECTICUT

New York City

NEW JERSEY

Trenton

Philadelphia

PENNSYLVANIA

Harrisburg

IOWA

Des Moines ★

Chicago ●

OHIO

Columbus ★

Baltimore

Annapolis

Dover

MARYLAND

DELAWARE

Washington, DC

Lincoln ★

ILLINOIS

Springfield ★

INDIANA

Indianapolis ★

WEST VIRGINIA

Charleston

Richmond ★

VIRGINIA

Topeka ★

MISSOURI

Jefferson City ★

Ohio River

Frankfort ★

KENTUCKY

KANSAS

STATES

Raleigh ★

NORTH CAROLINA

OKLAHOMA

Oklahoma City ★

Nashville ★

TENNESSEE

Columbia ★

SOUTH CAROLINA

ARKANSAS

Little Rock ★

Memphis ●

ALABAMA

Atlanta ★

ATLANTIC OCEAN

Dallas ●

MISSISSIPPI

Montgomery ★

GEORGIA

TEXAS

LOUISIANA

Jackson ★

Austin ★

Baton Rouge ★

Tallahassee ★

Houston ●

San Antonio ●

FLORIDA

Gulf of Mexico

Kilometers 0   500

SCALE

Miles 0   500

45°
40°
35°
30°
25°

95° 90° 85° 80° 75° 70° 65°

70°

15°

9

ATLAS

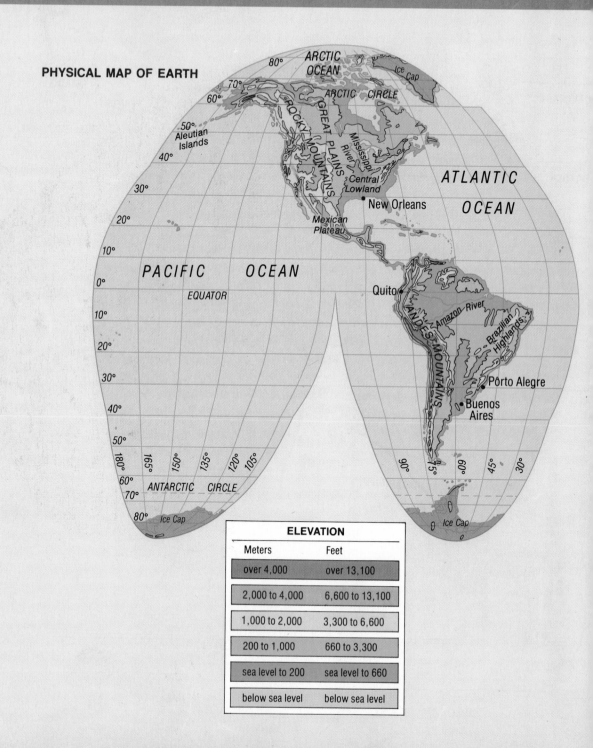

PHYSICAL MAP OF EARTH

ARCTIC OCEAN

Ice Cap

ARCTIC CIRCLE

80°

70°

60°

50°

Aleutian Islands

40°

30°

20°

10°

ROCKY MOUNTAINS

GREAT PLAINS

Mississippi River

Central Lowland

New Orleans

Mexican Plateau

ATLANTIC OCEAN

PACIFIC OCEAN

0°

EQUATOR

10°

20°

30°

40°

50°

60°

70°

80°

Ice Cap

ANTARCTIC CIRCLE

180° 165° 150° 135° 120° 105°

Quito

ANDES MOUNTAINS

Amazon River

Brazilian Highlands

Pôrto Alegre

Buenos Aires

90° 75° 60° 45° 30°

Ice Cap

ELEVATION	
Meters	Feet
over 4,000	over 13,100
2,000 to 4,000	6,600 to 13,100
1,000 to 2,000	3,300 to 6,600
200 to 1,000	660 to 3,300
sea level to 200	sea level to 660
below sea level	below sea level

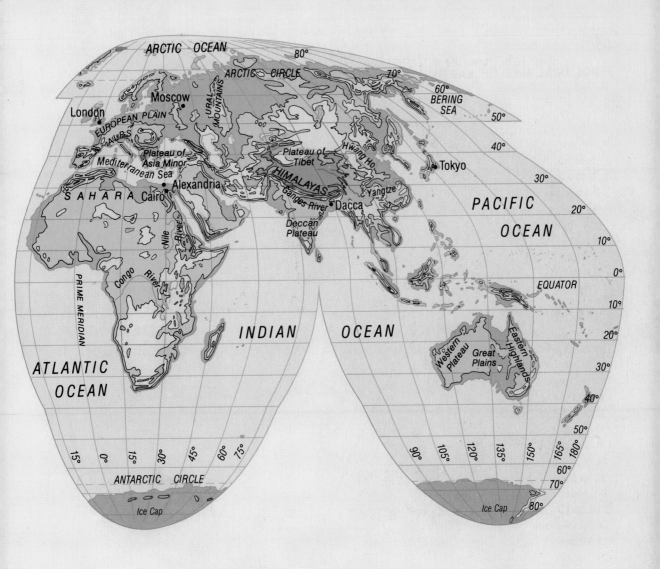

ARCTIC OCEAN

80°

ARCTIC CIRCLE

70°

60°

BERING
SEA

50°

40°

Moscow

URAL MOUNTAINS

London

EUROPEAN PLAIN

ALPS

Plateau of
Asia Minor

Mediterranean Sea

Plateau of
Tibet

Hwang Ho

30°

Tokyo

HIMALAYAS

Alexandria

SAHARA Cairo

Ganges River

Deccan
Plateau

Dacca

Yangtze

PACIFIC

20°

OCEAN

10°

Nile River

0°

Congo River

EQUATOR

10°

PRIME MERIDIAN

INDIAN OCEAN

20°

Western
Plateau

Great
Plains

Eastern
Highlands

30°

ATLANTIC

40°

OCEAN

50°

15° 0° 15° 30° 45° 60° 75°

90° 105° 120° 135° 150° 165° 180°

60°

ANTARCTIC CIRCLE

70°

Ice Cap

Ice Cap

80°

Kilometers 0   5000
SCALE
Miles 0   4000

11

ATLAS

POLITICAL MAP OF EARTH

1 Belize
2 Jamaica
3 Dominican Republic
4 Trinidad and Tobago
5 Antigua and Barbuda
6 Austria
7 Czechoslovakia
8 Hungary
9 Albania
10 Denmark
11 West Germany
12 East Germany
13 Netherlands
14 Belgium
15 Switzerland
16 Benin
17 Central African Republic
18 São Tomé and Príncipe
19 Djibouti
20 Equatorial Guinea
21 Gambia
22 Ghana
23 Guinea
24 Guinea-Bissau
25 Seychelles
26 Cyprus
27 Lebanon
28 Kuwait
29 Qatar
30 United Arab Emirates

31 Tuvalu
32 Nauru
33 Solomon Islands
34 Kiribati

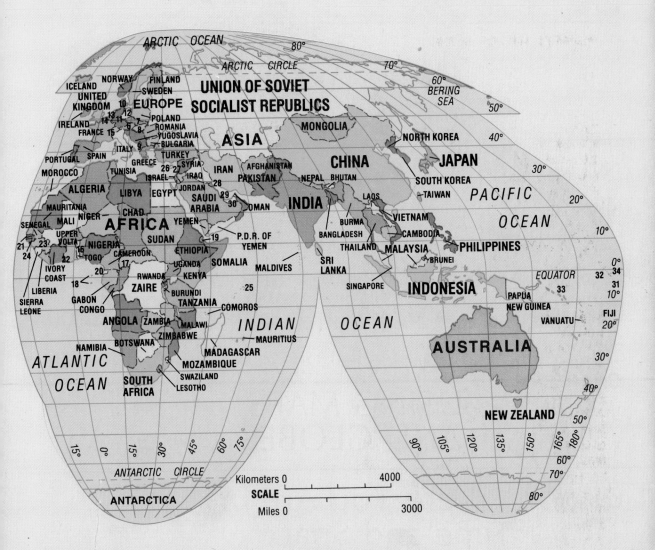

ARCTIC OCEAN 80°
ARCTIC CIRCLE 70°
60° BERING SEA
50°

ICELAND
NORWAY
FINLAND
SWEDEN
UNITED KINGDOM
EUROPE 10
7
IRELAND
13
14 11
12
POLAND
ROMANIA
FRANCE 15
6 8
YUGOSLAVIA
BULGARIA
ITALY 9
UNION OF SOVIET SOCIALIST REPUBLICS

MONGOLIA
NORTH KOREA 40°
ASIA
CHINA
JAPAN 30°
SOUTH KOREA
TAIWAN
PACIFIC 20°
OCEAN 10°

PORTUGAL
SPAIN
TURKEY
GREECE 26 27
SYRIA
IRAN
AFGHANISTAN
PAKISTAN
NEPAL BHUTAN
MOROCCO
TUNISIA
ISRAEL
IRAQ
28
ALGERIA
LIBYA
EGYPT
JORDAN
29
30
SAUDI ARABIA
OMAN
INDIA
LAOS
VIETNAM
MAURITANIA
NIGER
CHAD
YEMEN
BURMA
CAMBODIA
SENEGAL MALI
AFRICA
SUDAN
19
P.D.R. OF YEMEN
BANGLADESH
THAILAND
PHILIPPINES
UPPER VOLTA
21 23
16
NIGERIA
ETHIOPIA
MALAYSIA
BRUNEI
24 22
TOGO
CAMEROON
UGANDA
SOMALIA
SRI LANKA
IVORY COAST
17
20
RWANDA
KENYA
MALDIVES
EQUATOR 32 34
18
ZAIRE
BURUNDI
25
SINGAPORE
INDONESIA
33
31
LIBERIA
GABON
TANZANIA
PAPUA NEW GUINEA
10°
SIERRA LEONE
CONGO
COMOROS
VANUATU
FIJI
ANGOLA ZAMBIA
MALAWI
INDIAN OCEAN
20°
NAMIBIA
ZIMBABWE
MAURITIUS
AUSTRALIA
30°
BOTSWANA
MADAGASCAR
ATLANTIC
MOZAMBIQUE
40°
OCEAN
SOUTH AFRICA
SWAZILAND
LESOTHO
NEW ZEALAND 50°
60°
15°
0°
15°
30°
45°
60°
75°
90°
105°
120°
135°
150°
165° 180°
70°
ANTARCTIC CIRCLE
80°
Kilometers 0   4000
SCALE
ANTARCTICA
Miles 0   3000

13

CHAPTER 1 USING MAPS AND GLOBES

Lesson 1: Where You Are in Time and Space

FIND THE WORDS

history   historian   geography
geographer

Today, you are sitting in a classroom. Your room is in a school. Your school is in a community. Your community is part of a state. Your state is one of 50 divisions of your nation, the United States. Your nation is on the continent of North America. North America is one of seven continents on Earth. You can use a map or globe to find your location in space.

You are also at a point in time. What time is it now? What is the hour and minute? What is the day, month, and year? What is the century? Can you tell exactly where you are in time and space?

The United States also has a special location in space. It has existed for a certain period of time. This year, you are going to study the history and geography of the United States. **History** is the story of what happened in the past. When you study history, you learn about people and events that shaped your world. History also tells you what people in the past thought was important. People in the United States thought education was important. Otherwise, we might not have schools today. They thought rights and freedoms were important. Otherwise, we might not be free to say what we

Left: Education is important to people in the United States. *Right:* This blind girl uses hearing and touch to tell where she is in time and space.

think. We might not be allowed to meet, vote, or worship as we choose. We might have a government that told us what to do.

What is happening today is a result of what people did in the past. People had problems. They thought about those problems and came up with solutions. Then they acted. The actions of people in the past make up the history of our country.

We know about those actions because people kept written records. People who write or study records of past events are called **historians.** Historians do not re-port everything that happened in the past. They pass on records of the people and events they think are most important.

Most of the history in our nation took place in North America. Our continent is the stage on which our history was acted out. What is North America like? Why did so many people come to this continent to live? How did North America's land, climate, and resources affect what people did?

When you go to a new place, you need to get your bearings. You want to know where you are. You need to find your way around.

There are large areas of fertile soil in North America. The fertile land made farming easy for the people who settled in these areas.

To study the physical facts about a place is to study **geography.** What is the climate like where you are? What is the shape of the land like? What are the natural resources? For example, is the soil fertile? Is there enough water? What animals, plants, and minerals can you find? To learn these things, you need to know the terms and tools of geography. The word *geography* means "earth-writing." Experts who study places on Earth are called **geographers.**

Learning geography is like going on a treasure hunt. You can find a wealth of facts by using maps and globes. You can learn special terms to help you report what you find. For the rest of this unit, you will be setting the stage for history. You will explore the shapes, climates, and other features of the land.

REVIEW

WATCH YOUR WORDS

1. In ___ , we study what people did in the past.
   geography   history   math
2. In ___ , we study physical facts about places.
   history   division   geography
3. North America is one of seven ___ .
   countries   continents   nations
4. Experts who study physical facts about places on Earth are ___ .
   historians   pioneers   geographers
5. Experts who keep records of past events are ___ .
   historians   geographers   explorers

CHECK YOUR FACTS

6. Write your name and address. Include your street, town or city, state, nation, and continent.
7. How do people know about what happened in the past?
8. Where did most of our nation's history take place?
9. Name three things people study in geography.
10. How many natural resources can you name?

THINK ABOUT IT

Do you think people now and people in the past always thought the same things were important? Why, or why not?

TRY SOMETHING NEW

Be a historian. Start keeping a daily record of what happens around you. Find out what was different when your grandparents were your age.

Lesson 2: The Shape of the Land and Water

If you were to travel across our country, you would see many different **landforms,** or shapes of land. In some places, the land would be flat as far as you could see. In others, it would be high and rugged. And in still other places, it would be gently rolling.

Geographers define and describe all the landforms on Earth. The most important landforms are discussed below.

Plains are lands that are mostly flat. They may stretch for only a few miles or for thousands of miles. Plains are usually the most useful kind of land. Many plains have good soil for crops. Rivers flow slowly through the plains.

Many plains have good soil for farming.

LANDFORMS

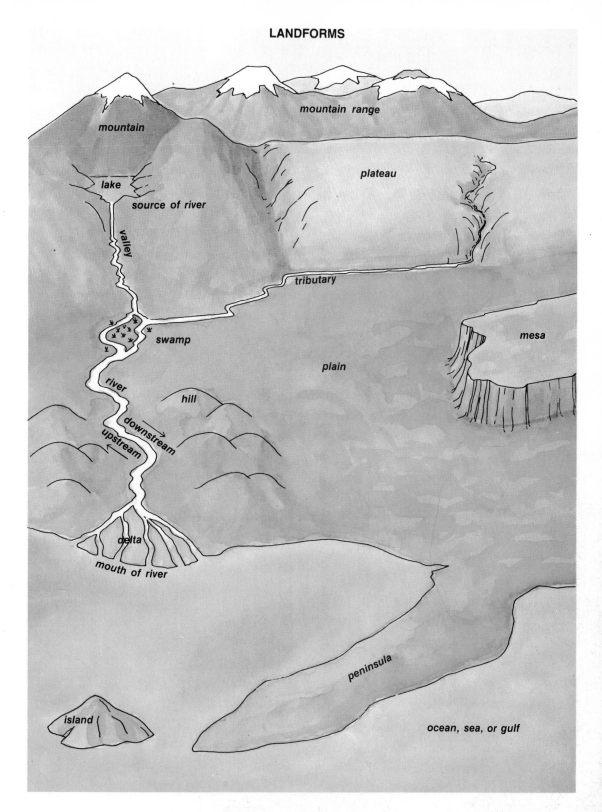

mountain range

mountain

plateau

lake

source of river

valley

tributary

mesa

swamp

plain

river

hill

downstream

upstream

delta

mouth of river

peninsula

island

ocean, sea, or gulf

Farming and travel are easy on the flat land. Often, plains are also lowlands.

Plateaus (pla TOHZ) are flat lands that are higher than the lands around them. They are also called tablelands. The flat top of a plateau is like a plain. Like plains, plateaus are often very useful lands. On plateaus, travel is easy.

Swamps are lowlands that are covered with water much of the time. Unless swamplands are drained, they are not very useful to people.

Hills are lands that rise higher than the land around them. In gently rolling hills, the land is often as useful as land on the plains. But in hilly areas, the land is steeper than on the plains. Rivers flow more quickly. Travel is often more difficult. A hill with steep sides and a flat top is called a **mesa** (MAY suh).

Mountains are areas of very high, steep land. A mountain is much higher than the land around it. Mountain areas are often beautiful. However, they are seldom

Mountain ranges are groups of mountains.

useful for planting crops. Usually, few people live on mountains. Mountains are often found in groups called **mountain ranges.** Huge groups of mountain ranges are called **mountain systems.**

Valleys are lowlands found between a group of hills or mountains. Rivers also form valleys between higher lands. In mountain areas, people often find much useful land in valleys. Many people live in some large river valleys.

Islands are pieces of land that are surrounded by water. **Peninsulas** are almost islands. They are pieces of land mostly surrounded by water.

Geographers also have terms to describe the water that covers seven-tenths of the Earth's surface.

Oceans are the huge bodies of water that cover most of Earth's surface. There are four oceans. Look at the map on pages 10 and 11. Name the four oceans.

Seas are much smaller than oceans. They are surrounded by land on two or more sides. A sea can be part of an ocean. Or it can be completely surrounded by land. Find the Bering Sea next to Alaska on the map on pages 8 and 9.

Gulfs are much the same as seas. A gulf is a large body of water surrounded by land on two or more sides. Find the Gulf of Mexico on the map on pages 8 and 9. Bays are also bodies of water mostly surrounded by land.

Montauk Point is at the tip of Long Island in New York. It provides a wonderful view of the Atlantic Ocean. The Atlantic is one of four oceans on Earth.

Rivers are bodies of water that carry water away from the land. The place where a river begins is its **source.** A river's source could be a lake or a spring. Most rivers flow into an ocean or a sea. The place where a river flows into another body of water is its **mouth.**

Sometimes, river water carries a great deal of soil. A river usually drops this soil at its mouth. This often forms a low, swampy plain shaped much like a triangle. Such an area is called a **delta.** Rivers that flow out through deltas often have many small mouths.

A river flows from a higher place to a lower place. The direction in which a river flows is called **downstream.** The direction opposite to the flow of a river is called **upstream.** Rivers usually have **tributaries** (TRIB yuh TEHR eez). These are smaller rivers or streams that flow into a larger river.

Lakes are bodies of water completely surrounded by land. Usually, the water in lakes is fresh. Fresh water has very little salt in it. Some large salty lakes are called seas.

REVIEW

WATCH YOUR WORDS

1. A____can be part of an ocean.
   lake   river   sea

2. The top of a____is like a plain.
   mountain   plateau   peninsula

3. A group of mountain ranges is a ____.
   mountain system   plateau   valley

4. ____flow into a river.
   Oceans   Lakes   Tributaries

5. The place where a river starts is its ____.
   mouth   source   tributary

6. The place where a river flows into another body of water is its____.
   source   mouth   tributary

CHECK YOUR FACTS

7. What is usually the most useful kind of land?

8. Name two kinds of land that are less useful for people and crops.

9. Why is the direction in which a river flows called *downstream?*

10. How do seas differ from oceans?

11. What kind of water do lakes usually have?

THINK ABOUT IT

12. What kind of land does your area have?

13. Are there any important bodies of water near where you live? If so, what are they?

Lesson 3: Weather and Climate

FIND THE WORDS

weather   climate

When you talk about the weather or the climate, you are talking about the air. You are speaking about how much heat and how much water is in the air.

The **weather** is the condition of the air at any moment. Suppose someone asks you about the weather today. In your answer, you tell what the air is like. You might say, "It's hot and raining." Or you might say, "It's cold and snowing."

Climate is different from weather. Knowing the climate does not tell you the condition of the air on any day. The **climate** is the average weather over a long period of time. Thus, you might describe the climate where you live this way: "Summers are hot and rainy. Winters are cold and snowy." This will not tell you the weather on any one day. But it tells you what to expect over time.

As you can imagine, there are many different climates on Earth. There are places on Earth where the weather is always hot. There are places where the weather is always cold. There are places where it rains every day. There are places where it might not rain at all for years. There are also places that are cold part of the year and hot part of the year. This is the way the climate is in most of the United States.

The chart on page 24 shows the way geographers group climates.

When you can talk about the land and climate of a place, you know a lot about that place. Look at the climate map of North America on page 25. What is the climate like where you live? Is it described the way you would describe it?

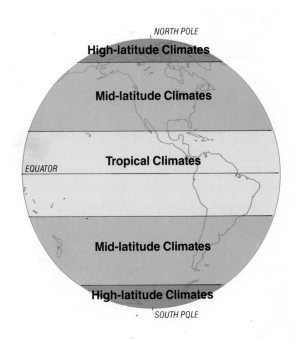

NORTH POLE

High-latitude Climates

Mid-latitude Climates

EQUATOR   Tropical Climates

Mid-latitude Climates

High-latitude Climates

SOUTH POLE

HIGH-LATITUDE CLIMATES

Climate	Winter	Summer	What is it like?
Ice cap	bitterly cold	cold	covered with permanent, thick ice
Tundra	bitterly cold, dry	cold, dry	always cold and dry; some hardy plants and animals

MID-LATITUDE CLIMATES

Climate	Winter	Summer	What is it like?
Mediterranean	mild, wet	warm, dry	a pleasant climate to live in
Humid subtropical	mild, wet	hot, wet	long summers and short winters
Marine	mild, wet	mild, wet	usually not too cold or too hot at any time of year
Continental	cold, wet	mild to hot, but wet	weather changes quickly; very hot in summer and cold in winter
Steppe (continental grasslands)	hot to cold, some rainfall	hot, some rainfall	weather changes quickly; enough rain for grasses to grow
Desert	hot to cold, but dry	hot and dry	not many plants grow except those that can store water

LOW-LATITUDE (TROPICAL) CLIMATES

Climate	Winter	Summer	What is it like?
Tropical grasslands (savanna)	hot, dry	hot, wet	always hot; covered with thick grasses and some trees
Rain forest	hot, wet	hot, wet	always hot with much rain; thickly covered with trees and smaller plants

Note: Highland areas have various local climates.

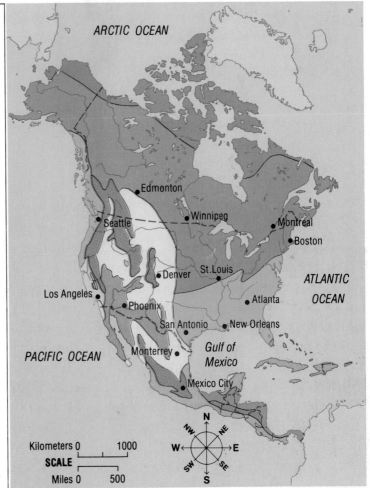

CLIMATES OF NORTH AMERICA

KEY

– –•– – National Borders
• Cities

CLIMATE KEY

Tundra: cold and dry all year

Continental: mild to hot wet summer, cold wet winter

Marine: mild wet summer, mild wet winter

Highlands: various local climates

Steppe (continental grasslands): hot summer, hot to cold winter, variable rainfall

Desert: hot summer, hot to cold winter, dry all year

Humid subtropical: hot wet summer, mild wet winter

Mediterranean: warm dry summer, mild wet winter

Tropical grasslands: hot wet summer, hot dry winter

Rain forest: hot and wet all year

Kilometers 0   1000
SCALE
Miles 0   500

REVIEW

WATCH YOUR WORDS

1. ____ is the average condition of the air over time.
   Weather   Climate   Humidity

2. ____ is the condition of the air at any moment.
   Weather   Climate   Temperature

CHECK YOUR FACTS

3. What two conditions of the air do you speak about in talking of the weather and climate?

4. There are (many/few) climates on Earth.

5. What is the climate like in most of the United States?

THINK ABOUT IT

Look at the climate chart. What kind of climate do you think you might like best?

Lesson 4: What Is a Globe?

FIND THE WORDS

globe   North Pole   South Pole
equator   hemisphere
Northern Hemisphere
Southern Hemisphere   parallel
lines of latitude   meridian
lines of longitude   grid system

Globes are models of Earth. They are round like Earth. They show where land and water are located on Earth's surface. They can also give you much more information. Globes can show where countries, cities, or mountains are located.

Globes are usually mounted on stands. The places where they are mounted are the North and South Poles. The **North Pole** is the farthest point north on the Earth. The

A globe is a model of the Earth. You can use a globe to locate everything from continents to cities.

South Pole is the farthest point south. Notice that the globe is tilted. The North Pole is not directly on top. This is done because Earth, itself, is tilted in relation to the sun.

Midway between the poles you will find a line that goes all around the globe. This line is the **equator.** It is an imaginary line. The equator divides the globe into halves, or **hemispheres** (HEM uh SFIRZ). The part of Earth between the equator and the North Pole is the **Northern Hemisphere.** The part of Earth between the equator and the South Pole is the **Southern Hemisphere.**

On most globes, you will see lines that run parallel to the equator. These lines are called **parallels** (PAR uh LELZ) or **lines of latitude** (LAT uh TOOD). You will also see lines that run north and south on the globe. They go through the North Pole and the South Pole. They are called **meridians** (muh RID ee unz) or **lines of longitude** (LON juh TOOD).

Parallels and meridians form a grid system all over the globe. A **grid system** is made up of lines that cross each other. This system is used to locate places on the Earth. Sailors in ships use it to find their way and to tell where

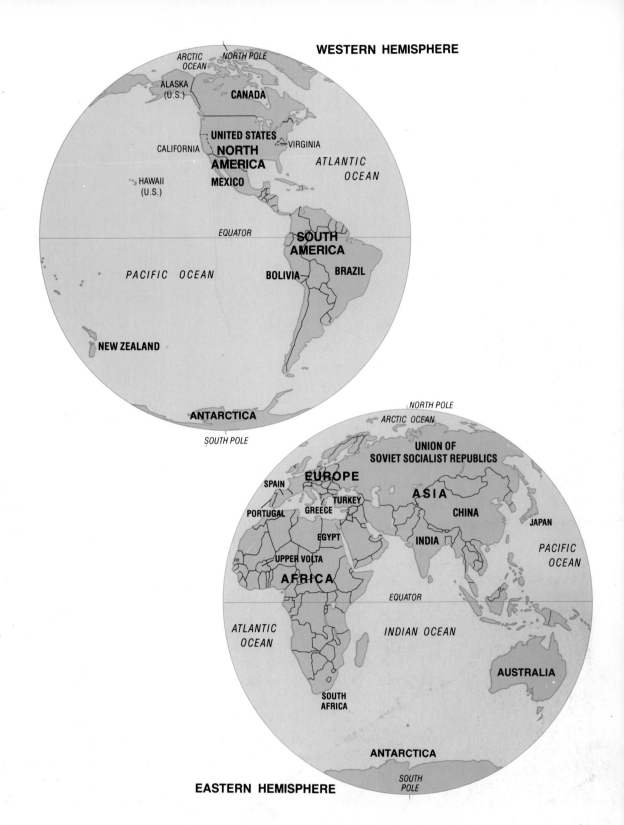

WESTERN HEMISPHERE

ARCTIC OCEAN

NORTH POLE

ALASKA (U.S.)

CANADA

UNITED STATES

NORTH AMERICA

CALIFORNIA

VIRGINIA

ATLANTIC OCEAN

HAWAII (U.S.)

MEXICO

EQUATOR

SOUTH AMERICA

BOLIVIA

BRAZIL

PACIFIC OCEAN

NEW ZEALAND

ANTARCTICA

SOUTH POLE

EASTERN HEMISPHERE

NORTH POLE

ARCTIC OCEAN

UNION OF SOVIET SOCIALIST REPUBLICS

EUROPE

SPAIN

ASIA

PORTUGAL

GREECE

TURKEY

CHINA

JAPAN

EGYPT

INDIA

PACIFIC OCEAN

UPPER VOLTA

AFRICA

EQUATOR

ATLANTIC OCEAN

INDIAN OCEAN

AUSTRALIA

SOUTH AFRICA

ANTARCTICA

SOUTH POLE

27

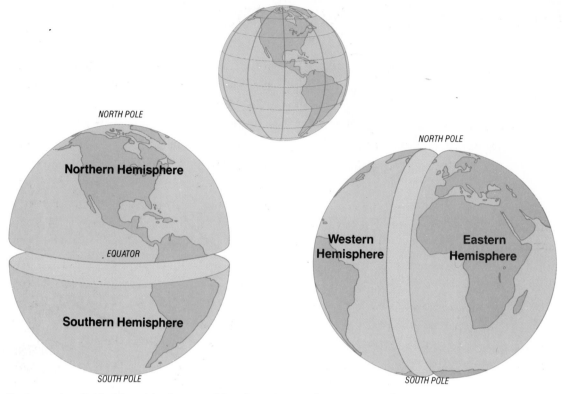

NORTH POLE

Northern Hemisphere

EQUATOR

Southern Hemisphere

SOUTH POLE

NORTH POLE

Western Hemisphere

Eastern Hemisphere

SOUTH POLE

Earth can be divided into Northern and Southern Hemispheres. It can also
be divided into Eastern and Western Hemispheres.

they are. In a later lesson, you will study this grid system.

Globes have a limited use, however. They cannot be put into books. They are also expensive. Each person in a class cannot have a globe to keep and to carry around. This is why we use maps.

REVIEW

WATCH YOUR WORDS

1. The ___ divides Earth into hemispheres.
   North Pole   globe   equator
2. ___ are the same as lines of latitude.
   Meridians   Lines of longitude   Parallels
3. ___ are models of Earth.
   Meridians   Parallels   Globes

CHECK YOUR FACTS

4. Why are globes tilted?
5. How are lines of latitude and longitude used?

THINK ABOUT IT

When is a map more useful to you than a globe? Think of times when you might need a map. Then make a list of those times.

Lesson 5: What Are Maps?

Maps are flat drawings of Earth or of parts of Earth. Because maps are flat, they cannot really show our round Earth accurately. Look at the drawing on pages 30–31. It shows the surface of a globe being peeled off. The pieces do not make a useful map. To have a useful map, we change the sizes or shapes of what we show on it. We have to change the sizes or shapes of pieces of land and bodies of water. There are many ways to do this. The way we choose depends on what we want our map to do. Remember, there is no way a flat map can accurately show the surface of Earth. Only a globe can do this. The way we change sizes or shapes on a map is the map's **projection** (pruh JEK shun).

One of the most famous projections is the **Mercator** (mur KAY tur) **projection.** As you remember, on a globe, the lines of longitude all cross at the poles. But on a Mercator map, the lines of latitude and longitude are both parallel. A Mercator map is very useful to ships. That is because the lines are true compass lines. But the land is greatly **distorted.** That means it is not shown accurately. On a Mercator projection, Greenland looks as big as South America. But Greenland is actually only about one-eighth the size of South America. Extra land has been added to Greenland on the map.

An **equal-area projection** keeps the land areas the right size, but it changes their shapes. Toward the edges of such a map, the land looks pushed in or squashed. To

FUN FACTS

The oldest known map is about 4300 years old. It is a clay tablet. It was found in Babylon, an ancient city in Asia. We are not sure about what the map shows. But it seems to show someone's farm in a big valley.

The Egyptians made maps about 3300 years ago. One of these maps shows the way to the gold mines that were to the south of the Nile River. It is the oldest treasure map in the world.

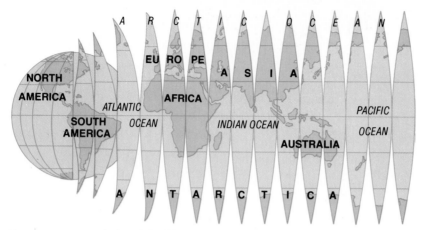

Suppose you peeled a globe like an orange. There would be many gaps. Mapmakers fill the gaps in different ways.

MERCATOR PROJECTION

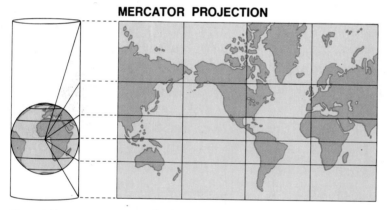

On a Mercator projection, lines of longitude do not meet at the poles. They remain parallel. Near the poles, extra land and water are added.

EQUAL-AREA PROJECTION

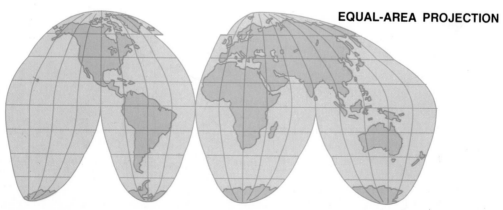

An equal-area projection changes the shape but not the size of land.

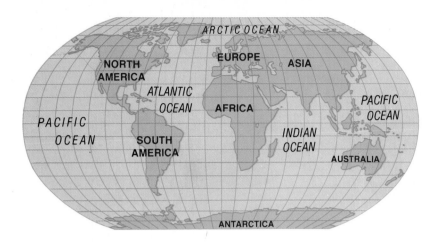

make the land on this kind of map even more accurate, the projection is often **interrupted.** That means there are gaps in it. This changes the shape of the oceans greatly. The lines of longitude curve toward the poles.

Try to pay attention to the projection on maps you use. Equal-area projections are most useful for seeing the size of something on Earth. Suppose, for example, that you wanted to compare the sizes of the plains in Europe and North America. You could not do this accurately with a Mercator map. In this book, most maps of Earth are equal-area projections.

REVIEW

WATCH YOUR WORDS

1. ___are flat drawings of Earth.
Globes   Areas   Maps
2. The way sizes or shapes are changed on a map is its___.
globe   area   projection
3. On a Mercator map, the land is ___.
distorted   interrupted   equal-area
4. An equal-area projection keeps land areas the right ___.
shape   color   size

CHECK YOUR FACTS

5. Why can maps not show Earth accurately?
6. How do the lines of longitude run on an equal-area projection? On a Mercator projection?

THINK ABOUT IT

Imagine you are making a long trip across a wilderness. You have only a map and a compass to guide you. What kind of map should you use? Why?

Lesson 6: Information on Maps

People who make maps are called **cartographers** (kahr TOG ruh ferz). Cartographers put information on maps in many ways. You should learn to read these different kinds of information. Then you can learn a lot from maps.

In order to put information on a map, cartographers use symbols. **Symbols** are signs that stand for something else. These symbols can be many different things. They can be lines, dots, or stars.

Cartographers are people who make maps.

They can also be little drawings. There is no limit to what the mapmaker can use. But everything the cartographer uses must be explained in the map key. The **key** always tells you what the symbols on a map mean.

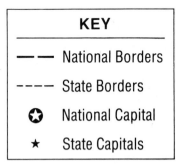

KEY

— — National Borders
---- State Borders
✪ National Capital
★ State Capitals

Most maps have a scale in the key or somewhere else. A **scale** tells you distances on a map. The scale is usually a line with kilometers and miles on it. It says that a certain distance on the map stands for a certain distance on Earth. By using the scale, you can figure out how far apart places on the map really are. Suppose a map scale says that 1 inch equals 100 miles. Suppose the distance between two places on the map is 2 inches. You then know that the places are 200 miles apart.

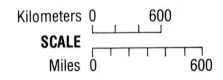

Kilometers 0   600

SCALE

Miles 0   600

Color can be used in many different ways on a map. Colors can help you tell land from water. They can show you where one state or nation ends and another begins. A map that shows nations or states is a **political map.** Color can also be used to show elevation on a map. **Elevation** is how high the land is above the surface of the oceans. The height of the ocean surface is known as **sea level.** Look at the scale on the right. It is a scale of colors used to show elevation. Choose a color from the scale. Then look at the map on page 44. Find some land that color. The color scale will tell you about how high that land is.

ELEVATION	
Meters	Feet
over 4,000	over 13,100
2,000 to 4,000	6,600 to 13,100
1,000 to 2,000	3,300 to 6,600
200 to 1,000	660 to 3,300
sea level to 200	sea level to 660
below sea level	below sea level

These are only three ways in which color can be used on a map. You will see other ways as we go along.

Many maps have a **compass** (KUM pus) also. The compass tells you directions on a map. Some maps have just a direction arrow pointing toward the North Pole. A compass will usually have at least the letter *N*. This stands for "north." The other directions will be shown on the compass with points and sometimes letters. The direction opposite to north is south. South is toward the South Pole. East is to the right of north. West is to the left of north. **East** is the direction in which we see the sunrise in the morning. **West** is the direction in which we see the sunset in the evening. North, south, east, and west are called the **cardinal** (KAHR duh nul) **directions.** Northeast, northwest, southeast, and southwest are called the **intermediate directions.**

FINDING NORTH

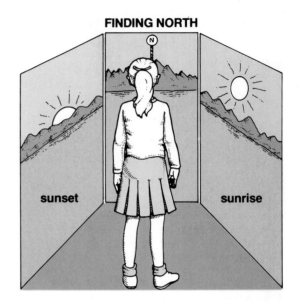

sunset   sunrise

REVIEW

WATCH YOUR WORDS

1. On a map, the ___ tells distance.
   symbol   key   scale

2. The map key lists the ___.
   cartographers   directions   symbols

3. The word ___ means "mapmaker."
   cartographer   geographer   historian

4. ___ is the height of the land.
   Elevation   Direction   Scale

5. ___ is the height of the surface of the ocean.
   Direction   Sea level   Latitude

CHECK YOUR FACTS

6. How do cartographers put information on a map?

7. How can you find out what the symbols on a map mean?

8. What part of a map can you use to find out how wide a nation is?

9. How can you tell which way is north on a map?

10. Describe two ways in which color can be used on a map.

THINK ABOUT IT

Suppose you were lost in the woods without a compass. How could you tell which way is north?

Lesson 7: Using Latitude and Longitude

In an earlier lesson, you read about the lines of latitude and longitude. Look at the globes below. As you remember, the lines of latitude—also called parallels—are great imaginary circles. They go around the globe parallel to the equator. They do not touch each other. The circles get smaller as they get closer to the North Pole and South Pole.

The lines of longitude, or meridians, circle the globe through the North and South Poles. All these lines touch at the poles. They are farthest apart at the equator.

The lines of latitude and longitude form a grid system all over the globe. This grid system is used to give the location of places on Earth. Sailors use it to describe their location at sea.

Every circle can be divided into 360 units called **degrees.** We write 360 degrees as 360°. On a globe, the equator is at 0° of latitude. The North Pole is at 90° north latitude. The South Pole is at 90° south latitude. The parallels between the equator and the poles are numbered between 0 and 90° north or south.

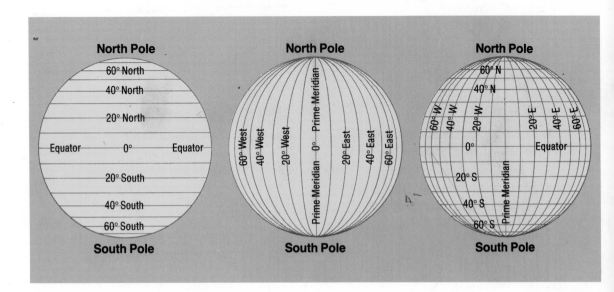

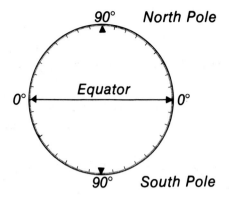

90° North Pole

Equator

0° 0°

90° South Pole

The meridians, or lines of longitude, are numbered from 0 to 180°. The **prime meridian** is a line that passes through Greenwich (GREN ich), England. This is the starting point for lines of longitude. The prime meridian is at 0° of longitude. All the meridians east of the prime meridian are numbered between 0 and 180° east longitude. All the meridians west of the prime meridian are numbered between 0 and 180° west longitude.

If you can read both sets of lines, you can locate any place on Earth. Look at the map on pages 10 and 11. Find New Orleans. It is located at about 90° west longitude. It is also located at about 30° north latitude. So you can describe the location of New Orleans as 90° west longitude, 30° north latitude. These two sets of numbers and directions are known as **coordinates** (koh OR duh nits).

Now look at Pôrto Alegre on the coast of Brazil in South America. It is located at about 50° west longitude, 30° south latitude. Did you find it?

There are several other cities on the map. If they are between the lines, do this: The space between two lines is 10°. Divide this space into 10 equal parts. Then try to guess the degree. If a place falls in the middle, add 5 degrees to the smaller number.

REVIEW

WATCH YOUR WORDS

1. The____is at 0° of longitude.
   equator   prime meridian   grid
2. A circle is divided into____.
   parallels   grids   degrees
3. Numbers and directions giving the latitude and longitude of a place are called____.
   meridians   coordinates   parallels

CHECK YOUR FACTS

4. Lines of longitude (do/do not) touch at the poles.
5. What line is at 0° of latitude?

THINK ABOUT IT

Imagine you are on a ship in the ocean. How do you think your latitude and longitude might be found?

Lesson 8: Special Maps

FIND THE WORDS

route   border   resource
product   distribution

Maps can give you many kinds of information. You know that a map can show directions, elevations, or the locations of nations and cities. Some of the other things that can be shown on maps are discussed below.

Routes

The path someone travels is called a **route.** In this book, you will see lines drawn on maps showing the routes of explorers in the past. These lines are made from records the explorers themselves left. They show you where the explorers started. They show the parts of Earth the explorers crossed.

Historical Maps

A **border** is a line dividing two nations or parts of nations. The borders of nations are not the same today as they were only 50 years ago. However, maps can show how the land was divided up in the past. They can show which country claimed which land. They

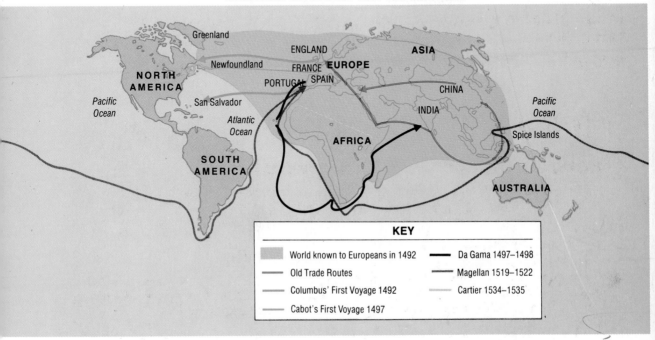

EUROPEAN DISCOVERY AND EXPLORATION

KEY

World known to Europeans in 1492
Old Trade Routes
Columbus' First Voyage 1492
Cabot's First Voyage 1497
Da Gama 1497–1498
Magellan 1519–1522
Cartier 1534–1535

THE THIRTEEN COLONIES ABOUT 1770

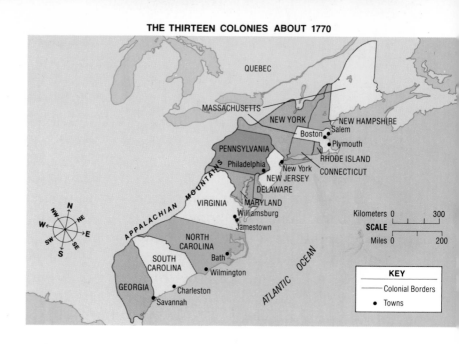

QUEBEC

MASSACHUSETTS

NEW YORK

NEW HAMPSHIRE

Boston
Salem
Plymouth

PENNSYLVANIA

Philadelphia

RHODE ISLAND
CONNECTICUT

New York

NEW JERSEY

DELAWARE

VIRGINIA

MARYLAND

Williamsburg

Jamestown

APPALACHIAN MOUNTAINS

NORTH CAROLINA

Bath

SOUTH CAROLINA

Wilmington

GEORGIA

Charleston

Savannah

ATLANTIC OCEAN

Kilometers 0   300
SCALE
Miles 0   200

KEY
— Colonial Borders
● Towns

POPULATION OF EARTH

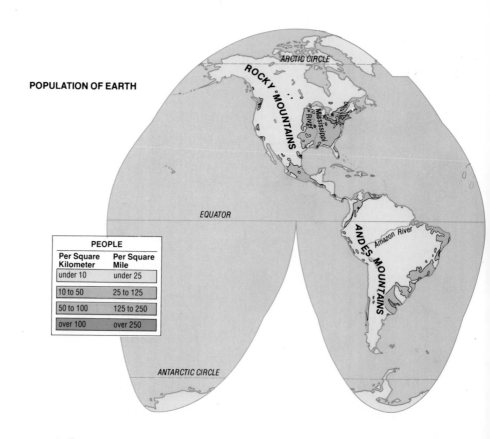

ARCTIC CIRCLE

ROCKY MOUNTAINS

Mississippi River

EQUATOR

ANDES MOUNTAINS

Amazon River

ANTARCTIC CIRCLE

PEOPLE	
Per Square Kilometer	Per Square Mile
under 10	under 25
10 to 50	25 to 125
50 to 100	125 to 250
over 100	over 250

can show what happened to the land as a result of wars or other events. You will find historical maps throughout this book. The map of the Thirteen Colonies shows the borders in about 1770.

Resource and Product Maps

A **resource** is anything people can use. A **product** is anything people gather or make. Maps can show the location of different resources on Earth. They can also show where certain products come from. For example, the map on page 40 shows many products and resources of the British Isles. A map can show the resources and products of a continent, nation, state, or city.

Distribution Maps

Distribution refers to the way things are spread or scattered over an area. Maps can show you the distribution of people on Earth. That is, maps can tell you where people live on the land. Maps can show the distribution of just about anything else on Earth. For example, they can show the location of crops, cattle, forests, and so on.

These are only a few things you can find on maps. See if you can find other kinds of maps not mentioned here.

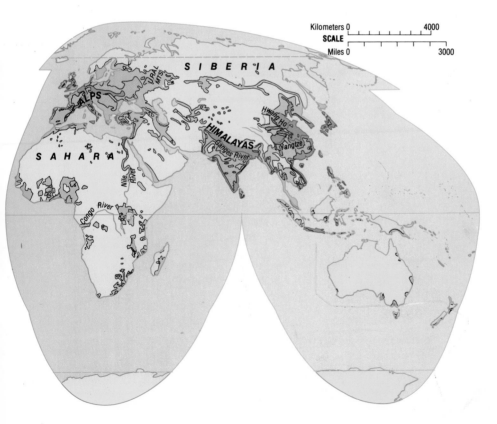

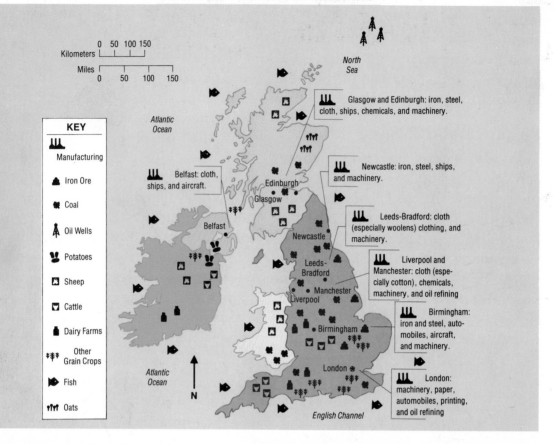

Glasgow and Edinburgh: iron, steel, cloth, ships, chemicals, and machinery.

Newcastle: iron, steel, ships, and machinery.

Leeds-Bradford: cloth (especially woolens) clothing, and machinery.

Liverpool and Manchester: cloth (especially cotton), chemicals, machinery, and oil refining

Birmingham: iron and steel, automobiles, aircraft, and machinery.

London: machinery, paper, automobiles, printing, and oil refining

Belfast: cloth, ships, and aircraft.

KEY

- Manufacturing
- Iron Ore
- Coal
- Oil Wells
- Potatoes
- Sheep
- Cattle
- Dairy Farms
- Other Grain Crops
- Fish
- Oats

Kilometers 0 50 100 150
Miles 0 50 100 150

Atlantic Ocean

North Sea

Edinburgh
Glasgow
Belfast
Newcastle
Leeds-Bradford
Manchester
Liverpool
Birmingham
London

Atlantic Ocean

N

English Channel

REVIEW

WATCH YOUR WORDS

1. The way in which something is spread or scattered over an area is its___.

   distribution projection route

2. A ___ is the line that divides two nations.

   distribution border route

3. Anything people can use is called a ___.

   resource product distribution

CHECK YOUR FACTS

4. What can maps show about explorers in the past?

5. National borders (were/were not) always the same.

THINK ABOUT IT

6. Name some things other than those mentioned in the lesson that distribution maps can show.

7. What sorts of things could cause national borders to change?

CHAPTER REVIEW

WATCH YOUR WORDS

1. ___ is the story of what happened in the past.
   Geography   History   Cartography

2. In ___ , we study physical facts about places.
   geography   history   cartography

3. ___ are shapes of the land.
   Globes   Projections   Landforms

4. A ___ is a flat drawing of Earth or part of it.
   globe   map   grid system

5. ___ are people who make maps.
   Motorists   Historians   Cartographers

CHECK YOUR FACTS

6. Why are people and events in the past important?

7. Name two kinds of flat lands.

8. Seas are (larger/smaller) than oceans.

9. What is the difference between weather and climate?

10. What kind of map is useful to pilots of ships?

11. An equal-area projection keeps land (size/shape) accurate.

12. What does the key on a map tell you?

13. Name the cardinal directions.

14. What line runs through 0° of longitude?

15. What divides nations or their parts?

CLOSE THE MAP GAP

Use the globe above to answer the questions. The top of the globe is north.

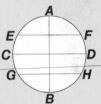

16. What is at point A?

17. What is at point B?

18. What is line CD?

19. What is the part of the globe above line CD?

20. If line AB is 0°, what is it?

THINK ABOUT IT

21. The United States was a new, weak nation in 1776. By 1918, it was one of the most powerful nations on Earth. Do you think the land and climate of North America had an influence on this?

22. What kind of land do you think you might like best to live on?

23. What kind of climate does your area have?

24. How could you tell someone the location of a place with no name?

25. Suppose you wanted to study plateaus of the world. What kind of map would you use to compare their sizes? To compare their heights?

CHAPTER 2
THE UNITED STATES AND NORTH AMERICA

Lesson 1: North America

FIND THE WORDS

**continent   region   national
capital**

You are one of the people who lives in North America. Your ancestors may have come here sometime in the last 500 years.

During that time, many people from all parts of the world came to North America. American Indians lived here before that time. American Indian peoples have lived in North America for thousands of years.

Have you heard the song that begins "Oh beautiful, for spacious skies"? Do you remember the rest of the words? This song is called "America, the Beautiful." It tells about the beauty of North America. It tells how big the land is, how wide the skies are, how rich the crops are.

North America is a **continent,** or large land mass, on Earth. There are three large nations on the continent of North America. They are Canada, the United States, and Mexico.

Because North America is so large, it has many different landforms. In some places, the land is as flat as a tabletop. In others, it is as jagged as the edge of a saw.

Some land in North America is covered with thick forests. Some land is covered with drifting sand. How do we study such a land?

We can begin by dividing the continent into seven **regions.** These are large areas where the landforms are similar. The seven regions are listed below:

Atlantic and Gulf coastal plains
Appalachian (AP uh LAY chun) Mountains
Central Lowland and Great Plains
Rocky Mountains
Great Basin
Pacific Coast Ranges and lowlands
Canadian Shield

Find each of these regions of North America on the map on the following page.

The United States is full of rich farming areas.

ARCTIC OCEAN

ASIA

Bering Sea

Beaufort Sea

BROOKS RANGE

ALASKA (U.S.)

Yukon River

ALASKA RANGE

Mt. McKinley

Mackenzie River

Great Bear Lake

Great Slave Lake

Hudson Bay

CANADIAN SHIELD

LAURENTIAN HIGHLANDS

CANADA

Lake Winnipeg

COAST MOUNTAINS

Vancouver

Seattle

Portland

Winnipeg

Montreal
Ottawa

St. Lawrence River

COASTAL PLAIN

San Francisco

CASCADE RANGE

Columbia River

Great Salt Lake

GREAT BASIN

SIERRA NEVADA

COAST RANGES

Denver

R O C K Y   M O U N T A I N S

Missouri River

GREAT PLAINS

GREAT LAKES

Milwaukee

Chicago

Toronto

River

Ohio River

APPALACHIAN MOUNTAINS

New York City

Washington, DC

ATLANTIC OCEAN

Los Angeles
San Diego

Mt. Whitney

Colorado River

Arkansas River

Rio Grande

CENTRAL LOWLAND

Dallas

Mississippi River

ATLANTIC COASTAL PLAIN

UNITED STATES

PACIFIC OCEAN

SIERRA MADRE OCCIDENTAL

Baja California

Gulf of California

GULF COASTAL PLAIN

Houston

MEXICO

SIERRA MADRE ORIENTAL

Gulf of Mexico

Miami

DOMINICAN REPUBLIC

BAHAMAS

PUERTO RICO (U.S.)

CUBA

HAITI

JAMAICA

WEST INDIES

MEXICAN PLATEAU

Mexico City

Veracruz

Yucatán Peninsula

BELIZE

Caribbean Sea

HONDURAS

GUATEMALA

EL SALVADOR

NICARAGUA

Isthmus of Panama

COSTA RICA

PANAMA

Panama Canal

SOUTH AMERICA

ELEVATION

Meters	Feet
over 4,000	over 13,100
2,000 to 4,000	6,600 to 13,100
1,000 to 2,000	3,300 to 6,600
200 to 1,000	660 to 3,300
sea level to 200	sea level to 660
below sea level	below sea level

KEY

- - - National Borders

★ National Capitals

• Cities

SCALE

Kilometers 0   600

Miles 0   600

N NE E SE S SW W NW

The elevation key on the map tells how high some of these regions are. The color green stands for the lowlands. This land is usually found along seacoasts. The highest land is colored brown. Look at the key. How many meters high is this land? Now look at your map and find the brown areas. What regions of North America have the highest land?

The other key on your map gives the symbols that stand for cities, national capitals, and national borders. **National** means "of a nation." A **capital** is the city where the center of government is. Thus, a national capital is the city where the nation's government meets. The key has a symbol for national capitals. Find the capital of the United States.

National borders are the lines on a map that divide one nation from another. They show where one nation ends and another begins. Find the symbol for national borders in your key. Now look at the map. With your finger, trace the border between Canada and the United States. Then find and trace the border between the United States and Mexico.

Notice that the land regions of North America do not stop at national borders. Landforms do not change suddenly as you go from one country into another. For example, the Great Plains stretch from Canada through the United States and into Mexico. The coastal plains lie along the seacoasts of both the United States and Mexico.

In the next two lessons, you will learn about the land and resources of the seven main regions of North America.

REVIEW

WATCH YOUR WORDS

1. A____is the center of government.
   continent   region   capital

2. North America can be divided into
   ____.
   continents   regions   capitals

3. North America is a____.
   continent   region   nation

CHECK YOUR FACTS

4. What group has been in North America for thousands of years?

5. Landforms (do/do not) change at national borders.

THINK ABOUT IT

In what region of North America do you live?

Lesson 2: Eastern and Central Regions of North America

FIND THE WORDS

fertile   dairy   coal   prairie
petroleum   transporation   herd
beef   hide   graze

Along the east coast of North America is a narrow plain. This plain begins far up the coast and becomes wider as you travel south. Look at the map on page

44. Trace the coastal plain with your finger. The coastal plain stretches along the Atlantic Coast and Gulf Coast of the United States.

The coastal plain is low and flat. In some places, there are large swamps. The swamps are thick with plants. There are also many wild animals in the swamps.

There is a lot of plant life in swamps.

LIVING RESOURCES OF NORTH AMERICA

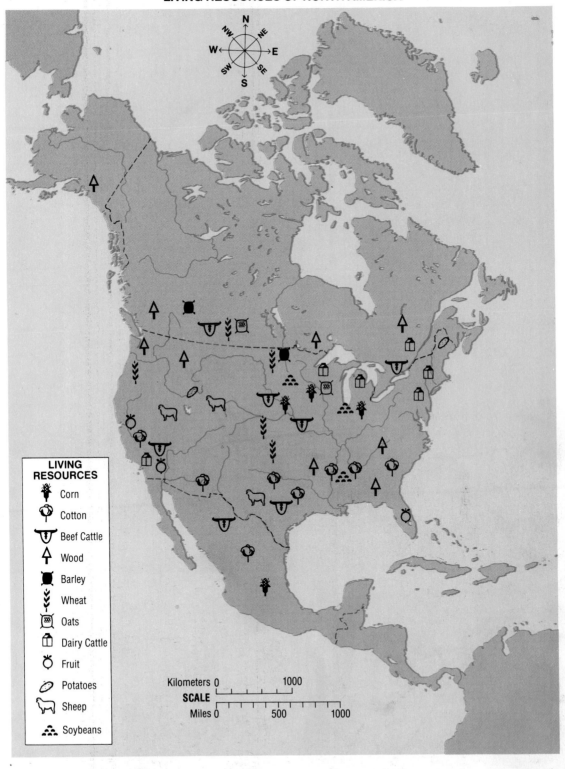

LIVING RESOURCES

- Corn
- Cotton
- Beef Cattle
- Wood
- Barley
- Wheat
- Oats
- Dairy Cattle
- Fruit
- Potatoes
- Sheep
- Soybeans

Kilometers 0   1000

SCALE

Miles 0   500   1000

NONLIVING RESOURCES OF NORTH AMERICA

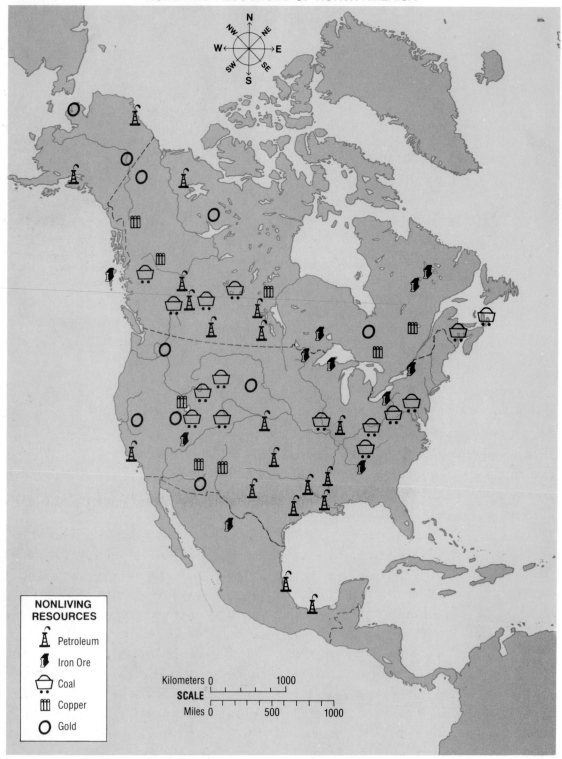

NONLIVING
RESOURCES

- Petroleum
- Iron Ore
- Coal
- Copper
- Gold

SCALE

Kilometers 0   1000

Miles 0   500   1000

These are the Appalachian Mountains. They begin in Canada. They reach all the way to Georgia and Alabama. The mountains are millions of years old. The weather has worn them down.

Much of the coastal plain is **fertile** land. That means it is good for growing crops. In the north, farmers grow vegetables and raise **dairy** cattle. These are cattle that provide milk. In the south, farmers grow crops such as fruit, vegetables, cotton, and rice.

Some of the largest cities in North America are found on the coastal plain. Many of the cities on the plain are near important or famous waterways.

West of the coastal plain are the Appalachian Mountains. These mountains begin in Canada. They reach all the way to Georgia and Alabama. The Appalachians are old even for mountains. They were formed millions of years ago. Since then, they have been worn down by the wind and the weather. Today, most of the mountains have rounded tops. The valleys between them do not have steep sides.

In parts of the Appalachians, the land is not good for farming. People farm only thin strips in the valleys where the land is flat. Farmers here grow barely enough for themselves to eat. However, much coal is found in the ground in these mountains. **Coal** is black and rocklike. It is made up of the remains of plants that lived long ago. Coal is used for fuel and is very valuable today.

Stretching across the center of North America are the Central Lowland and the Great Plains. This is one of the largest areas of flat land in the world. It stretches from northern Canada to the Gulf of Mexico. Originally, much of the northern and western part of this area was prairie (PREHR ee). A **prairie** is a large area of flat or rolling grassland. It has fertile soil and few trees.

The plains east of the Missouri River are called the Central Lowland. Here is some of the most fertile land in the world. On these plains, the farmers grow corn, soybeans, and wheat. These crops feed people in North America and around the world. The Central Lowland is also rich in petroleum. **Petroleum** is a thick, dark liquid found under the earth. It is used as a fuel.

Many of the large cities in the United States are located in the Central Lowland. Cities are often built on level land because transportation is much better there. **Transportation** is the movement of people or goods. Building roads, railroads, and airports on level land is fairly easy.

To the west of the Missouri River are the Great Plains. Less rain falls here than on the Central Lowland. Much of the land is covered with grass. Great **herds,** or groups, of cattle are raised on these plains. They are **beef** cattle,

These farm machines are harvesting wheat on the Great Plains.

which means they provide meat. Their **hides,** or skins, are used to make leather. Herds of sheep are also raised on the plains. These sheep provide both meat and wool. Both the cattle and the sheep **graze** on the plains. That means they eat the grass and other plants that grow there. In addition, farmers grow large amounts of wheat on the Great Plains.

REVIEW

WATCH YOUR WORDS

1. ____are made into leather.
   Herds   Hides   Dairies

2. Herds____on the Great Plains.
   beef   hide   graze

3. The movement of people and goods is____.
   petroleum   grazing
   transportation

4. ____cattle provide milk.
   Beef   Dairy   Herd

5. ____ lands are good for growing crops.
   Fertile   Dairy   Coal

CHECK YOUR FACTS

6. What is the difference between dairy cattle and beef cattle?

7. The Appalachians are (young/old) mountains.

8. What is coal used for?

9. What is the dividing line between the Central Lowland and the Great Plains?

10. Name an important crop grown on the Great Plains.

THINK ABOUT IT

Why are many of the cities of the coastal plain near waterways?

Lesson 3: Western, Southern, and Northern Regions of North America

FIND THE WORDS

mining   logging   arid   factory
irrigation

West of the Great Plains are the Rocky Mountains. The Rocky Mountains were formed later than the Appalachian Mountains. Compared to the Appalachians, the Rockies are new. Because the Rockies are newer, they are not as worn down as the Appalachians. The Rockies are high mountains with jagged peaks, steep sides, and deep valleys.

Some of the people living in the Rocky Mountains earn their living by mining and logging. **Mining** is taking minerals out of the ground. **Logging** is cutting down trees for wood. The Rocky Mountains also attract visitors who come there for sports and vacations.

West of the Rockies in the United States is a large area of high land. It is called the Great

The Rocky Mountains are high and have steep sides.

Many rivers flow into the Great Salt Lake.

Sand dunes are a common sight in the desert.

Basin. This land receives little rainfall. Much of it is desert. It is **arid**, or dry. Find this area on the map on page 44. The rivers here do not flow toward the sea. Many flow into the Great Salt Lake. There are few big cities in this part of North America.

Along the Pacific Coast of North America, we find mountains, valleys, and coastal plains. Some of these mountains are close to the ocean. They are called the Pacific Coast Ranges. Other mountains separate the Coast Ranges from the Great Basin. Find the names of these mountains on the map on page 44.

The plains are narrow along the Pacific Coast. But look at the map closely. Between the mountain ranges are some large valleys, especially in California. These lands are heavily farmed. Some of the important crops of these valleys are grapes, oranges, and lettuce. What large cities are found along the Pacific Coast of North America?

Two mountain ranges continue south into Mexico. They are similar to the Pacific Coast Ranges and the Rockies. These mountains cover much of Mexico's land. Mexico is divided into four areas by its mountains. Find these areas on the map on page 44 as you read about them.

The central plateau (pla TOH) is the part of Mexico where most people live. It is the high, flat land between Mexico's two mountain ranges. The soil is fertile. Farmers grow much of Mexico's food there. Mexico City, the capital of Mexico, is located in this area.

The southern area is mostly mountains and swamplands. The Yucatán (YOO kuh TAN) Peninsula in the south is low and flat. Many of Mexico's Indians live in the Yucatán. It is a poor area with few roads and factories. A **factory** is a place in which people make goods with machines. Most of the people of the Yucatán live on small farms. The main city in the south is the port of Veracruz (VER uh KROOZ).

The western area, except for Baja (BAH hah) California, is much like the central plateau. It has good farmlands. It also has many mines and factories. Tourists from all over the world visit the beaches along the Pacific Coast.

The northern area of Mexico borders on the United States. This area is much like the southwestern United States. Large areas of northern Mexico receive little rainfall. Cattle ranches are found here. So are iron, lead, and silver mines. Irrigation has made some of this land into good farmland. **Irrigation** means supplying land with water that comes from somewhere else.

Baja California is a peninsula in northwestern Mexico. It is about 1223 kilometers (760 miles) long. It separates the Gulf of California from the Pacific Ocean. Baja California has many mountains. There are also coastal plains. The land is generally too dry and poor for crops. The seacoast is popular with tourists. The land is rich in silver, lead, copper, and gold.

Oranges are one of the important crops that grow in California's valleys.

These are ruins of an old civilization in the Yucatán.

The last main region of North America that we will study is the Canadian Shield. It is also known as the Laurentian (lor REN chun) Plateau. This is a large area of rocky hills covered with forests. It forms the central land mass of North America. It has the shape of a giant shield. It stretches from Newfoundland in the east to the Beaufort (BOH furt) Sea in the northwest. It extends south through Wisconsin and Minnesota. Few people live in this northern region. But the land is rich in minerals such as nickel, copper, and silver. There are also many streams and lakes in the Canadian Shield. Many Canadians and Americans vacation there.

REVIEW

WATCH YOUR WORDS

1. ____land is dry.
   Mining   Logging   Arid

2. ____ is supplying land with water that comes from somewhere else.
   Mining   Logging   Irrigation

3. In a ____ , goods are made by machine.
   peninsula   factory   mine

CHECK YOUR FACTS

4. Compared with the Appalachians, the Rockies are (new/old) mountains.

5. In what area of Mexico do most of the people live?

THINK ABOUT IT

Suppose you wanted to open a resort. A resort is a place for tourists to come. What parts of North America would be good for this?

Lesson 4: Climates of North America

FIND THE WORDS

temperature   precipitation
season

"People talk about the weather, but they never do anything about it." You may have heard that say-ing. Well, people cannot do much to change the weather. But they have to talk about it. Weather is very important to people. It often determines what they wear, how they work, and where they go. It can even make the difference between life and death. You have

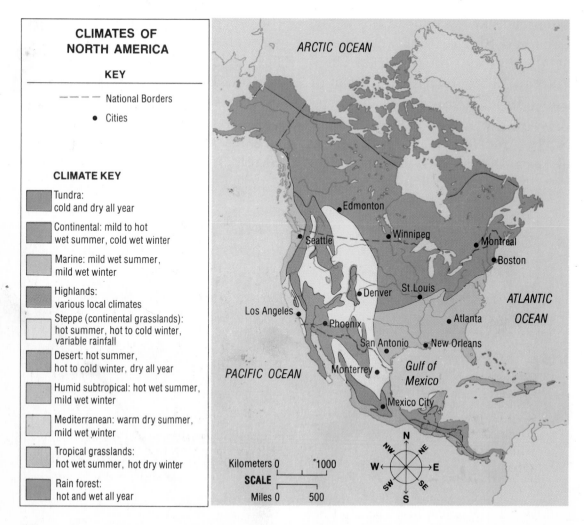

CLIMATES OF NORTH AMERICA

KEY

- - - - National Borders

● Cities

CLIMATE KEY

Tundra:
cold and dry all year

Continental: mild to hot
wet summer, cold wet winter

Marine: mild wet summer,
mild wet winter

Highlands:
various local climates

Steppe (continental grasslands):
hot summer, hot to cold winter,
variable rainfall

Desert: hot summer,
hot to cold winter, dry all year

Humid subtropical: hot wet summer,
mild wet winter

Mediterranean: warm dry summer,
mild wet winter

Tropical grasslands:
hot wet summer, hot dry winter

Rain forest:
hot and wet all year

ARCTIC OCEAN

Edmonton

Seattle   Winnipeg   Montreal
                        Boston

Denver   St.Louis   ATLANTIC
Los Angeles   OCEAN

Phoenix   Atlanta

San Antonio   New Orleans

PACIFIC OCEAN   Monterrey   Gulf of Mexico

Mexico City

SCALE
Kilometers 0   1000
Miles 0   500

N NW NE W E SW SE S

read that weather is the condition of the air at any moment. You have also learned that climate is the average weather conditions over time.

When we talk about weather or climate, we are talking mainly about two things. First, we are talking about the **temperature.** This is how much heat is in the air. Second, we are talking about the **precipitation** (pri SIP uh TAY shun). This is the amount of water that falls from the air. This water can be in the form of rain, snow, sleet, hail, or fog.

When you describe the weather, you tell people about temperature and precipitation. You might say, "It's cold and snowy." Or, "It's hot, and the sun is shining." When you describe the climate, you are saying what the weather is like during a season of the year. A **season** is a period of the year with similar weather. Winter, summer, spring, and fall are the seasons. Thus, to describe the climate, you might say, "The winters are very cold, and it snows a lot." Or, "The summers are very hot, and it doesn't rain much."

Look at the climate map of North America on page 56. It shows 10 different climates. Look at the key to the map. Notice that the climate is described for both winter and summer. It is not described for spring and fall. The weather in spring is partly like summer and partly like winter. How could the climate for fall be described?

REVIEW

WATCH YOUR WORDS

1. ___ is how much heat is in the air.
   Temperature   Precipitation
   Season

2. ___ is how much water falls from the air.
   Temperature   Precipitation
   Season

3. A period of the year that has similar weather is a ___.
   temperature   precipitation
   season

CHECK YOUR FACTS
Look at the Map

4. What is the largest climate area in North America?

5. What area has no set climate?

6. What kind of climate does Los Angeles have?

THINK ABOUT IT

What is the weather today? Describe it in terms of both temperature and precipitation.

Lesson 5: Rivers and Lakes of North America

FIND THE WORDS

**drain   river system
drainage basin**

Most rivers carry water from the land to the oceans. Rivers are very important to people. River valleys often have much fertile land. Here, people farm and often build cities. Rivers also provide a way to go from place to place. Before many roads were built, rivers were one very important means of transportation.

You have probably heard of the Mississippi, the Missouri, and the Ohio rivers. You may know about the St. Lawrence, the Colorado, and the Rio Grande (REE oh GRAND). These are just a few of the rivers that flow in North America. Find these rivers on the map of North America on page 44. These rivers **drain** a large part of North America. A river can drain a land area. That means it carries away all the water that runs off that land.

Find the Great Lakes on your map. They are the largest group of lakes with fresh water in the world. The Great Lakes are very deep. They are connected to the

The Mississippi River begins in the northern part of the United States. This picture was taken in Wisconsin.

Atlantic Ocean by the St. Lawrence River. Many ships travel these lakes, carrying people and goods. There are many important cities on the shores of the Great Lakes.

Notice that many rivers of North America flow into one another. The Missouri River flows into the Mississippi River. The Ohio and the Arkansas (AHR kun saw) rivers also flow into the Mississippi. Such a group of rivers is called a **river system.**

The land area drained by a group of rivers is called a **drainage basin.** Rain and sometimes snow fall in a drainage basin. Much of this water is caught and carried away by the river system. Some drainage basins are very small. Others are very large.

The landforms in each area determine which way the rivers flow. The mountains divide the land. Rivers on different sides of mountains will flow in different directions. Find rivers that begin in the Rocky Mountains. Into what bodies of water do they flow?

Rivers are also affected by the climate. Where rain or snow is heavy, rivers are usually larger. There are probably more rivers in

LONGEST RIVERS IN NORTH AMERICA

Rivers	Length in km	Length in miles
Mackenzie	4,072	2,530
Mississippi	3,627	2,254
Missouri	3,576	2,222
St. Lawrence	2,935	1,824
Rio Grande	2,913	1,810
Yukon	2,781	1,728
Arkansas	2,240	1,392
Colorado	2,240	1,392
Columbia	1,875	1,165
Saskatchewan	1,862	1,157
Peace	1,846	1,147
Snake	1,661	1,032
Red	1,629	1,012

Lakes provide many opportunities for recreation, such as sailing.

such places, too. Do you remember where the dry areas in North America are? Check the climate map on page 56. See how many of the largest rivers are located in the dry areas.

REVIEW

WATCH YOUR WORDS

1. A group of rivers that flow into one another is a____.
   drain   river system
   drainage basin

2. A group of rivers carry water from a____.
   drain   river system
   drainage basin

CHECK YOUR FACTS

3. List some ways in which rivers are important.

4. What is the largest group of lakes with fresh water?

5. What determines which way rivers flow?

THINK ABOUT IT

Look at the chart of large rivers. The Mackenzie appears to be the longest river in North America. But one large river in the chart flows into another river. If these two were considered one river, that river would be the longest. Which two rivers are these? You should be able to find them on the map of North America on page 44.

CHAPTER REVIEW

WATCH YOUR WORDS

1. North America is a____.
   capital   region   continent
2. ____land is good for growing crops.
   Dry   Swamp   Fertile
3. ____ is supplying land with water from somewhere else.
   Mining   Logging   Irrigation
4. ____ is the amount of water that falls from the air.
   Temperature   Precipitation   Drainage
5. Rivers____the land.
   hide   swamp   drain

CHECK YOUR FACTS

6. What are the three large nations in North America?
7. What divides one nation from another?
8. What kind of cattle provide milk? What kind provide meat and hides?
9. Name some older mountains in North America. Name some newer ones.
10. What large body of water is found in the Great Basin?
11. Name two large peninsulas found in Mexico.
12. What large plateau is located in northern North America?
13. What two things make up weather and climate?

14. What river drains the Great Lakes?
15. What affects the size and number of rivers?

USE YOUR MAPS

16. Look at the map of North America on page 44. What are the capitals of Canada and Mexico?
17. Name three large cities on the Great Lakes.
18. What three oceans border on North America?
19. Look at the climate map on page 56. In what climate areas are these cities located: Mexico City, Boston, Winnipeg?
20. What is the coldest climate area? What is the driest? What is the hottest and wettest?

THINK ABOUT IT

21. What is the national border nearest to where you live?
22. What kinds of crops or animals are raised near where you live?
23. What mountains are the nearest to where you live?
24. What is the climate like in your area? Describe both the temperature and precipitation in both summer and winter.
25. Name the ocean, river, and lake nearest to where you live.

UNIT REVIEW

WATCH YOUR WORDS

Use the words below to fill in the blanks. Use each term only once.

Cartographers	interrupted	Mountains	projection
climate	key	North Pole	rivers
degrees	lakes	Northern Hemisphere	scale
distorted	latitude	oceans	South Pole
Globes	longitude	Plains	Southern Hemisphere
Hills	Maps	prime meridian	symbols

The land has many shapes. ___ are mostly flat. ___ rise higher than the land around. ___ are the highest land of all. Besides land, Earth has large bodies of water called ___ . On land, the ___ and ___ provide water. The ___ , or average weather conditions, of an area is very important.

___ are models of Earth. On Earth, the ___ is at the top, and the ___ is at the bottom. The equator divides Earth into the ___ and the ___ . Lines of ___ run parallel to the equator. Lines of ___ run east and west of the ___ . Both are numbered in ___ .

___ are flat drawings of Earth. The way they show Earth is their ___ . On a Mercator map, the land is ___ . On an equal-area map, the projection is often ___ . ___ make maps. They use ___ to show things. These are listed in the ___ . The ___ shows distance on a map.

CHECK YOUR FACTS

1. How do we know about the actions of people in the past?

2. Travel across plains is (easy/hard).

3. Usually, (many/few) people live in mountain areas.

4. Knowing about the climate (does/does not) tell you what the weather will be like today.

5. Why are globes tilted?

6. What divides Earth into the Northern Hemisphere and Southern Hemisphere?

7. What are the other names for parallels and meridians?

8. Maps (can/cannot) show the Earth accurately.

9. How can you tell what the symbols on maps mean?

10. How many degrees are there in a circle?

11. What kind of map shows you how things are spread over Earth?

12. How many large nations are there in North America?

13. The land regions of North America (do/do not) stop at national borders.

14. Which mountains are older, the Appalachians or the Rockies?

15. Why are cities often built on level land?

16. In the Great Basin, the rivers (do/do not) flow to the oceans.

17. In what part of Mexico do most people live?

18. The Canadian Shield (does/does not) extend into the United States.

19. The Great Lakes have (fresh/salt) water.

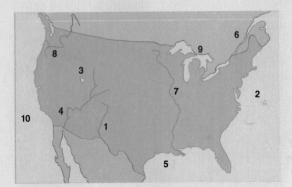

CLOSE THE MAP GAP

20. The numbers on this map stand for important bodies of water in North America. Match these numbers to the bodies of water listed below.

> Pacific Ocean
> Mississippi River
> Gulf of Mexico
> Atlantic Ocean
> Columbia River
> Rio Grande
> St. Lawrence River
> Great Salt Lake
> Colorado River
> Great Lakes

USE YOUR MAPS

21. Look at the map of the Earth on pages 10 and 11. What islands extend west from the coast of Alaska?

22. What circle passes through Alaska and Canada?

23. Look at the map of North America on page 44. What two gulfs border on Mexico?

24. What river flows through Alaska?

25. Look at the map of North American climates on page 56. Name three large climate areas in the United States.

THINK ABOUT IT

26. Tell exactly where you live, including the town, county, state, nation, and continent.

27. What kind of land do you think you might like best to live on?

28. What kind of climate does your area have?

29. Suppose you wanted to tell someone the location of a place with no name. How could you do it?

30. What do you know about the elevation of your area?

TRY SOMETHING NEW

31. Get a map of your local area. Measure the direct distance between your home and your school. Measure the distance you actually travel to get from one to the other.

32. Draw a map to show where an imaginary treasure is buried. Show and label important landmarks like roads, buildings, parks, rivers, and so on. Include a key, scale, and compass.

33. Get some travel brochures about Canada or Mexico. Pick out some interesting places that you would like to visit. Using a map, plan a trip that would take you to each one.

PUT IT ALL TOGETHER

34. Draw a map of North America. Show the borders of the United States, Canada, and Mexico. Label the three countries. Show and label the national capitals. Show and label important natural features. These should include oceans, other large bodies of water, and a few major rivers and mountain ranges.

THE BEGINNING OF THE
UNITED STATES

CHAPTER 1 SETTLING NORTH AMERICA

Lesson 1: The First People of the Americas

FIND THE WORDS

time line   ancestors

All people have a past. This is true for groups as well as individuals. People study their past for many reasons. They want to know where they came from. They want to know how they got to be the way they are. They hope that if they get to know themselves better, they can make better plans for their future.

An American writer once said, "Those who cannot remember the past are condemned to repeat it." This means that we should try to learn from past mistakes. If we do not, we may make the same mistakes again. It is also true that we can learn from past successes.

As you have learned, history is what happened in the past. **Time lines** can help you learn history. They are charts that show important events in the order in which they happened. Time lines give you a clear idea of what happened over a certain period of time. In this book, you will read about important events in American history. See where these events fit on the time lines in your book.

Here is a time line showing some early events in North and South America.

It is thought that the first people in North America came from Asia. They came sometime between 20,000 and 40,000 years ago. How do you think they got here?

Look at the map on page 68. The northeastern tip of Asia is about 80 kilometers (50 miles) from the northwestern tip of North America. People may have crossed from Asia to North America by raft or boat. They may even have walked across during the Ice Age. The level of the ocean was much lower then. The area between the two continents was sometimes dry land. The earliest Americans probably came in small groups over a period of many thousands of years.

We know that the first Americans were good stonecutters and

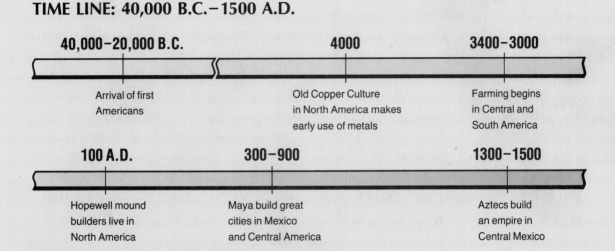

TIME LINE: 40,000 B.C.–1500 A.D.

40,000–20,000 B.C.
Arrival of first
Americans

4000
Old Copper Culture
in North America makes
early use of metals

3400–3000
Farming begins
in Central and
South America

100 A.D.
Hopewell mound
builders live in
North America

300–900
Maya build great
cities in Mexico
and Central America

1300–1500
Aztecs build
an empire in
Central Mexico

ROUTE OF THE FIRST NORTH AMERICANS

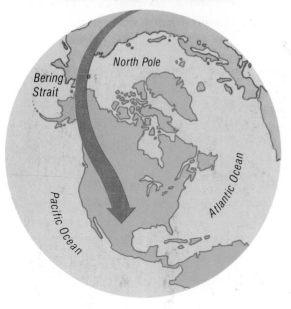

daring hunters. In Texas and New Mexico, stone and ivory spearheads have been found in the bones of animals. Some of these animals died more than 10,000 years ago. People chipped stone to make tools and weapons such as axes and spear points. They decorated some pieces with beautiful carvings. With these weapons, they hunted wild animals. Some of the animals were larger than any now living in the Americas.

Groups of people gradually moved south and east. We know this because remains of their camps have been found. They gathered around campfires for warmth and protection at night.

They lived on the meat of the animals they killed. They also ate wild fruits and vegetables. They fished in the rivers and along the coasts. Some people found places they liked in North America. They decided to stay. Others moved on to Central and South America.

Wild fruits and vegetables were not always easy to find. About 5000 years ago, people in Central and South America began to plant corn. Later, they learned to plant beans, squash, cotton, and potatoes. This was the beginning of farming in the Americas.

Can you imagine how farming might change a people's way of life? Farming people can settle in one place. They can do this because their crops give them a supply of food. Then they have more time to discover new ways of doing things. For example, they usually learn how to raise certain animals for food or skins. They may learn to make baskets of reeds or pots of clay. Settled people may begin to make cloth from cotton, from other plants, or from the hair of animals. Some discover how to melt down metals such as copper or gold. They use the metals to make tools and jewelry.

Early people in Central and South America learned how to do these things. Farming began there about 5000 years ago. Knowledge of how to grow corn and other crops slowly spread north. Traders probably carried knowledge about farming into what is now Mexico and the United States. Sometimes traders traveled great distances to exchange goods. They also spread ideas from one culture to another.

The people who came to the Americas from Asia were the ancestors of today's American Indians. **Ancestors** are members of a person's family who lived long ago. Groups of early American Indians created their own arts and followed their own customs. Over thousands of years, many native cultures came to exist in North and South America.

You will study some of these cultures in the lessons that follow. You will see how they developed.

You will also see how the coming of Europeans changed the lives of all American Indians.

American Indians now share North America with people from all over the Earth.

REVIEW

CHECK YOUR FACTS

Look at the Time Line

1. When did farming begin in Central and South America?
2. About how many years did the Mayan culture last?

Look at the Lesson

3. Where did the first Americans come from?

4. What crops did the early farmers plant?
5. How did knowledge about farming spread in the Americas?

TRY SOMETHING NEW

Make a time line that shows the important events in your own personal history.

Lesson 2: Early Cities of North America

FIND THE WORDS

astronomer   mathematician
hieroglyphic   temple

Did you know that cities were built in North America more than 1600 years ago? At that time, an American Indian people called the Maya (MAH yah) began to build stone cities in Central America. Many Mayan cities have been found in Guatemala (GWAH tuh MAH luh) and on the Yucatán (YOO kuh TAN) Peninsula in Mexico. The Mayan culture was like no other. It was the most advanced culture in the Americas for about 600 years. It compared well with cultures in Europe, too.

The Maya possessed great knowledge and important skills. They were expert **astronomers,** people who study stars. They were excellent **mathematicians,** people who study numbers. The Maya used the number zero long before it was used in Europe. They developed a calendar as accurate as the one we use today.

The Maya used **hieroglyphics** (HY ruh GLIF iks), a complicated kind of picture writing.

They were also fine stone cutters. They carved writing and numbers into standing slabs of

Some early peoples of the Americas carved great statues of stone.

This is the Temple of Warriors found in the Yucatán. It was built by the Maya and the Toltecs.

stone. They also carved scenes showing their way of life. All this stonecarving was done without metal tools.

We know very little about how the Mayan government was organized. Most of the people lived in villages and farmed. Some helped build the great stone cities. There were also craft workers, merchants, and traders. And there were slaves. The ruling class was made up of priests and nobles.

The Maya had an organized religion with many priests. Only members of ruling-class families could become priests. A special place was created for religious ceremonies. At the center of each Mayan city was a high pyramid with a flat top. On top of the pyramid was a temple. A **temple** is a place where people worship a god or gods. Steep steps were cut in the stone leading to the top of the pyramid. Mayan priests climbed these steps. They held religious ceremonies at the top.

The Maya were peaceful farming people. They grew corn, potatoes, and tobacco. The peasants worked hard. They did not use animals to pull or carry loads. They had no plows or wheels.

Around 900 A.D., the great age of the Maya ended. No one knows what happened. The great cities of the south were deserted. But Mayan cities did survive in the Yucatán.

Then another people rose to power in Mexico. These people were the Toltecs (TOHL teks). They gained power over the Maya in the Yucatán. The Toltecs were fierce fighters. They were very different from the peaceful Maya.

After conquering the Maya, the Toltecs settled among them. The Toltecs and the Maya influenced one another. The Toltecs added new elements to Mayan cities. The two groups built cities together.

Their most beautiful cities are near the middle of the Yucatán.

Sports were popular among the Maya and the Toltecs. They played a ball game something like kickball or rugby. This game was played on a long court. Points were scored by kicking the ball through stone rings on opposite walls of the court. A ball court like this can be seen today at Chichén Itzá (chee CHEN eet SAH) in Mexico.

In the 1400s, the Toltecs were conquered by fierce Aztec warriors. The Aztecs built an empire that ruled several million people.

The Aztecs made this stone calendar.

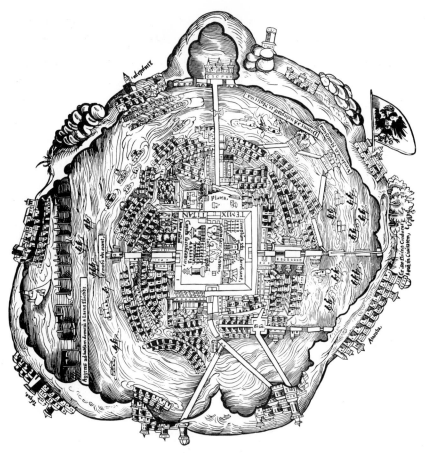

This is a map of Tenochtitlán. It was the capital city of the Aztecs.

They were the first people to control all of central Mexico. Their way of life was warlike and highly organized. The Aztecs made beautiful objects of gold and precious stones. They built great stone pyramids with temples on top. There, people worshiped the sun and other Aztec gods. The Aztecs also adopted the Mayan calendar. They made a great round calendar stone which still exists today.

The capital city of the Aztecs was Tenochtitlán (teh NOCH teet LAHN). It was founded in 1325. Tenochtitlán was a large city built on islands in a shallow lake. It was located where Mexico City is today. Tenochtitlán was built mostly of stone. Four long roads connected the island city to the land around the lake. Open spaces in the roads allowed canoes on the lake to pass through. Wooden bridges crossed the open spaces. The city also had floating gardens where vegetables, fruits, and flowers were grown.

Tenochtitlán had two central markets. All kinds of goods made in the countryside were sold there. Food products, gold and silver jewelry, lead, brass, copper, bones, shells, and feathers were sold. The Aztecs also sold colored cotton cloth, pots, pitchers, tiles, and vases of glazed and painted clay.

The Aztecs were the last great American Indian civilization to flourish in Mexico. The Aztecs built their empire between 1428 and 1519. So this great empire lasted only about 100 years. Then, in 1519, the Spanish came to Mexico. A small Spanish army easily conquered the Aztecs. The Spanish had guns and cannons. The Aztecs did not have such weapons. Also, many Aztecs died from European diseases.

War and invasion had happened before in central Mexico. But the Spanish conquest was different. The arrival of the Spanish was the end of rule by the native peoples in Mexico.

This old drawing shows fighting during the conquest of Mexico.

REVIEW

WATCH YOUR WORDS

1. A(n) ____ is a place where a god or gods are worshiped.
   astronomer   hieroglyphic   temple
2. A person who studies the stars is a(n) ____.
   astronomer   hieroglyphic
   mathematician

CHECK YOUR FACTS

3. Where did the Maya live?

4. What group conquered the Maya?
5. What group conquered the Toltecs in the 1400s?

THINK ABOUT IT

People of different cultures learn from one another. The Aztecs and the Toltecs learned much from the Maya. List some foods and some customs that the United States has borrowed from other lands.

Lesson 3: Other Early Cultures of North America

FIND THE WORDS

evidence   pestle   adobe
stockade   tribe   confederacy

In the area that is now the United States, there were many ancient peoples. Signs of their cultures have been found throughout the country. The things they left behind them are **evidence,** or visible proof, of how they lived.

Some of the earliest examples of metalwork anywhere in the world have been found in Wisconsin. They are copper spearheads and tools. They were made by an ancient group of people called the Old Copper Culture. We know that these people lived 5000 to 7000 ears ago near the Great Lakes. The tools are evidence that these early people knew much about working with metal.

The ancient Cochise (KOH chees) people lived where Arizona, New Mexico, and Mexico now meet. This area is a desert. Once, however, it had a large lake. The Cochise people lived in this region for thousands of years. They began to grow corn about 4000 years ago. They used **pestles,** or grinding stones, to grind the corn in stone bowls. Later, they also grew beans and squash.

The Cochise were probably the ancestors of the modern Pueblo (PWEB loh) people. About 500 years ago, Pueblo people began to dig irrigation ditches to water the land. They changed the course of streams. They made ponds to store water. That way, they could grow more crops.

The Pueblo people are best known as builders. Their homes, called pueblos, were often several stories high. They were built of **adobe** (uh DOH bee), which is sun-baked clay. Ladders were used to reach entrances in the roof. Pueblos look somewhat like apartment buildings. Some pueblos were built on the sides of cliffs 900 years ago. Early pueblos like this can still be seen in the Southwest. Modern Pueblo people still live in that region today.

About 1900 years ago, the Hopewell mound builders lived in the Ohio and Mississippi valleys. The Hopewell people built large, high mounds of earth. We are not sure what these mounds were for. Most were used as burial places.

Modern Pueblo people still live in pueblos in the Southwest.

Some were forts. Some were shaped like animals. All may have served some religious purpose.

The Hopewell Culture started as a community of farmers. Slowly, it grew into several communities that agreed to help and protect one another. The Hopewell people were great traders in art objects, sea shells, wood, copper, and food. Their communities stretched south from Wisconsin to the Gulf of Mexico. They extended west from New York to Kansas.

Another mound-building people are now known as the Temple Mound Culture. These people lived along the Mississippi River valley about 500 years ago. Their villages were surrounded by high wooden fences. The Temple Mound people built temples 33 meters (100 feet) high. These temples were shaped like pyramids with flat tops. The Temple Mound people had much in common with the earlier Maya of Mexico. They may have had contact with early Mexican cultures through trade.

One example of an early culture that survived into modern times is the Natchez Culture. The Natchez people lived near where the city of Natchez, Mississippi, is today. They had a highly developed class system and religion. Their king and high priest was called Great Sun. The king's

The Hopewell people built large, high mounds of earth. This is the Great Serpent Mound in Ohio.

mother, if she was alive, or his sister, was the Woman Sun. She chose the king's successor from among her sons or brothers when the king died. The Natchez were the strongest tribe along the lower Mississippi River when Europeans arrived. They were defeated by the French in the early 1700s. A few Natchez survivors are found today living among other tribes in the Southwest.

The Europeans arriving in the New World found many American Indians living along the Atlantic Coast. These native people belonged to Woodlands cultures.

The Woodlands peoples lived in villages. For defense, a village was often surrounded by a **stockade,** a fence made of wooden posts. Families lived in various kinds of houses within the stockade. There was usually an open area in the center of the village.

The Woodlands peoples were organized into groups known as **tribes.** In some places, tribes formed larger groups that were called **confederacies.** There was almost constant warfare among the various groups. Many people were killed in these wars.

The Woodlands tribes got food by gathering wild plants and by hunting and fishing. They also farmed in a way that made it impossible to stay in one place permanently. They cleared fields for farming by cutting down some trees and burning the rest. The ashes enriched the soil, but only for a few years. The richness of the soil was soon used up. As a result, the people had to move often. For this reason, and because of the constant warfare, the number of people remained small.

Here, early Indian women plant seeds while men prepare the ground.

REVIEW

WATCH YOUR WORDS

1. A(n)____is a grinding stone.
   hieroglyphic   adobe   pestle
2. ____is sun-baked clay.
   Stockade   Adobe   Pestle
3. A(n)____is a group of tribes.
   stockade   adobe   confederacy
4. A(n)____is a fence of wooden posts.
   stockade   adobe   pestle
5. The Woodlands peoples were organized into groups called____.
   stockades   mounds   tribes

CHECK YOUR FACTS

6. Where did the people of the Old Copper Culture live?

7. List three crops that the Cochise people grew.
8. What kind of homes did the Pueblo people build?
9. Name two cultures that built mounds.
10. Why did the Woodlands people move from place to place?
11. Give two reasons why the number of Woodlands people remained small.

TRY SOMETHING NEW

Find out what early peoples lived in your state. Has any evidence of these people been found? Use your library to find out. If you can, visit a museum.

Lesson 4: Europeans Find the Americas

"Wednesday, October 10th, 1492. Steered west-south-west day and night, and made 59 leagues progress. Here the men lost all patience. They complained of the length of the voyage. But the Admiral encouraged them the best he could. He told them their voyage would make them rich. And he added that they had come so far, they could not turn back. They had no choice but to go on.

"At two o'clock on Friday morning, land was discovered. They found themselves near a small island, where they saw people on the beach. The Admiral landed in a small boat with a party of his men. They found very green trees, many streams of water, and many kinds of fruit. The Admiral planted a flag on the beach and claimed the land for the King and Queen of Spain."

The "Admiral" in this story is the Italian explorer Christopher Columbus. The story comes from

The day is October 12, 1492. Columbus and his crew see the New World ahead.

his diary. This voyage, in 1492, is the earliest recorded discovery of the New World by Europeans.

There is evidence that people from Europe and Asia may have come to the Americas long before. Some people from these parts of the world were great sailors. Probably the first European visitors to North America were the Norwegian (nor WEE jun) Vikings. We know they reached Iceland and Greenland in the 900s. Led by Leif Ericson (LEEF ER ik sun), they explored the northern coast of North America in 1003. Years later, some English sailors may have come as far as the Grand Banks. This is a rich fishing area off the coast of Nova Scotia (NOH vuh SKOH shuh) in Canada. They may have come to catch fish that fed there.

But for the next several hundred years, Europe showed no interest in exploring the New World.

In the 1400s, changes began to take place that increased interest in exploration. For example, scientists developed tools that helped sailors cross the oceans. One example is the compass. Such tools helped sailors know where they were and in what direction they were going. They no longer had to stay close to land to keep from getting lost. Still, sailing out of sight of land was very frightening to sailors. At that time, ships were very small.

Another important change was the growth of powerful states in Europe. France, England, Spain, and Portugal were becoming stronger. Leaders could give more

The Vikings explored the northern coast of North America in ships like this one.

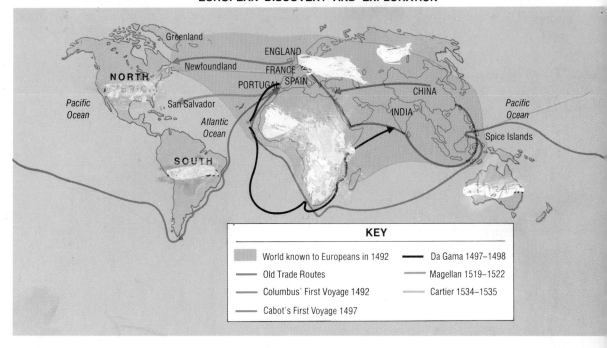

Greenland

ENGLAND

Newfoundland FRANCE

NORTH PORTUGAL SPAIN

Pacific Ocean CHINA

San Salvador INDIA Pacific Ocean

Atlantic Ocean

Spice Islands

SOUTH

KEY

World known to Europeans in 1492 — Da Gama 1497–1498

— Old Trade Routes — Magellan 1519–1522

— Columbus' First Voyage 1492 — Cartier 1534–1535

— Cabot's First Voyage 1497

attention to other parts of the world.

Europeans wanted the silk and spices that were found in India and China. In the 1400s, India was called "the Indies." Trade routes to the Indies were over land. It took many months, and even years, to carry goods over mountains, deserts, and plains. The goods were often damaged along the way or stolen by robbers. European kings and queens wanted to find better trade routes to the Indies. They provided ships and money to explorers so a sea route could be found.

The Portuguese were the first Europeans to encourage exploration overseas. Prince Henry of Por-

tugal opened a special school to train sailors and mapmakers. The Portuguese looked for a route sailing south and then to the east around Africa.

Christopher Columbus had a different idea. He believed he could find a shorter route to Asia by sailing west instead of east. He shared the belief of many that the world was round. But he also thought the world was much smaller than it is. Many people thought Columbus was a fool. But Queen Isabella of Spain was more farsighted. She gave him the support he needed. She agreed to pay for Columbus's voyage.

In 1492, Columbus set sail with three small ships. These were the

This is a reproduction of Columbus's cabin on the *Santa Maria.*

Niña (NEE nyuh), the *Pinta* (PEEN tah), and the *Santa Maria* (SAHN tuh muh REE uh). Columbus and his sailors traveled 33 days across the Atlantic Ocean without seeing land. Finally, on October 12, they arrived at an island about 640 kilometers (400 miles) from the coast of Florida. It is still called San Salvador, the name Columbus gave to it. They also explored the islands of Hispaniola (HIS pun YOH luh), nearby Puerto Rico, and Cuba.

The people Columbus found on these islands were the Taino (TY noh). But Columbus called them "Indians" because he thought he was in the Indies. He returned to Spain with some of these peaceful Taino people. He also brought tobacco and a little gold. Queen Isabella and King Ferdinand were not satisfied with this cargo. They sent Columbus on three more voyages to the New World.

Columbus never found the riches he was looking for. He died in 1506, poor and unhappy. To the end, he believed he had found the best route to the Indies.

Over the next 100 years, many other explorers followed Columbus. In 1497, another Italian, John Cabot, sailed from England to Newfoundland. He hoped to find a northern route to the Indies, but he failed. Amerigo Vespucci (ah MAIR i goh ves POO chee) traveled to the New World in the years that followed. He was one of the first to realize that Columbus had discovered a new world. He wrote stories about the new land. A German mapmaker studied information that the explorers had brought back. He drew maps of this new world in 1507. The mapmaker called the new world America, after Amerigo Vespucci.

Ferdinand Magellan (muh JEL un) was the first to succeed in what Columbus had hoped to do. In 1519, he sailed west to the Indies. Magellan was a Portuguese explorer paid by the Spanish king. He reached the Pacific Ocean by sailing around the southern tip of South America. He then crossed the Pacific to the Spice Islands in present-day Indonesia.

Magellan and his crew met with great difficulties in their travels. All but one of his five ships were destroyed during the voyage. Magellan himself was killed in a conflict with the people who lived in the Philippines. In 1522, the remaining ship arrived back in Spain. It was the first ship to sail all the way around the world. The goods it brought back to Spain were worth more than enough to pay for the whole voyage. They gave the king a large profit.

REVIEW

CHECK YOUR FACTS

1. Columbus and his crew (were/were not) the first Europeans in the New World.
2. Why were Europeans looking for ocean trade routes in the 1400s?
3. How did the early Portuguese plan to sail to the Indies? Which way did Columbus decide to go?
4. After whom was America named?
5. Whose expedition was the first to sail around the world?

THINK ABOUT IT

Columbus thought the Earth was smaller than it is. He also thought that he had sailed west to the Indies. How are these two beliefs connected?

Lesson 5: More Spaniards Come to the Americas

FIND THE WORD

mission

The news of a new world to explore spread quickly throughout Europe. The Spanish rulers heard about a rich empire in North America where Mexico is today. They sent Hernando Cortés (hur NAHN doh kor TEZ) to Mexico to seek gold. Thus, Spain was the first nation to seek riches in the Americas.

With only 500 people, Cortés conquered the great Aztec empire between 1519 and 1521. The Aztecs were fine warriors, but the Spanish had many advantages. They had guns and cannons, iron armor, swords, and horses. The Aztecs had never seen these things. The Aztecs also had enemies among the people they ruled. These people thought Cortés would free them from having to pay taxes to the Aztec emperor, Montezuma II (MON tuh ZOO muh). So they helped Cortés and the Spanish soldiers.

Probably the greatest disadvantage the Aztecs had was a story that had been handed down from generation to generation. According to this story, the ancestors of the Aztecs had once worshiped a god named Quetzalcoatl (ket SAHL KWAHT ul). He had been defeated by other gods hundreds of years before. When he went away, he promised to return one day in great white birds that flew over the water. They would come from the direction of the rising sun. Then Quetzalcoatl would rule the Aztecs again.

In 1519, the Aztec emperor Montezuma heard that warriors had come to Mexico. They had come from the east in big ships

TIME LINE: 800s–1565

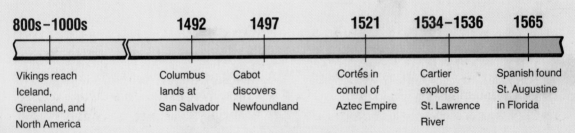

800s–1000s	1492	1497	1521	1534–1536	1565
Vikings reach Iceland, Greenland, and North America	Columbus lands at San Salvador	Cabot discovers Newfoundland	Cortés in control of Aztec Empire	Cartier explores St. Lawrence River	Spanish found St. Augustine in Florida

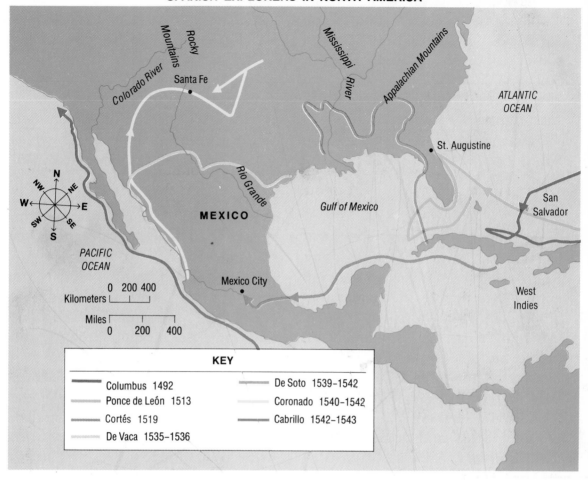

Rocky Mountains

Colorado River

Santa Fe

Mississippi River

Appalachian Mountains

ATLANTIC OCEAN

St. Augustine

Rio Grande

MEXICO

Gulf of Mexico

San Salvador

PACIFIC OCEAN

0 200 400
Kilometers

Miles
0 200 400

Mexico City

West Indies

KEY

▬▬ Columbus 1492	▬▬ De Soto 1539–1542
▬▬ Ponce de León 1513	▬▬ Coronado 1540–1542
▬▬ Cortés 1519	▬▬ Cabrillo 1542–1543
▬▬ De Vaca 1535–1536	

with sails like white wings. Montezuma was not sure what to do. He thought the Spanish might be the ancient rulers of the Aztecs. Montezuma waited. In the end, he decided to fight. The Aztecs fought well, but it was too late. They were defeated.

Over the next 15 years, Spanish conquerors took over rich empires in South America. From all these places, the Spanish sent gold and silver back to Spain. This made Spain the richest nation in all of Europe.

Spanish explorers were eager to find other rich empires. So they traveled north from Mexico into what is now the United States. The stories of great, hidden riches spread.

Panfilo de Narváez (PAHN fee loh duh nahr VAH ays) explored what is now Florida in 1527. Afterward, he sailed his ships along the Gulf of Mexico. There, near what is now Galveston, Texas, his ships were wrecked. Four men survived the wreck and reached shore. They were Cabeza de Vaca (kuh BAY zuh duh VAH kuh), two other Spanish sailors, and a Black man named Estebanico (ES tuh VAH nee koh). For 6 years, they wandered across Texas. Finally, they reached Mexico City. They brought American Indian tales of seven "Cities of Gold."

Francisco Coronado (fran SIS koh KOR uh NAH doh) was another Spaniard who looked for a rich empire like that of the Aztecs. Beginning in 1540, he spent 2 years exploring parts of Texas and Kansas. Some of Coronado's explorers discovered the Grand Canyon. But they found no cities of gold.

In 1541, Hernando de Soto explored Florida and areas that are now Alabama, Arkansas, and Mississippi. He and his party were the first Europeans to see the Mississippi River. The American Indians called this great river "The Father of Waters." De Soto got as far north as the present site of Memphis, Tennessee. He died near the great river he had found.

In 1565, the Spanish founded St. Augustine in Florida. This was the first permanent European settlement in the United States.

Roman Catholic priests from Spain were important to all the Spanish settlements. They came to the New World to teach Roman Catholic beliefs and Spanish culture to the American Indians. They built **missions,** or religious communities. There, they lived and taught the people.

The Spanish brought their laws, language, and religion to the New World. In Lima, Peru, and in Mexico City, Mexico, universities were built in 1551. The first printing press in North America was set up in Mexico City in 1539.

De Soto and his party were the first Europeans to cross the Mississippi.

St. Augustine was the first European settlement in what is now the United States.

REVIEW

CHECK YOUR FACTS

1. Cortés conquered the Aztecs with a (large/small) force.
2. Who was the Aztec ruler when Cortés arrived?
3. What Spanish expedition found the Mississippi River?
4. What did the Spanish priests build?
5. Where were universities set up in Spanish America?
6. Where was the first printing press in North America?

THINK ABOUT IT

Was the part of the United States in which you live ever explored or settled by the Spanish?

Lesson 6: Other Europeans Come to North America

FIND THE WORDS

colony   Puritan
indentured servant

By the late 1500s, other European countries began to make discoveries in the New World. The French, the Dutch, and the English explored farther north than the Spanish. They began to settle North America. Soon, there were Spanish, French, Dutch, and English colonies on the continent. A **colony** is a group of people who settle in a distant land. In that land, they are still ruled by their parent country.

The French found furs and fish rather than gold. They explored areas that are now parts of Canada and the United States. Jacques Cartier (KAHR tee AY) led French groups that explored the Atlantic Coast and the St. Lawrence River in 1534–1535. Under Samuel de Champlain, the French founded a settlement at Quebec in 1608. Montreal was founded in 1641. French explorers traveled in canoes through the Great Lakes and down the Mississippi River.

As the French traveled, they set up small trading posts along their way. They traded for furs with the American Indians. These native peoples trapped the animals in the great forests that covered much of the continent. The French were also active in the Grand Banks off the coast of North America. There they caught huge amounts of fish. They dried their catch in the sun. Then they took the fish back to France. These activities brought the French a good profit.

Dutch explorers from the Netherlands sailed to the Middle Atlantic coast. Henry Hudson was an English captain who made an important voyage while working for the Dutch. Hudson explored the fine harbor that is now called New York Harbor. He also sailed up the Hudson River, which was named for him. Soon, the Dutch began founding settlements in that area. They made money in trade.

The English also wanted a share of the riches being made in the New World. The first English voyages to America took place soon after Columbus's discovery. In 1497, John Cabot, an Italian, led an English voyage that discovered Newfoundland. That large island, off the coast of North America, is now part of Canada.

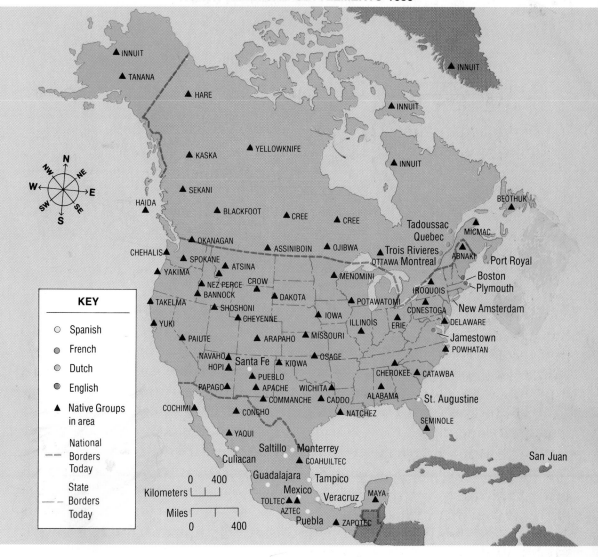

KEY

○ Spanish
◐ French
◑ Dutch
◉ English
▲ Native Groups in area
--- National Borders Today
-- State Borders Today

0   400
Kilometers

Miles
0   400

The first English settlement in the New World was organized by Sir Walter Raleigh in the 1580s. Raleigh sent three groups of colonists to Roanoke Island, now part of North Carolina. He named the area "Virginia." The first two groups of colonists were men. They went back to England. The third group included men, women, and children. These colonists simply disappeared. No one knows what happened to them. They are known as the "Lost Colony."

The fate of Raleigh's colony did not long discourage English settlement in the New World. Many English nobles and merchants had

La Salle was a French explorer. He led an exploration of the Mississippi River.

heard of the great amounts of gold being shipped to Spain from America. They soon learned that the French and Dutch were also making money in the New World. The English wanted wood and tar for building ships. They wanted to grow crops that could not be grown in England.

The merchants and nobles asked the English king to grant them land to settle. The king gave them land both south and north of the Dutch claims in North America. The merchants and nobles then formed companies that outfitted ships to carry settlers to the New World. There, they meant to start English colonies. You will learn about each of these colonies in the next chapter.

In the following years, many English people settled in North America. The trip to North America was hard and dangerous. And life in the colonies was hard and dangerous, too. Why were so many English people willing to face these dangers? For one thing, England had too many people. John Winthrop, a leader in the colonies, remembered how difficult life had been in England. He said that a human was "of less value among us than a horse or sheep." Most of the people in England were poor. Work was hard to find. Food, land, and shelter were getting very expensive. In the New World, land could be had for almost nothing. People who worked hard could make a good living.

Many people came to the colonies from English prisons. Some of these prisoners had been criminals. Others had been put in prison because they could not pay back money they owed. The English authorities were glad to be rid of them. They were accepted in the colonies because the new settlements needed workers.

Many homeless children were also sent to work in North America. In England, large numbers of poor children were living on London streets. Hundreds of these children were put on ships bound for the colonies. The children had nothing to say about this. But most people did not think it was wrong. They thought the children should be glad to do useful work in the New World.

Some American Indians of the Northeast lived in villages like this one.

STRANGE FACTS

Sir Walter Raleigh did not have much luck with his colonies. He sent one group of men to Roanoke Island in 1585. They soon sailed back to England. A second group was sent. All but 15 of them went back home, too. These 15 were never heard from again.

Raleigh sent a third group to America in 1587. This group included 17 women and 9 children. Within a month after the colonists landed, Virginia Dare was born. She was the first English child born in North America.

Virginia's grandfather, John White, returned to England. He had to get food and other supplies for the group. But England was being attacked by the Spanish Armada. This was a great fleet of ships. Not until 1590 was White able to get back to Roanoke Island. When he returned, the colonists had disappeared. The word *Croatoan* was carved on a post. No one knew for sure what the word meant. No one has ever found out what happened to the Lost Colony.

Some people left England for religious reasons. The **Puritans** (PYOOR uh tuns) wanted to "purify" the Church of England, which was very powerful. They believed that the church should not have rich buildings and ceremonies. It should be plain and simple. At that time, most European nations did not allow citizens to worship as they pleased. The Church of England gave the Puritans a great deal of trouble. Some Puritans were thrown into prison. As a result, some of them left England. Other religious groups left for similar reasons. They wanted to worship and live according to their beliefs.

Many of the people who wanted to come to the colonies could not afford to pay for the trip. One way to solve this problem was to come as an indentured servant. An **indentured** (in DEN churd) **servant** signed a contract, or indenture, with a company or a wealthy person. The servant agreed to work without pay for a set time. This was usually about 7 years. In return, the employer paid for the voyage and provided food and shelter for the servant. At the end of the 7 years, the servant was free.

We have seen that people came to North America for many different reasons. Some came in search of more freedom. Others were trying to escape poverty or even find riches. For most, the hardship and danger must have been worth the risk. European settlers continued to arrive throughout the seventeenth century, and the colonies steadily grew.

REVIEW

WATCH YOUR WORDS

1. A(n) ____ was a person who agreed to work in return for the trip to America.
   Puritan   colonist
   indentured servant

2. A(n) ____ is a person who settles in a distant land.
   Puritan   colonist
   indentured servant

CHECK YOUR FACTS

3. What two kinds of goods did the French obtain in North America?

4. Who explored New York Harbor?

5. What are some reasons people left England for the colonies?

THINK ABOUT IT

Do you live in a state that was ever part of a colony? Which colony?

CHAPTER REVIEW

WATCH YOUR WORDS

1. ____ are members of a person's family who lived long ago.
   Astronomers   Ancestors   Puritans

2. Symbols used in picture writing are ____ .
   hieroglyphics   pestles   adobes

3. Ancient peoples have left ____ of their culture.
   missions   colonies   evidence

4. A(n) ____ is a religious community.
   mission   colony   indenture

5. A(n) ____ is a group of people who settle in a distant land.
   mission   colony   adobe

CHECK YOUR FACTS

6. The first people came to America from Asia (all at once/gradually).

7. Name the three great American Indian cultures of Mexico.

8. Where was Tenochtitlán located?

9. What brought the great American Indian cultures to an end?

10. What were the pueblos made of?

11. Columbus (did/did not) believe he had found a new world.

12. Who led the Spanish conquest of Mexico?

13. Which group of explorers discovered the Grand Canyon?

14. Which group of explorers discovered the Mississippi River?

15. What European people explored the St. Lawrence River?

USE YOUR MAPS

16. Look at the map on page 68. What body of water was crossed by the early people who came from Asia to the Americas?

17. Look at the map on page 81. List three continents that were unknown to Europeans in 1492.

18. Look at the map on page 85. Who led the expedition that explored the west coast of Mexico?

19. Look at the map of North American settlements on page 89. Which American Indian groups lived near Santa Fe? What Spanish settlement was in the present-day southeastern United States?

20. What was the English settlement in the South in 1630? What were the two English settlements then in New England?

THINK ABOUT IT

21. Suppose Ireland was as close to Newfoundland as it is to Great Britain. Tell how the early history of the Americas might have been different.

22. Do the Maya remind you of any ancient people of the Old World? Who are they?

23. What would it have meant if Columbus had found Asia after sailing west for 33 days?

24. Many French people came to the New World in the years after 1492. Where would you expect to find their descendants living today?

25. Suppose the United States decided to start colonies in space. Who do you think would go to live there? What hardships would they face?

2 THE ENGLISH IN NORTH AMERICA

Lesson 1: The Founding of Virginia and Maryland

FIND THE WORDS

representative   burgess

In 1607, the Virginia Company founded the colony of Jamestown in Virginia. Jamestown was to be the first successful English colony in North America. One hundred and twenty men had signed on with the Company to set up this colony. Some of the men came from wealthy families. They were not used to working with their hands. Others were workers. They knew how to make useful things out of wood or iron. At first, there were no women in the colony.

Jamestown did not begin well. The colonists chose a swampy spot about 48 kilometers (30 miles) up the James River. The place was full of mosquitoes (muh SKEE tohz) that carried diseases. The water was salty and dirty. To add to these problems, winter was coming. The colonists had to have shelter and food. The supplies of food the colonists brought from England had quickly run out. But most of the men only wanted to search for gold. They did not want to clear fields, plant crops, or build homes. There was nobody to give orders about work. A few colonists did manage to build a small fort, some shelters, and a storehouse.

This is a drawing of Jamestown in 1607. Notice the ships on the left. They were called the *Discovery*, the *Susan Constant*, and the *Godspeed*. These ships brought colonists from England.

Among these colonists was Captain John Smith. He made friends with the local Powhatan (POW uh TAN) people through Pocahontas (POH kuh HON tus), the daughter of a chief. The Powhatan people supplied the colonists with food that first winter. Otherwise, all the colonists probably would have died. Even so, when spring came, only 40 of them were alive.

The following year, Captain Smith became the leader of the colony. More settlers arrived, including the colony's first women. Captain Smith made sure that everyone did his or her fair share of the work. He told the colonists,

"He who will not work, will not eat." Soon, the colonists put up more buildings and planted good crops. But Captain Smith had to go back to England. While he was gone, the settlers began to quarrel again. People stopped working. And so, during the winter of 1609–1610, the colonists had little food. Over 400 colonists died in that "starving time."

Soon after, Sir Thomas Gates arrived to serve as governor of the colony. Over the next few years, he made the colonists live under strict military rules. They were marched to the fields by the beat of a drum. Twice a day, they were

This old map shows Jamestown and other plantations along the James River.

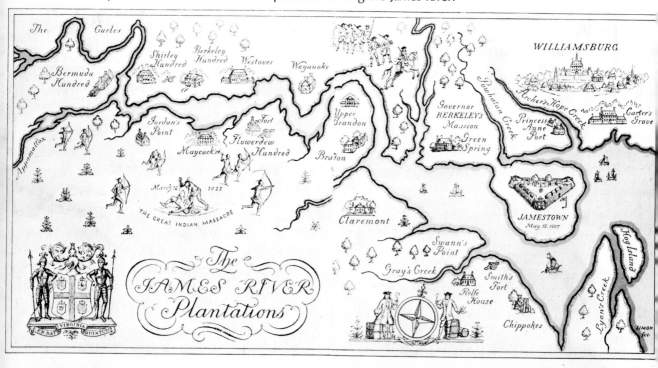

marched to church the same way. People who broke the rules or did not work were punished. In this way, the colony survived.

Life in Jamestown gradually improved. There were several reasons for this. In 1616, the Virginia Company decided to divide some of its land among the colonists. Each family was given land to farm. Once they were landowners, the colonists were willing to work very hard. There was no longer a need for strict rules.

At last, the colonists found a way to make money. A colonist named John Rolfe planted a new kind of tobacco. Virginia tobacco became popular in London. Soon, England was buying all the tobacco Jamestown could produce. It was so valuable, it was even planted in the streets of the colony! This new source of wealth pleased the owners of the Virginia Company. It also brought more settlers to Jamestown.

Among these settlers were women. Most were already married to male colonists. In 1614 John Rolfe got married, too, but not to an English woman. He married the American Indian princess Pocahontas. Then, in 1619, ships began to bring unmarried women from England to Jamestown. Most were poor women looking for a better life. The Company gave them a place to live and work until they married. Then the bridegroom repaid the Company for the cost of the bride's voyage. As more women came, family life became more settled. The colonists began to think of Jamestown as home.

Another thing that changed life in Jamestown was government. Before, only the governor of the colony and his council of advisers made the laws. Then, in 1619, the Virginia Company gave the white male landowners a voice in running the colony. These colonists elected representatives from among themselves. A **representative** (REP ri ZEN tuh tiv) is a person who is chosen to speak or act for a group. In the colony of Virginia, the elected representatives were called **burgesses** (BUR jis ez). The Virginia burgesses formed a group that helped make laws for the colony. This group was called the House of Burgesses. This was the start of self-government in America. But life in Virginia was still hard. Disease killed hundreds of people every year. Other colonists were killed when they came into conflict with American Indians. The Indians were becoming more and more angry as the English took their land.

In spite of these difficulties, the colony of Virginia began to grow. In addition, other colonies were founded in the South. Maryland

TIME LINE: 1607–1681

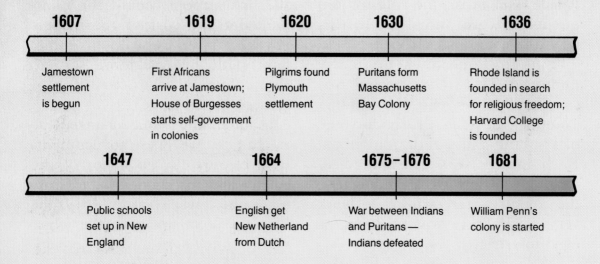

1607 Jamestown settlement is begun

1619 First Africans arrive at Jamestown; House of Burgesses starts self-government in colonies

1620 Pilgrims found Plymouth settlement

1630 Puritans form Massachusetts Bay Colony

1636 Rhode Island is founded in search for religious freedom; Harvard College is founded

1647 Public schools set up in New England

1664 English get New Netherland from Dutch

1675–1676 War between Indians and Puritans — Indians defeated

1681 William Penn's colony is started

was the first of these. In the years to come, the colonies of North Carolina, South Carolina, and Georgia would also be set up.

Maryland was founded in 1634, when 200 Roman Catholic settlers landed at Chesapeake Bay. The Calvert family had received this colony from the English rulers. The Calverts were Roman Catholics. They made Maryland a safe place for Catholics and for Protestants as well. The soil of the new colony was rich, and the climate was mild. Tobacco soon became an important crop.

REVIEW

WATCH YOUR WORDS

1. Define a *representative*.
2. How does a representative differ from a ruler?

CHECK YOUR FACTS

3. In what year was Jamestown founded?
4. What early leader said the colonists had to work if they wanted to eat?
5. What crop brought wealth to Jamestown?
6. With what group did self-government begin in Virginia?
7. What was the second permanent colony in the South?

THINK ABOUT IT

Why do you think most of the first Virginia colonists only wanted to search for gold?

Lesson 2: Life on the Southern Plantations

FIND THE WORDS

cash crop   indigo   planter
plantation   slave

In the Southern colonies, the main way of making a living was raising crops to sell. The South had large areas of rich soil. It had a mild climate. There were many months between the last frost of spring and the first frost of fall.

These conditions made it possible to produce large crops to sell to other countries, especially to England. A crop grown to be sold is called a **cash crop.** Tobacco was the main cash crop in the South. Two others were rice and **indigo** (IN duh goh), a blue dye taken from various plants. Much later, cotton became a cash crop.

The people who owned the farms on which cash crops were

This old drawing shows what a plantation was like. High on the hill is the owner's house. Below are other plantation buildings.

raised were called **planters.** Most planters were small farmers. They had little money and only a few workers to help them. A few planters were wealthy and owned large amounts of land. They were able to raise huge crops on their large farms. These large farms were called **plantations** (plan TAY shuns). To run their plantations, wealthy planters needed many, many workers.

In the beginning, most plantation workers were indentured servants. These included both Whites and Blacks. The first Africans arrived in Jamestown in 1619. Like all indentured servants, they worked until their contracts were over. Then they became free. Some became landowners, themselves. But as time passed, planters stopped using indentured workers. It was cheaper to use the Africans who were then being brought to the colonies as slaves. A **slave** is a person who is owned by another person.

These Black people were captured in parts of western Africa. There, they were put in chains and sold to slave traders. The slave traders brought them to America in ships. The conditions on these slave ships were horrible, and many of the Africans died. When the survivors arrived in America, they were sold to buyers

Rich planters used Africans as slaves to work on their plantations. Slaves worked long hours in the fields. These slaves are picking cotton.

WHERE WE ARE IN TIME AND PLACE

FROM THE LOST COLONY TO THE CONSTITUTION

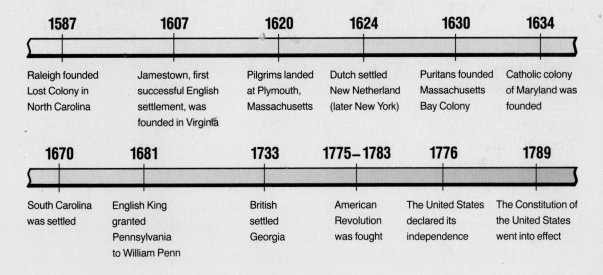

1587	1607	1620	1624	1630	1634
Raleigh founded Lost Colony in North Carolina	Jamestown, first successful English settlement, was founded in Virginia	Pilgrims landed at Plymouth, Massachusetts	Dutch settled New Netherland (later New York)	Puritans founded Massachusetts Bay Colony	Catholic colony of Maryland was founded

1670	1681	1733	1775–1783	1776	1789
South Carolina was settled	English King granted Pennsylvania to William Penn	British settled Georgia	American Revolution was fought	The United States declared its independence	The Constitution of the United States went into effect

THE THIRTEEN COLONIES ABOUT 1770

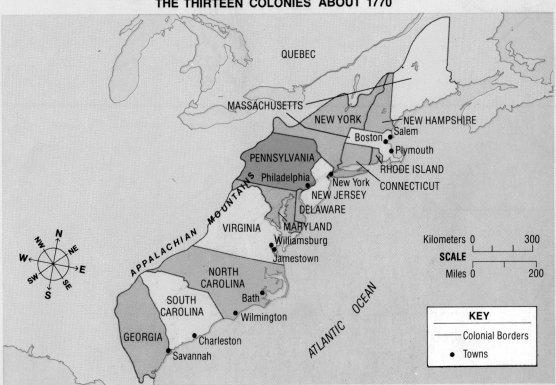

QUEBEC

MASSACHUSETTS

NEW YORK · NEW HAMPSHIRE

Boston · Salem

Plymouth

PENNSYLVANIA

RHODE ISLAND

Philadelphia · New York · CONNECTICUT

NEW JERSEY

DELAWARE

VIRGINIA · MARYLAND

Williamsburg

Jamestown

NORTH CAROLINA

Bath

SOUTH CAROLINA

Wilmington

GEORGIA · Charleston

Savannah

ATLANTIC OCEAN

APPALACHIAN MOUNTAINS

N NE E SE S SW W NW

Kilometers 0 ___ 300
SCALE
Miles 0 ___ 200

KEY
— Colonial Borders
● Towns

101

in slave markets. Usually, the buyer owned a slave for life.

After 1640, the colonies began to pass laws about slavery. Some laws declared that the children of slaves were also slaves. Other laws made it hard for any Black people to live as free men and women. By the 1700s, most Blacks in the Southern colonies were slaves. They did most of the work on the large plantations.

The planters tried to have almost everything needed on the plantation grown or made there. A small part of the land would be used to plant food for the planter's family and the slaves. The rest would be planted with tobacco, rice, or indigo to be sold for cash. After the harvest, the cash crop was prepared for sale on the plantation. Most plantations were near rivers and had their own docks. In this way, the crop could be loaded directly onto ships and sent to market.

In many ways, a plantation was like a small village. Life centered around the planter's house.

As the English colonies developed, people did many different kinds of work. Refer to this map as you study the English colonies.

THE BRITISH COLONIES ABOUT 1770

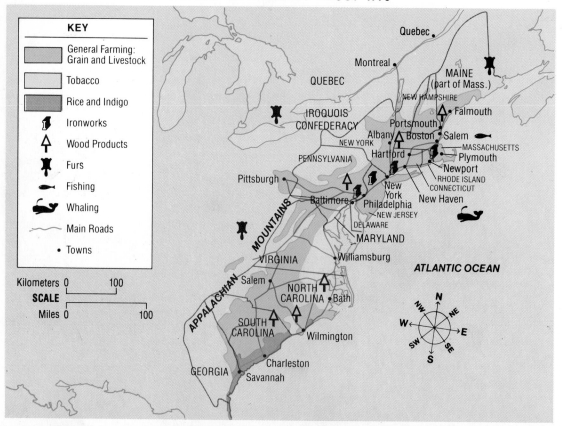

Often, this house was very large. But there were many other buildings nearby. There were stables for horses, a kitchen, laundries, and rooms for weaving and spinning. Sometimes, there was a schoolhouse for the planter's children. Sometimes, there was a mill for grinding grain. Farther away, often hidden behind trees, were slaves' cabins, storage buildings, and cattle pens.

George Mason, a Virginia planter, described how one plantation worked:

"My father had among his slaves carpenters, barrel makers, blacksmiths, leather tanners, shoemakers, spinners, weavers, and knitters. His woods supplied timber for the carpenters and barrel makers, and charcoal for the blacksmiths. His cattle were killed for his own use and for sale. They supplied skins for the tanners and shoemakers. His sheep gave wool for the weavers and spinners. His carpenters built and repaired all houses, barns, and stables on the plantation."

Slaves working in the fields brought in the crops. Slaves working at trades kept the plantation running smoothly.

REVIEW

WATCH YOUR WORDS

Find the word that completes the sentence. Choose words from the list below.

1. A(n) ___ is a person owned by another person.

2. Some plants yield a blue dye called ___.

3. A(n) ___ is grown to be sold.

4. The ___ owned the farms on which cash crops were raised.

5. Large farms were called ___.
cash crop   indigo   planters
plantations   slave

CHECK YOUR FACTS

6. Name three important crops grown in the Southern colonies.

7. What were most plantations like?

8. At first, what kind of workers were used on the plantation?

9. When did the first Africans arrive in Jamestown?

10. Name five different jobs that people on plantations did.

THINK ABOUT IT

People on plantations produced most of the things they needed. How was a plantation like a city of today? How was it different?

Lesson 3: The Founding of New England

In 1620, a tiny ship called the *Mayflower* sailed from England for the New World. Crowded together in the small ship were 102 passengers. Thirty-one passengers were children.

Half of the *Mayflower's* passengers were Pilgrims. The **Pilgrims** were a group of English Protestants. They believed that religious worship should be plain, simple, and strict. Their beliefs led them to separate from the Church of England. Thus, they were called **separatists** (SEP ur uh tists). In England, they had suffered because of their religious beliefs. So they had set sail for Virginia. There, they planned to start their own churches. They wanted to worship as they pleased.

After the *Mayflower* had sailed for 6 weeks, it ran into storms in the Atlantic. The ship was blown off course. Instead of arriving in Virginia, the Pilgrims landed in Massachusetts. They anchored their ship off the sandy coast of Cape Cod. For 4 weeks, most of the people stayed on the ship. Small groups set out to explore the area.

It was almost winter. The Pilgrim leaders knew that everyone's help was needed. Otherwise, the group would not survive. Since they were far from Virginia, they decided to stay there and set up their own government.

The Pilgrims wrote a now-famous agreement called the Mayflower Compact. They agreed that all the male Pilgrims would make the rules and laws for the settlement. They would pick their own leaders and make "just and equal laws." Women had few rights and were not allowed to sign the agreement. Still, this was the first time European colonists had decided to rule themselves.

The Pilgrims now sailed to an area Captain John Smith had explored some years before. Smith had named the place "Plymouth" (PLIM uth) on a map. People believe the Pilgrims landed at Plymouth Rock, a large rock on the coast. At Plymouth, the Pilgrims set up the first permanent English colony in New England.

During the first icy winter in Plymouth, half the *Mayflower's* passengers died. Many others became sick. The food the settlers had brought with them was almost used up. Winter was no time to plant a crop. Then, in early spring, an American Indian named Samoset (SAM uh SET) visited the Pilgrims. Samoset spoke English. He had learned the language from early explorers of the area. Samoset helped the Pilgrims communicate with the Wampanoag (WAM puh NOH ahg) people who lived 64 kilometers (40 miles) away.

That spring, the Wampanoag people showed the Pilgrims how to hunt wild turkey and deer. They showed the newcomers where to fish. They taught them how to plant corn and how to get sap from maple trees. The Pilgrims had a fine harvest of corn in the fall. And they were very thankful. They made a feast and invited the Wampanoag people who had helped them. This was the first Thanksgiving.

The next settlers to arrive in New England were another group of English Protestants called the Puritans. Like the Pilgrims, these people were very religious. However, they did not want to separate from the Church of England.

The Puritans received a charter from the English king to start the Massachusetts Bay Company. This **charter** was a paper that gave the Company the right to run the colony. It also listed the rules by which the Company would govern. The Puritans voted to take their charter with them to the New World. The charter and the government of the Company would be in Massachusetts. Then, the king could not so easily change the

The Pilgrims celebrated the first Thanksgiving with the Wampanoag people.

For many years, Puritans carried their guns to church. They feared attacks by American Indians.

charter or tell the Company what to do. In most other colonies, the charter and at least some of the government remained in England. So, from the beginning, the Puritans had more freedom to govern themselves than most early colonists had. Between 1630 and 1634, more than 10,000 Puritans came to Massachusetts. They settled eight small towns. The largest group founded the town of Boston.

REVIEW

WATCH YOUR WORDS

1. The ___ set up the first permanent English settlement in New England.
   Pilgrims   Puritans   Wampanoag

2. The English king gave the Massachusetts Bay Company a ___.
   compact   charter   government

3. People who leave one church to start a different church are called ___.
   Pilgrims   Puritans   separatists

CHECK YOUR FACTS

4. In what year did the Pilgrims come to America? Where did they land?

5. What important agreement did the male Pilgrims make?

6. Name three things the Wampanoag people taught the Pilgrims.

7. What was the main religious difference between the Pilgrims and the Puritans?

8. How did the Puritans achieve so much self-government?

THINK ABOUT IT

9. What might have happened if the Wampanoag people had not helped the Pilgrims?

10. How were the Pilgrims like the early settlers of Jamestown? How were they different?

Lesson 4: Religion in Colonial New England

John Winthrop, a Puritan leader, became the first governor of the Massachusetts Bay Colony. Winthrop sailed from England in 1630. Aboard the ship, he gave a sermon about his hopes for the new colony:

"We have joined together to find a place to live under a proper form of civil and church government. In cases like this, the group is more important than any individual. Our purpose is to improve our lives in order to serve the Lord.

"We have entered into a contract with God. Now if God should hear us and bring us in peace to the place we desire, then He has accepted our contract. And He will expect us to follow it strictly. If we sink into sinful ways, the Lord will surely break out in anger against us."

The Puritans wanted to set up a kind of holy city in the New World. In this model society, everyone would live according to the teachings of the church.

The government of the Massachusetts Bay Colony was founded on these principles. The rules of the government and the church were closely tied together. Only adult males who belonged to the church could vote. Only male Puritans could be elected to serve in the government. No person could speak against the church. Yet everyone had to pay taxes to support the church.

This made life difficult for some of the people who settled in the Massachusetts Bay Colony. People of other religious beliefs were sometimes called the "devil's agents." Even Puritans had problems. They could not speak out against a Sunday sermon, for example. Merchants were sometimes brought to court because, according to the church, they were charging unjust prices. Many people who believed or simply lived differently were forced to leave the colony.

Roger Williams, a minister, was one such person. Williams said that the government should have no power over religious matters. Some people in the Massachusetts Bay Colony agreed with him. Governor Winthrop was afraid Williams's ideas might

John Winthrop was the first governor of the Massachusetts Bay Colony.

divide the colony. So he forced Williams to leave.

In 1635, Williams and his followers moved south to the area around Narragansett (NAR uh GAN sit) Bay. They bought some land from the Narragansett Indians and started the colony of Rhode Island. In Rhode Island, colonists did not have to be church members in order to vote. Colonists did not have to support any one church. Rhode Island became the first colony to have full freedom of religion.

Anne Hutchinson was also one of the founders of Rhode Island. She, too, was forced to leave Massachusetts for her religious beliefs. Hutchinson arrived in Massachusetts with her husband and children in 1634. While she lived in Boston, she organized meetings for women. There, she discussed sermons that ministers had given.

Anne Hutchinson introduced her own religious ideas into these talks. She felt that each person should be free to think for herself or himself in religious matters.

This painting shows Puritans worshiping.

This was considered a dangerous idea in Massachusetts. Anne Hutchinson was put on trial in 1638. She was found guilty of questioning the authority of the ministers. So she and her family were forced to leave the colony. Roger Williams invited her to live in Rhode Island. She then started a settlement there.

At first, most of the settlers in New England had clustered around Boston. The people of Rhode Island were not the only ones, however, to settle other areas. Later, people began to move inland. Some settlers moved west to the fertile Connecticut River valley. Another group of Puritans from London started a colony at New Haven on Long Island Sound. In 1662, the English king granted a charter that brought these two groups together to form Connecticut. Colonists also moved north from Massachusetts to found New Hampshire. By 1679, there were four New England colonies—Massachusetts, Rhode Island, Connecticut, and New Hampshire.

Anne Hutchinson believed in religious freedom. The people of Massachusetts thought this was a dangerous idea. They made her leave the colony.

REVIEW

CHECK YOUR FACTS

1. Who was the first governor of the Massachusetts Bay Colony?

2. How were the government and the church closely tied together in Massachusetts?

3. Name two people who rebelled against Puritan rules.

4. Name the first colony to practice religious freedom.

5. What two areas were joined to form Connecticut?

6. List the four New England colonies in 1679.

THINK ABOUT IT

The Puritans had been treated badly in England because of their religious beliefs. When they were in power in New England, how did they treat those who disagreed with them?

Lesson 5: Education and Trade in Colonial New England

The church was the center of life in the towns of New England. On Saturday afternoon, everyone began to get ready for Sunday. All work stopped. Even cooking was not allowed until sundown on Sunday. People spent much time in prayer. On Sunday, everyone went to hear long sermons in church.

On other days, the church was often used as the town hall. Villagers would meet there to pass laws, make decisions, or solve community problems.

The Puritans thought everyone should be able to read the Bible. Because of this, education was very important in New England. As early as 1647, public schools had been set up. Every community with more than 50 people had to hire a schoolteacher. In class, the children learned the Puritan religion along with their lessons. Here is part of the alphabet from the *New England Primer.* This was often the children's first schoolbook.

In *Adam's* Fall
We Sinned all.
Thy Life to mend
This *Book* attend.
The *Cat* doth play
And after slay.

A *Dog* will bite
The Thief at night.
An *Eagle's* flight
Is out of sight.
The Idle *Fool*
Is whipped at
school.

Sometimes, a woman ran a school in her home. A school like this was called a **dame school.** *Dame* means "lady." The dame was the schoolmistress. Children would come to learn the alphabet, spelling, reading, and arithmetic. As the children studied, the teacher usually went about her household chores. Often, she was also teaching older girls to weave or spin. This was not unusual. It was said that New England people were used to doing "twenty different things well"!

The Puritans believed in hard work. And they had to work hard to live in New England. The soil was thin and rocky. The time between frosts, when crops could grow, was often short. These conditions made farming difficult.

In the spring and summer, farmers worked the rocky soil to raise wheat and corn. Sometimes, there was a little extra to sell, but not often. The farmers also bred cattle and pigs. During the long

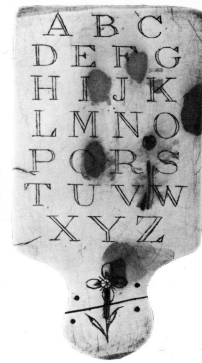

Left: Some Puritan women ran schools in their homes. *Right:* This is the kind of book a child used to learn to read.

winters, they trapped animals for fur and sometimes for food.

Because farming was so difficult, many New Englanders looked for other ways to make a living. Many turned to the sea. Thick forests supplied plenty of wood for building ships. Wood that can be used to build things is called **timber.** Timber sawed into boards or planks is called **lumber.** At first, most ships built in New England were used for fishing. The waters of the Atlantic Coast were some of the richest fishing grounds in the world. A **fishing ground** is a part of an ocean, river, or lake where many fish are found. Many New

Boston was a busy center of trade in 1764. This watercolor shows the harbor crowded with ships.

New England merchants bought fish and shipped it to the West Indies.
These men are packing salted herring into barrels for shipment.

Englanders made their living by catching fish or spearing whales. The fish were then dried and salted to keep them from spoiling. Before long, New England was selling dried, salted fish to other countries.

Sometimes, New Englanders would even sell their ships. With so much timber in the forests, they could easily build more. It was not long before shipbuilding became an important activity.

Some people built the ships out of timber. Others made ropes and sails for the ships. Still others made wooden barrels in which to pack fish, grain, and other goods. All these people were practicing different trades. **A trade** is a way of making a living by doing skilled work with the hands.

The word *trade* has another meaning. It also stands for the business of buying and selling goods. In time, most of the ships built in New England were used by merchants for trade. **A merchant** (MUR chunt) is a person who buys goods in order to sell them for a profit. The New England merchants bought fur, timber, cattle, and grain from the farmers. They bought fish from the fishers. Then they shipped fish and grain to the West Indies. There, they traded these foods for sugar. Then they sent the sugar to England, along with fur and timber. In England, they traded for manufactured goods. There, they filled their ships with woolen cloth, furniture, and glass. Then, they set sail for New England. In New England and the other colonies, the merchants sold the manufactured goods. Then, once again, they loaded their ships with local goods to sell outside the colonies.

Sometimes, New England merchants traded for molasses (muh LAS iz) in the West Indies. Molasses is a thick syrup that is left over after sugar is purified. New Englanders made the molasses into rum, an alcoholic drink. The rum was then used to trade for slaves in Africa. The slaves were sold in the West Indies and the Southern colonies.

By the 1700s, New England was becoming a region of merchants, sailors, fishers, small farmers, and people who practiced trades. It was a region with many different kinds of jobs.

REVIEW

WATCH YOUR WORDS

Match the word with the meaning.

1. dame school
2. fishing ground
3. merchant
4. trade
5. timber

A. the business of buying and selling
B. a school run in a woman's home
C. wood used for building
D. a person who buys and sells goods
E. a good place to catch fish

CHECK YOUR FACTS

6. What was the center of life in New England's towns?

7. Why was education important in New England?
8. What subjects did New England children study in school?
9. What kinds of things did the people of New England do to earn a living?
10. What kinds of things did New Englanders sell to other countries? What kinds of things did they buy in England?
11. What is molasses?

THINK ABOUT IT

Southern planters raised only a few crops. At the same time, New Englanders were farming, fishing, and trading. Which situation is more favorable? Why?

Lesson 6: The Founding of the Middle Colonies

FIND THE WORDS

port   patroonship
assembly   trial by jury
Quaker   breadbasket

New York, Pennsylvania, New Jersey, and Delaware were called the Middle Colonies. These four colonies were located in the middle, between the Southern colonies and the New England colonies. The Middle Colonies were founded later. They had fewer people than the other colonies had.

New York and New Jersey first belonged to the Dutch. The Dutch claimed the territory when Henry Hudson explored it for them in 1609. They named their colony New Netherland. In 1624, they set up their first permanent settlement at Fort Orange (later called Albany).

Then, in 1626, the Dutch bought Manhattan Island from the Manhattan Indians for goods worth $24.00. On the southern tip of this island, they founded a fur-trading post. They called it New Amsterdam. New Amsterdam was a good port. A **port** is a place where ships take on and unload people and goods. From New Amsterdam, Dutch ships sailed in all directions, trading goods. New Amsterdam was the capital of New Netherland for 38 years.

The Dutch traded for furs with American Indian peoples in the north. Then they shipped the furs down the Hudson River to New Amsterdam. Dutch ships also sailed along the Atlantic coast. They picked up food and rum from New England. They took aboard tobacco from the Southern colonies. Then, ships filled with these goods sailed from New Amsterdam to Europe and the West Indies. From Europe, Dutch ships brought tea, cloth, and other goods.

To help bring settlers to New Netherland, the Dutch set up a system of patroonships (puh TROON SHIPS). A patroon was someone who brought 50 settlers to New Netherland. Such a person was then given a large piece of land called a **patroonship.** The patroon got a share of everything the farmers raised on the patroonship. Patroons made all the laws. And a patroon acted as the final judge in almost all matters.

In 1644, the English captured New Netherland. The colony's

115

Dutch trading ships sailed out of New Amsterdam.

Dutch governor, Peter Stuyvesant (STY vuh sunt), had ruled harshly for 17 years. He swore that he would die before giving up to the English. In fact, he gave up quietly without firing a shot. The Dutch settlers were glad to be rid of Stuyvesant. New Netherland now belonged to the Duke of York, a brother of the English king. New Netherland and New Amsterdam got a new name. What do you think it was?

At first, few English people came to New York. The people of the colony had little voice in the government. Many English people did not want to go to a colony that did not have self-government. Without more settlers, the Duke of York made little profit. Also, the people already in the colony were asking for an assembly (uh SEM blee). The kind of **assembly** they wanted was a group of representatives. At last, the duke allowed an assembly to meet. The assembly immediately passed a Charter of Liberties. It gave the colonists the same rights as all English citizens. These included the right to **trial by jury.** This right applied to a person who was being tried in a court. Such a person could only be found guilty or not guilty by others who were his or her equals.

The Duke of York gave what is now New Jersey to two friends named Carteret and Berkeley. The rules they made for their colony included religious freedom.

In 1681, the king of England gave William Penn a large piece of land in America. It lay between New Jersey and Maryland. Penn

William Penn wanted a colony where all people could live together in peace.

received it in payment for a debt the king owed his father.

William Penn was a member of the Society of Friends. The Friends were called **Quakers** by others. They were a small group of Protestants whose beliefs caused them trouble wherever they lived. Friends believed that all people were equal and good. They lived simply. They refused to fight in wars against other human beings. William Penn wanted a colony where people of all nations and

Farms in the Middle Colonies produced large amounts of wheat, corn, and oats.

religions could live together in peace.

With high hopes, Penn and other Friends sailed for America. Penn's new colony was as large as England. There were many rivers and lots of rich soil. The land was covered with trees. Penn called his colony Pennsylvania, which means "Penn's woods." Pennsylvania then included the land that later became Delaware.

William Penn sent pamphlets to Europe describing his new colony. He told about its religious freedom. He described its excellent farmland. Thousands of English Friends came to Pennsylvania.

Many thousands of German farmers also arrived. There were Swedish, Finnish, French, and Dutch settlers as well. Later, people came from Scotland and Ireland.

Farms in Pennsylvania, New York, and New Jersey soon produced large amounts of wheat, corn, and oats. These crops were shipped to New England, the South, and the West Indies. The Middle Colonies became the breadbasket of the New World. A **breadbasket** is an area that produces large amounts of grain.

Several towns of the Middle Colonies became centers of business and trade.

REVIEW

WATCH YOUR WORDS

1. To encourage settlement, the Dutch set up a system of____.
   trials by jury   patroonships   assemblies

2. A(n) ____ is a group of representatives.
   colony   patroonship   assembly

3. Members of the Society of Friends are called____.
   Quakers   patroons   Dutch

4. The Charter of Liberties established the right to____.
   trial by jury   patroonship   assembly

5. A ____ is an area that produces a large amount of grain.
   colony   charter   breadbasket

CHECK YOUR FACTS

6. What European people first owned New York and New Jersey?

7. What did these Europeans name the colony and city of New York?

8. Why did few English people come to New York at first?

9. Who was the founder of the colony of Pennsylvania?

10. How did the Middle Colonies differ from the Southern and New England colonies? Name two ways.

THINK ABOUT IT

Which do you think settlers would prefer, to work on a patroonship or to own their own land? Why?

Lesson 7: Philadelphia

FIND THE WORDS

export   import   cobblestone
epidemic   bifocal   volunteer
postmaster

In the 1700s, most colonists were farmers. But cities were growing quickly. And this rapid growth was bringing a new way of life to the colonies.

Philadelphia grew quickly under the English Friends. Like New York, it became a center of trade. Farmers sent their crops to Philadelphia. From there, merchants **exported** them, or shipped them overseas for sale. More and more

This is a drawing of Chestnut Street in Philadelphia in 1799.

119

people came to Philadelphia from Europe. Soon there were ministers, bakers, bricklayers, and well-educated teachers. Skilled workers designed and made clothes, furniture, and houses. Barbers cut hair off people's heads. And wigmakers found fancy ways to put hair back on.

Printing presses and bookstores appeared throughout the city. Some of these were owned by women. Cornelia Bradford owned and ran the *Philadelphia Mercury*. This was the third-largest newspaper in the colonies. Trade with Europe kept people in touch with European ideas. Newspapers printed news from the Old World. Books were **imported,** or bought, from Europe. These books let Americans know what educated Europeans were thinking.

Growing cities like Philadelphia faced problems that people who lived in towns and on farms did not have. Heavy traffic from horse-drawn carriages forced the cities to surface their streets with **cobblestones,** or paving stones. Otherwise, the streets became rivers of mud when it rained. Or, they became clouds of dust in dry weather. With so many people living so close together, cities needed sewers. And they needed rules to protect people's health. Even so, diseases could spread quickly and

Early printing presses were run by hand.

widely, causing an **epidemic** (EP uh DEM ik). Epidemics of smallpox or typhoid (TY foid) often killed thousands of people. Fires were yet another danger. Crowded wooden buildings burned quickly. A fire could destroy whole sections of a city. Fire companies were needed.

One important Philadelphian did much to help meet the needs of the city. His name was Benjamin Franklin. Ben Franklin was

Bookstores in Philadelphia sold books imported from Europe.

Ben Franklin invented bifocal glasses.

born in 1706 to a poor family in Boston. When he was 17, Franklin sailed to Philadelphia. There, he became a printer. Later, he owned his own newspaper. He also published *Poor Richard's Almanac*. This little booklet gave information about the weather, farming, and business.

Ben Franklin was interested in science. In an experiment, he proved that lightning is electricity. He flew a kite on a wire during a storm. Lightning hit the kite and produced a spark at the end of the wire.

Ben Franklin had a curious and practical mind. He developed a stove that could heat a room better than an open fireplace. It came to be called the Franklin stove. He also invented **bifocal** (by FOH kul) glasses. With them, a person who needed glasses could read things up close and could also see things far away.

Franklin talked to people and wrote about the problems of the city. In this way, he helped bring street lighting and paving to Philadelphia. He organized fire companies made up of **volunteers** (VOL un TIRZ), people who gave their time for free. He also started the first hospital and lending library. People could borrow books from a lending library instead of buying them. In 1751, Franklin helped found the Academy of Philadelphia. This later became the University of Pennsylvania. Franklin also served Philadelphia as **postmaster,** the person in charge of the mails.

Franklin learned a great deal about all the colonies and about Europe. He was loved and admired by many colonists. He became a representative for several colonies in London. Well-informed leaders like Benjamin Franklin would play an important role when the colonies broke away from Great Britain.

REVIEW

WATCH YOUR WORDS

1. The person in charge of the mails is the____.
   volunteer   postmaster   merchant

2. ____give their time for free.
   Volunteers   Postmasters
   Merchants

3. The rapid spread of a disease over a wide area is a(n)____.
   bifocal   typhoid   epidemic

4. ____ glasses let one see things up close and far away.
   Bifocal   Typhoid   Franklin

5. To buy goods from abroad is to ____ them.
   volunteer   export   import

CHECK YOUR FACTS

6. What sort of work did most colonists do in the 1700s?

7. In what way was Philadelphia like New York?

8. How did the colonists learn about what was going on in Europe?

9. List some of the problems of colonial cities.

10. Where did Benjamin Franklin live for most of his life? Name two things he invented.

THINK ABOUT IT

Imagine that you lived in colonial times. Would you have preferred living on a farm or in a city? Give reasons for your answer.

CHAPTER REVIEW

WATCH YOUR WORDS

1. The House of Burgesses was a group of ___ .
   slaves   Pilgrims   representatives

2. A blue dye called ___ was produced in the colonial South.
   molasses   cobblestone   indigo

3. The English separatists who founded Plymouth were the ___ .
   Quakers   Pilgrims   Puritans

4. A ___ is a person who buys goods in order to sell them for a profit.
   merchant   patroon   planter

5. To sell goods abroad is to ___ them.
   volunteer   export   import

CHECK YOUR FACTS

6. What was the first successful English colony in North America? When was it founded?

7. To what religious group did many early settlers of Maryland belong?

8. What were the differences between indentured servants and slaves?

9. What important agreement did the Pilgrims make?

10. How did the Pilgrims and Puritans differ?

11. Who was John Winthrop?

12. What did colonial New Englanders do on Sunday?

13. Name the four Middle Colonies.

14. What European people founded the colony that later became New York?

15. What was the main city in the colony of Pennsylvania?

KNOW YOUR PEOPLE

Match the name with the clue.

16. Cornelia Bradford
17. Anne Hutchinson
18. William Penn
19. Pocahontas
20. Captain John Smith
21. Peter Stuyvesant

A. led the Jamestown colony.
B. was a founder of Rhode Island.
C. was the governor of New Netherland.
D. founded the colony of Pennsylvania.
E. owned the *Philadelphia Mercury*.
F. married the colonist John Rolfe.

USE YOUR MAP

22. Look at the map of the British colonies on page 102. In 1770, how did most colonists make a living?

23. What barrier seems to have blocked westward movement?

24. What colony had two separate parts?

25. In what four colonies was tobacco grown?

26. Where were rice and indigo grown?

THINK ABOUT IT

27. Suppose you were founding a colony in the New World. List some rules you would make to guide it through the beginning.

28. How did religion affect the founding of the Southern colonies, New England, and the Middle Colonies?

29. Why was the House of Burgesses so important?

UNIT REVIEW

WATCH YOUR WORDS

Use the words below to fill in the blanks. Use each term only once.

adobe	colonies	missions	Quakers
assembly	epidemics	patroonships	slaves
bifocal	exported	Pilgrims	temples
Burgesses	imported	plantations	Timber
cash crops	indentured servants	postmaster	trade
charter	Merchants	Puritans	volunteer

Before the first Europeans arrived, American Indians had built great ___ in Central America. Farther north, American Indians built houses of___. When the Spanish came, their priests founded ___ . Other European nations soon set up ___ in the New World.

Jamestown was the first successful English colony. There, self-government began in English America with the House of ___ . Soon, Southern planters were growing ___ like tobacco, rice, and indigo on large farms called___. At first,___ did the work. Later,___ were brought in from Africa.

In New England, the___came to Plymouth and the___to Massachusetts Bay. The Bay Colony brought its ___ from England.

New England had a varied economy. ___ from the forests was used to make ships for fishing. ___ also used ships for ___ in North America, the West Indies, Africa, and England.

New Netherland had large pieces of land called ___ . After the English took over, the Duke of York finally allowed a(n) ___ to meet. Pennsylvania was settled by members of the Society of Friends, also called ___ . Philadelphia, like New York, became a trading center. There, goods were ___ and ___ . Cities had problems with___of disease. In Philadelphia, Benjamin Franklin invented ___ glasses and founded ___ fire companies. He was also the___.

CHECK YOUR FACTS

1. How did people first reach North America?
2. Name three great American Indian cultures of Mexico.
3. Where was Tenochtitlán?
4. Who were probably the ancestors of the Pueblo people?
5. How did the first Americans get the name *Indians*?
6. How did America gets its name?
7. Who led the Spanish conquest of Mexico?
8. Coronado (did/did not) find cities of gold.
9. Besides Spain, what three European nations explored and settled North America?
10. What organization founded the colony of Jamestown?
11. Name an important early leader of Jamestown.
12. What family founded Maryland?
13. Name three cash crops of the Southern colonies.
14. What two groups of English Protestants founded New England?

15. Who was the first governor of the Massachusetts Bay Colony?

16. What colony was founded by Roger Williams and Anne Hutchinson?

17. Why was education important to the Puritans?

18. Who gave the Dutch their claim to New Netherland?

19. What religious group settled the colony of Pennsylvania?

20. Name a very important leader of Philadelphia in the 1700s.

CLOSE THE MAP GAP

21. Draw a map of North America. Show the areas of Spanish, French, Dutch, and English settlement.

22. Add England and the West Indies to your map. Use red arrows to show the patterns of New England's trade.

23. Use green arrows to show the patterns of Dutch trade starting from New Netherland.

USE YOUR MAPS

24. Look at the map on page 81. What continents did the Europeans know about in 1492?

25. Look at the map on page 85. What explorer reached Mexico City? What explorer crossed the Mississippi River? Who crossed the Rio Grande?

26. Look at the map of North American settlements on page 89. What American Indian group lived in what became New York? What group lived in Florida?

27. Look at the map of the British colonies on page 102. Where were fishing and whaling important?

THINK ABOUT IT

28. Why do farming peoples tend to have more advanced cultures than hunting peoples?

29. Why was the discovery and use of metal so important to many ancient peoples?

30. Do you think the New World should have been named *Columbia?* Why or why not?

31. Unlike the Spanish, the English did not find gold in their colonies. What effects do you think this had on the British colonies?

32. Why do you think slavery was not widespread north of Maryland?

TRY SOMETHING NEW

33. Write an advertisement in which you try to get Europeans to come to the New World. Stress the disadvantages of remaining in Europe and the advantages of a new life in America.

34. Draw a map of a plantation. Show the main house, the other buildings, the slave quarters, the fields, and a river and dock. Label each item.

35. Imagine that you are on trial in colonial Massachusetts because of your religious beliefs. List some arguments you would use to defend yourself.

PUT IT ALL TOGETHER

36. Make a chart entitled "The British Colonies." Down the left side, list the main colonies. Across the top, list important facts. These should include the following: date the colony was founded, founding group, religion, economy, main towns. Then add any other categories that you think are important.

1 THE STRUGGLE FOR INDEPENDENCE

Lesson 1: Trouble in British America

FIND THE WORDS

revolution   tax   Parliament
raw material
manufactured goods   smuggle

In the 1750s, a British traveler wrote these words about the American colonies: "There are so many differences among the Amer-

icans! There are big differences in way of life, religion, and wealth. If the Americans are left to themselves, they will be fighting each other from one end of the country to the other."

But what the British traveler did not know was that the American colonists had even bigger differences with Britain. Twenty-five

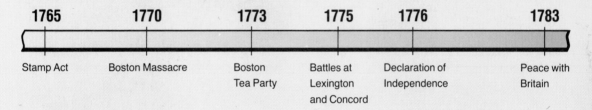

1765	1770	1773	1775	1776	1783
Stamp Act	Boston Massacre	Boston Tea Party	Battles at Lexington and Concord	Declaration of Independence	Peace with Britain

years later the American colonies joined together and declared themselves free of British rule. Few Americans wanted war. But they could not find a peaceful way to solve their problems with the British government.

The American colonists fought and won a war called the American Revolution. A **revolution** is a war in which the people of a country overthrow the government. The Americans then started a new government and a new nation called the United States of America.

Why did the colonists take such serious steps? The colonists' main complaint had to do with the **taxes** they had to pay to Britain. These were amounts of money added to the price of goods coming into or out of the colonies. The colonists had not agreed to pay these taxes. All taxes were set by the British **Parliament,** the law-making group. But Parliament had no American representatives in it.

The Americans would not accept "taxation without representation." "We have been making our own laws for almost 100 years," said the Americans. "Now Parliament wants to make laws for us."

Britain passed laws taxing sugar, cloth, wine, and other goods. Then, in 1765, Parliament passed the Stamp Act. This law said that the colonists had to buy tax stamps. These stamps had to be pasted on all newspapers, birth certificates, wills, and other important papers. Many Americans became very angry about this tax. . They refused to pay it. They warned others not to pay it. Some Americans burned the tax stamps when they arrived from Britain. Others chased the tax collectors out of town. Finally, the colonies joined together and sent a message to Britain. They asked that the stamp tax be stopped.

The British did not agree. Britain had fought a long war with France. Part of this war had been

The colonists refused to buy these tax stamps.

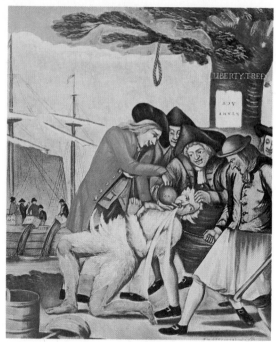

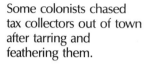

Some colonists chased tax collectors out of town after tarring and feathering them.

fought in the American colonies. It was called the French and Indian War. It seemed fair to the British that the American colonies should help pay for it.

The British government did not want to use taxes only to raise money. Some taxes were also meant to encourage the colonies to trade with Britain and not with other countries. Britain, like other European countries, looked on its colonies as sources of wealth. The British wanted the colonies to produce raw materials. A **raw material** is a product that has not been improved by manufacturing. The colonies were to sell raw materials only to Britain. And, in turn,

the colonies were to buy all of their manufactured goods from Britain. **Manufactured goods** are products made in factories with machines. This trade would help make British manufacturers and merchants, and Britain itself, rich.

However, the colonies did not do exactly what the British government wanted. New England, in particular, did not produce many raw materials. The New Englanders often traded with other countries. Both New England and the Middle Colonies produced some manufactured goods. The South was the closest to what Britain wanted. But many Southerners were unhappy. They felt the British paid low prices for raw materials and charged high prices for manufactured goods. Many Southerners were deeply in debt to British merchants.

In the end, the Stamp Act could not be enforced. Britain did away with it in 1766. But Parliament wanted to show that it had the right to tax the colonies. So it placed a tax on tea, glass, and other goods. It also said Americans could buy tea only from Britain. Many Americans stopped drinking tea rather than pay the tax on it. Some continued to bring it in from countries other than Britain. They had to **smuggle** it in, or sneak it past the authorities.

The British king was furious. He tried to force the colonies to obey. British soldiers were sent to the colonies to search for smuggled goods. Feelings among the colonists had been divided. There were still many who did not question Britain's right to pass these tax laws. But few Americans liked

This engraving shows the British firing on colonists during the Boston Massacre. The engraving was done by Paul Revere.

having British soldiers searching their homes and stores.

Small fights broke out between the soldiers and Americans in the cities. In March of 1770, a crowd in Boston began to poke fun at some soldiers. Some of the colonists threw stones. The soldiers became angry and fired their guns into the crowd. Five Americans were killed. It was a terrible event that the colonists called the Boston Massacre. As a result of the Boston Massacre, feelings became more tense. The colonists would not easily forget that Americans had been killed by the British.

Patrick Henry was one of the first Americans to speak in favor of a revolution.

REVIEW

WATCH YOUR WORDS

1. ____are made in a factory.
   Taxes   Manufactured goods
   Raw materials

2. ____have not been improved.
   Imports   Manufactured goods
   Raw materials

3. In a ____, the people overthrow the government.
   Parliament   revolution   tax

4. Parliament added____to goods.
   smuggling   revolution   taxes

5. To ____ goods is to sneak them past the authorities.
   smuggle   manufacture   tax

CHECK YOUR FACTS

6. What is the war the colonists fought against Britain called?

7. What was the main problem between Britain and the colonies?

8. When was the Stamp Act passed by Parliament?

9. What did Parliament do after it ended the stamp tax?

10. What important event took place in March 1770?

THINK ABOUT IT

The British government wanted the American colonies to help pay for their own defense. The colonists wanted to be taxed only by themselves. Which side do you think was right? Why?

Lesson 2: The American Revolution Begins

FIND THE WORDS

quarter   Continental Congress
boycott

Late in 1773, something happened in Boston that had two important results. It hardened the feelings of the British against the Americans. It also united the colonists more than ever before.

In December, British ships entered Boston harbor loaded with tea. The Americans tried to send it back, but this was not allowed. The British tea was cheaper than the Dutch tea the Americans usually smuggled into the colonies. But it had a tax on it. If the Americans bought the British tea, it would mean that they agreed that Britain could tax them. Some of the people of Boston decided to protest against this tax.

On the night of December 16, 1773, they dressed up like American Indians with feathers and war paint. They climbed aboard the ships and broke open all 342 chests of tea. Then they threw the tea into the harbor. As they worked through the night, a crowd watched from the shore. There was no damage to the ships or any other trouble. One man wrote, "It was the stillest night that Boston enjoyed for many months." The British, however, were angered by what was called the Boston Tea Party.

The Boston Tea Party was a protest against the tax on tea.

Now the British government decided to punish Massachusetts. It closed the port of Boston to all ships. Parliament passed laws that forced the colonists to **quarter** the British troops. This meant the colonists had to let the troops stay in their homes. These things made other colonies worry. If Britain could punish Massachusetts, it could do the same to them.

In September of 1774, representatives from all the colonies met in Philadelphia to talk about the problem. This was the first meeting of the **Continental Congress.** The members decided to support the city of Boston. They agreed to **boycott,** or stop buying, British goods. A boycott—a refusal to use or buy something—is a form of peaceful protest. The Continental Congress also agreed to raise a volunteer army. The volunteers were supposed to protect the colonies if Britain used force to break the boycott.

In April of 1775, British soldiers were ordered to march out of Boston. They were to take guns and supplies the colonists had stored near the towns of Lexington and Concord. On the night of April 18, Paul Revere and William Dawes learned that British soldiers were lined up along the Charles River. They rode all night to warn the towns.

In Lexington, a group of armed Americans waited on the village green. Soon, the British soldiers were facing them, only a few yards away. A shot was fired—no one knows by whom. Eight Amer-

The colonists objected to British troops being quartered in their homes.

This painting shows Americans fighting the British at Lexington. The battles at Lexington and Concord started the American Revolution.

icans were killed. At Concord, farmers shot back at the British soldiers. The British soldiers had a hard time returning to Boston that night. All along the way, farmers fired on them from behind rocks and trees.

With the battles at Lexington and Concord, the American Revolution had begun.

REVIEW

WATCH YOUR WORDS

1. Parliament forced the colonists to ___British troops.

   quarter   smuggle   boycott

2. The colonists agreed to ___ British goods.

   quarter   import   boycott

CHECK YOUR FACTS

3. What were the two important results of the Boston Tea Party?

4. What two things did the Continental Congress decide to do to support Boston?

5. Name the two Massachusetts towns in which the American Revolution began.

THINK ABOUT IT

Do you think that destroying the tea in Boston was the right thing to do? Why, or why not?

Lesson 3: War and Independence

FIND THE WORDS

trench   barricade   grenadier
independence   declaration

The Second Continental Congress met in Philadelphia in May of 1775. Samuel and John Adams of Massachusetts, Benjamin Franklin of Philadelphia, and Thomas Jefferson of Virginia were among the representatives. The colonists had not yet decided to break away from Britain. But they realized they needed a regular army to defend themselves against the British soldiers. They also needed a leader to raise and train such an army. George Washington of Virginia had served as a colonel in the French and Indian War. The members of Congress respected his military experience. They chose him to be commander in chief of the new Continental Army.

Before Washington could take command of the army, he heard the news of the first major battle. In June 1775, British ships had arrived in Boston harbor with more troops. A battle began when 3000 American volunteers came to the defense of Boston.

The Americans took up positions near a place called Bunker Hill. From there, they could watch the ships in the harbor. The night before the battle, the Americans dug **trenches,** or defensive ditches. They also set up **barricades,** defensive barriers. And they hid behind bushes and trees to stop the British from going around behind the barricades.

The next day, three British generals led 2000 soldiers against the Americans. The British soldiers marched shoulder to shoulder. Their best fighters, called **grenadiers** (GREN uh DIRZ), were in

The Battle of Bunker Hill proved that Americans could stand up to the British.

Left: Deborah Sampson joined the army disguised as a man.
Right: Molly Pitcher fought at the Battle of Monmouth.

the lead. The British thought that by attacking in such large numbers, they would make the Americans afraid. They hoped that the Americans would give up. The fighting began and went on all day. The Americans did not give up. When they ran out of bullets, they loaded their guns with scraps of metal, glass, and rocks. Many soldiers on both sides were killed or wounded.

Still, the British had better guns and more bullets. At day's end, they won the Battle of Bunker Hill. But the Americans won the glory. This battle made it clear to everyone that the Americans would not be easy to beat.

One of the Americans who fought at Bunker Hill was a Black man named Salem Poor. Poor was later praised for his bravery by several of his officers. About 5000

Black Americans served in the American army during the Revolutionary War.

Women also fought in the Revolution. Deborah Sampson joined the army disguised as Robert Shurtleff. She was 20 years old. She fought in several battles and was wounded in a battle near Tarrytown, New York. Her identity was discovered when she was put in a hospital in Philadelphia. Margaret Corbin fought beside her husband in a battle at Harlem Heights in New York in 1776. When her husband was killed, Margaret Corbin began firing his cannon. She fought with great bravery until she was wounded three times. Other women also helped the army.

By the middle of 1776, it seemed clear that Britain would never give the colonies the rights they wanted. Members of the Second Continental Congress decided that the colonies should declare their **independence.** That meant they would be free from British rule. This would be done in a document called a **declaration.** This document would give the reasons why the colonies wanted to be independent. On July 4, 1776, the Declaration of Independence was approved by the representatives of the colonies.

Throughout 1775 and 1776, George Washington and his army had many problems. There were not enough supplies. Tired and hungry Americans were fighting fresh and well-equipped British troops. The Continental Army lost several battles. George Washington was desperate. He wrote to Congress: "Ten more days will put an end to the existence of our army." By the middle of December 1776, the war seemed lost.

Then, on Christmas night, 1776, Washington led a surprise attack. He and his soldiers crossed the freezing Delaware River while the enemy were celebrating the holiday. The plan worked. The Americans defeated the enemy soldiers at Trenton and Princeton in New Jersey. At last, the Americans had a reason to be hopeful.

REVIEW

WATCH YOUR WORDS

1. The____were British soldiers.
   barricades   continentals
   grenadiers

2. A____is a defensive ditch.
   barricade   trench   grenadier

3. A____is a defensive barrier.
   barricade   trench   declaration

CHECK YOUR FACTS

4. Who was chosen to command the Continental Army?

5. Where was the first major battle of the war?

THINK ABOUT IT

The Americans lost most of the major battles of the Revolution, yet they won the war. What are the reasons for this?

Lesson 4: An American Victory

FIND THE WORD

treaty

In 1777, the Americans had one of their biggest victories. General Burgoyne, a British officer, tried to capture the Hudson Valley of New York. His plan was to cut off New England from the rest of America. Then Britain could win the war easily. Burgoyne marched his army south from Canada. He was to be joined by British troops from New York City, led by General Howe. Burgoyne's army was large and slow. The British had trouble moving their heavy equipment along the winding, hilly roads in the wilderness. The Americans, led by Horatio Gates and others, made the going harder. They chopped down trees to block the roads. They destroyed bridges. The colonists fought like the American Indians. They attacked in small groups. They fired at the British from hiding places in the forest. The British were not used to fighting this way. They were angry and confused. When the British reached Saratoga, they were surrounded by Americans, most of whom they could not see.

Americans fought part of the Revolution at sea.

139

THE REVOLUTIONARY WAR

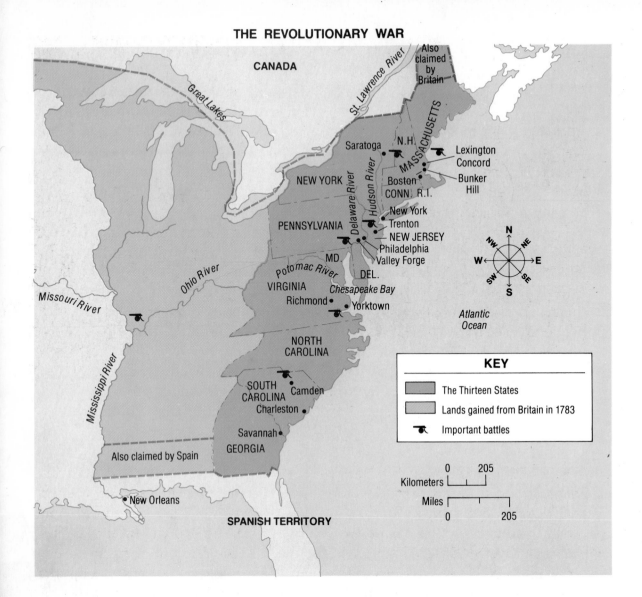

CANADA

Also claimed by Britain

St. Lawrence River

Great Lakes

MASSACHUSETTS

N.H.

Saratoga

Lexington
Concord

Boston
Bunker Hill

NEW YORK

CONN. R.I.

Hudson River

Delaware River

New York
Trenton
NEW JERSEY
Philadelphia
Valley Forge

PENNSYLVANIA

MD.

Ohio River

Potomac River

DEL.

Chesapeake Bay

VIRGINIA

Richmond

Yorktown

Missouri River

NORTH CAROLINA

Atlantic Ocean

Mississippi River

SOUTH CAROLINA

Camden

Charleston

Savannah

GEORGIA

Also claimed by Spain

New Orleans

SPANISH TERRITORY

N NE E SE S SW W NW

KEY

The Thirteen States

Lands gained from Britain in 1783

Important battles

Kilometers 0 205

Miles 0 205

After fierce fighting, Burgoyne surrendered in October 1777. Howe's army never arrived to help. On his own, General Howe had decided to capture Philadelphia instead.

The victory at Saratoga was a turning point for the Americans. As a result of this battle, France agreed to join the war against Britain. France had a strong army and navy.

Howe's troops spent the winter of 1777–1778 in Philadelphia. They were warm and well fed. Washington and his soldiers did not have such an easy winter. Only 32 kilo-

Washington and his army suffered from cold and hunger at Valley Forge.
Here, Washington reviews his ragged soldiers.

meters (20 miles) away, in Valley Forge, they suffered terrible cold and hunger. The men did not have enough warm clothes. Many were barefoot. Over 3000 died that winter from cold and disease. The women who traveled with the army tried to find food for the soldiers. They nursed the sick. They sewed and washed clothes. They buried the dead. During this "winter of despair," many soldiers lost heart and went home. But Washington did not give up. He continued to drill his soldiers. By spring, the worst had passed.

In 1778, the tide turned in favor of the Americans. The French navy captured British ships on their way to North America. This made it hard for the British to get fresh troops and supplies. Captain John Paul Jones won a series of naval victories over the British. In addition, George Rogers Clark led an army to victory against the British in the Ohio Valley.

Now the British sent their largest army into the South. In 1780, General Cornwallis and about 8000 British troops invaded the South.

In the summer of 1781, Cornwallis moved his army to Yorktown, Virginia. This was a costly mistake. Yorktown was surrounded by water on three sides. The French navy defeated the British fleet that was guarding the coast. The British could neither get supplies nor escape by sea.

American and French troops moved in. Cornwallis was trapped. His soldiers were exhausted. On October 19, 1781, Cornwallis surrendered his army to George Washington at Yorktown.

This was the final defeat for Britain. The war in America had lasted 6 years. The British were

In this painting, a British fort surrenders to George Rogers Clark.

At Yorktown, American and French troops fought together to defeat the British. This painting shows General Rochambeau of France at Yorktown.

tired of it. King George III and Parliament decided to bring the soldiers home.

Two years after the surrender at Yorktown, the British and the Americans made a formal peace. They signed a **treaty,** or agreement, in Paris, France, in 1783. The United States of America had won its independence.

REVIEW

CHECK YOUR FACTS

1. Why was the American victory at Saratoga so important?
2. What was the winter of 1777–1778 like for General Howe's army? For General Washington's army?
3. Who led the Americans to victory in the Ohio Valley?
4. What was the final British defeat?
5. When and where was the peace treaty signed?

THINK ABOUT IT

Do you think the Americans could have won the Revolutionary War without French help? Why, or why not?

Lesson 5: The Leaders of the Revolution

FIND THE WORDS

Committee of Correspondence

The American Revolution did not take place only on the battlefield. Before the war and during it, Americans needed leaders. These leaders and their ideas helped shape what people thought and did about the British. The leaders helped people make up their minds about new ideas such as independence. Some wrote well or made good speeches. Others stood out because of their personal qualities, such as firmness, courage, and fairness.

Samuel Adams of Boston was one of the leaders of the Revolution. Samuel Adams wanted to unite the colonies against the British. He wrote articles and made speeches. He did everything he could to make the colonists act. Adams started a **Committee of Correspondence** in Massachusetts. This group wrote to similar groups in other colonies. These committees shared news about the British and told each other of their own plans. Adams was also the head of a group of Americans called the Sons of Liberty. The Sons of Liberty did many things to protest British laws and taxes. One such protest was the Boston Tea Party. They also held parades. They sang songs and danced around the Liberty Tree, a big elm near Boston. Sometimes, they would coat a British official with tar and feathers. Not everyone agreed with Samuel Adams and his followers. Many people thought they went too far.

Many women worked against British rule. They formed boycott

Samuel Adams was one of the leaders of the American Revolution.

groups against merchants who supported Britain. They formed anti-tea leagues. These groups tried to get people to use drinks made from other plants in place of tea. Some women organized the Daughters of Liberty. The Daughters of Liberty joined the Sons of Liberty in street marches and meetings. They read newspapers out loud to people who could not read. Groups of women would spin yarn and weave cloth. They used the cloth to make uniforms and bandages for soldiers.

Mercy Warren was a writer of poems and plays who used her pen against the British. She made fun of them in her plays. She criticized the British in letters to her friend Abigail Adams. Then she had the letters printed in the newspapers for all to read. Once she wrote: "Be it known unto Britain even American daughters are politicians and patriots. They

In this painting, Americans raise a liberty pole. It was a symbol of liberty.

will aid the good work with their efforts."

Thomas Paine was another patriot who used his pen against the

Left: Mercy Warren was a writer who published letters criticizing the British.
Right: In Common Sense, Thomas Paine listed reasons why America should be independent.

145

John Adams felt that a declaration of independence should be written.

British. In January 1776, he published a small book called *Common Sense.* In it, he listed reasons why the colonies should be independent. He wrote that Britain could no longer rule the colonies. Britain was too far away. North America was too big to be ruled by a little island. Paine said other countries would trade with the colonies as long as "eating is the custom in Europe." Because *Common Sense* was well written, many people read it. It helped thousands of people decide that the colonies must be independent.

John Adams, a cousin of Samuel Adams, was a good speaker and writer. He worked hard and long for what he believed in. John Adams spoke out early and often against the British. As a young lawyer in Boston, he wrote newspaper stories and petitions against British laws and taxes. After the Stamp Act, he decided that independence was the only way to solve the colonies' problems. Together with Benjamin Franklin, he convinced the Continental Congress that a declaration of independence should be written.

Abigail Adams asked her husband to "remember the ladies" in the country's new laws.

Abigail Smith Adams was married to John Adams. She had heard that the Continental Congress might declare independence. So Abigail Adams wrote the following letter to her husband.

"I long to hear that you have declared independence. And by the way, in the new code of laws . . . I wish you would remember the ladies, and be more generous . . . to them than your ancestors. Do not put such unlimited power in the hands of husbands. Remember, all men would be tyrants if they could. If particular care and attention is not paid to the ladies, we are determined to stir up a rebellion and will not regard ourselves as bound by any laws in which we had no voice or representation."

The person who wrote the Declaration of Independence was Thomas Jefferson. A lawyer and planter from Virginia, Jefferson was also a fine writer. He believed that people could govern themselves and that they had a right to do so. The declaration said "all men are created equal." It said they have certain rights, given by God, which no one can take away. Among these rights, it continued, are "life, liberty, and the pursuit of happiness." The Declaration went on to say that governments draw their powers from the peo-

Thomas Jefferson wrote the Declaration of Independence.

ple. When government is no longer fair and just, it said, the people have a right to change it. The Declaration of Independence gave people faith that independence was fair and right. They needed that faith during the years of war.

Once the fighting had started, Americans had no greater leader than George Washington of Virginia. Congress chose him to lead the army because he had more military experience than most Americans. It was also hoped that he would help bring the American people together.

Everywhere, people admired Washington's courage and steadiness. These qualities were worth a

George Washington was a great leader. Even after the worst defeats, he would not surrender. This gave Americans the courage to keep fighting.

great deal to a people at war. Washington's job was difficult. He had to make an army out of groups of shopkeepers and farmers. This had to be done in a short time and with very little money. As a general, Washington did make mistakes. The Americans lost more battles than they won. But Washington saw that his job was more than winning. It was to keep on fighting, no matter how badly the war was going. Even after the worst defeats, with his army hungry and in rags, Washington would not surrender. This set an example for other Americans. It raised their spirits. It gave them courage to keep on fighting.

Every age has its leaders. They are people who believe in something. They are the men and women who help people make their beliefs come true.

REVIEW

CHECK YOUR FACTS

1. What committee did Samuel Adams start? What group did he lead?
2. Name two writers who used their pens well against the British.
3. How did American women work against British rule? Name three ways.
4. Name the person who wrote the Declaration of Independence.
5. What did George Washington feel was more important than winning battles?

THINK ABOUT IT

When we read of the American Revolution, we study about a few great leaders. Yet the war was fought by thousands of ordinary people. Most of them have been forgotten. Which do you think are more important, the leaders or the ordinary people? Why?

Lesson 6: How the Americans Won

FIND THE WORDS

ammunition   Loyalist   slogan

Few people thought the Americans could win the Revolutionary War. In 1776, the British had the world's strongest navy. They had far more money and soldiers than the Americans did. The British had factories that could produce guns, ammunition, and clothing for war. **Ammunition** includes bullets and shells fired from guns.

The Americans seemed easy to defeat. They had no army or navy. They showed few signs that they could work well together. Many Americans wanted to keep their ties with Britain. Some fought against the colonial army. These people were called **Loyalists.** Some Loyalists escaped to Canada. Many other Americans did not care who won the war. They sold supplies to both sides.

Yet, 6 years after the fighting began, the United States had won its independence. How had this come about?

The British actually had many disadvantages. The war was not popular in Britain. Many British people agreed with the goals of the colonists. Also, Britain fought several wars in Europe not long before the American Revolution. In addition, Britain had been fighting wars in its colonies all over the world. These wars were expensive. The British people did not want to continue paying for them with high taxes.

The British navy had too few sailors and ships for all the jobs the government wanted done. The army could not get enough men to join. The British had to hire soldiers from other nations to help them fight. This, too, cost money. Britain also had to worry about enemies close at hand. France and Spain might invade Britain.

Britain had another important disadvantage. The American war was fought 4800 kilometers (3000 miles) away. Supplies and orders took a long time to arrive in North America. European soldiers were not used to the hot summers and cold winters of the Northern colonies. They did not like marching where there were no roads.

The Americans had some important advantages. The war was fought in their homeland. People will fight very hard to protect their own families, homes, and land. The Americans were used to the climate and land. They had learned from the American Indians how to fight in the wilderness.

The Americans had a fine leader in George Washington. They also had many friends in Europe. Some of these friends came to America to fight. Americans needed the skills of these European leaders. The Marquis de Lafayette (mahr KEE duh LAH fee ET) came from France to lead part of Washington's army. Thaddeus Kosciusko (tha DEE uhs KOS ee US koh) from Poland and the German Baron von Steuben came to help train Washington's soldiers. These foreign friends admired what the Americans were doing.

The turning point in the war came in 1778. It was then that the French agreed to send soldiers and ships to help the Americans. Without French help, the Americans might not have won.

Perhaps the greatest advantage the Americans had was their desire to be free and independent of Britain. People like Thomas Jeffer-

This portrait shows George Washington, the Marquis de Lafayette, and Tench Tilghman. Tench Tilghman told the Continental Congress about Cornwallis's surrender to Washington.

Some Europeans came to help the Americans fight. The Baron von Steuben, *left*, came over from Germany. Thaddeus Kosciusko, *right*, came from Poland to help train Washington's soldiers.

son and Thomas Paine had written of this desire in exciting words. Patrick Henry, a great speaker from Virginia, had given the Americans a **slogan,** or inspiring phrase. In the Virginia Convention, he gave a speech that became famous. It ended with these stirring words: "Give me liberty, or give me death!"

REVIEW

WATCH YOUR WORDS

1. The ____ were Americans who supported the British.
   Canadians   Loyalists
   Continentals

2. ____ includes bullets and shells.
   Slogan   Revolution   Ammunition

CHECK YOUR FACTS

3. What was the outlook for the Americans in 1776?

4. The war (was/was not) popular in Britain.

5. What may have been the Americans' greatest advantage?

THINK ABOUT IT

Pretend you are a Loyalist during the American Revolution. What arguments will you use to persuade your friends to support Britain?

CHAPTER REVIEW

WATCH YOUR WORDS

1. A ___ is a war in which people change their government.
   boycott   slogan   revolution
2. The ___ is the law-making body in Britain.
   Parliament   Continental Congress
   Committee of Correspondence
3. The British forced the colonists to ___ troops in their homes.
   boycott   grenadier   quarter
4. The colonists agreed to ___ British goods.
   boycott   smuggle   barricade
5. A ___ is an agreement made between nations.
   declaration   treaty   revolution
6. Sam Adams started the ___.
   Parliament   Continental Congress
   Committee of Correspondence
7. ___ includes bullets and shells fired from guns.
   Revolution   Ammunition   Trench
8. The ___ were Americans who wanted to stay under British rule.
   Sons of Liberty   grenadiers
   Loyalists
9. A ___ is an inspiring phrase.
   declaration   slogan   treaty
10. The American Revolution began because the British government put ___ on the colonies.
    taxes   slogans   treaties

CHECK YOUR FACTS

11. The colonies (did/did not) have representatives in Parliament.
12. Why did the colonists destroy British tea?
13. What was the first major battle of the American Revolution?
14. What American victory brought France into the war?
15. Who wrote *Common Sense*?

USE YOUR MAP

16. Look at the map on page 140. What was the western border of the new nation?
17. What divided the United States from Canada along much of the border?
18. What two areas were in dispute with other nations?
19. In what states were the battles of Camden and Yorktown fought?
20. In what state were the battles of Lexington and Concord fought?

THINK ABOUT IT

21. Suppose you were a third party trying to make peace between Britain and the colonies *before* 1776. What would you suggest to help solve the problem?
22. Suppose you were forced to let enemy soldiers live in your home. How would you feel about it?
23. What do you think the colonists hoped to gain by boycotting British goods?
24. Most of the early fighting of the Revolution was in the North. Yet a Southerner, Washington, commanded the army. What reasons can you think of for this?
25. How would the war have been changed if the armies of Burgoyne and Howe had joined?

CHAPTER 2 GOVERNING THE NEW NATION

Lesson 1: The First Government

During the Revolutionary War, the 13 American colonies were all working for the same goal. They had to win the war. When the fighting was over, the differences between the colonies became important again. The colonies were now states in one nation. Some states earned money from farming. Others were centers for manufacturing and trade. Some states had slaves, while others did not. Some states claimed large areas of land to the west. Others had no western lands. In the years after the

Under the Articles of Confederation, each state could issue its own money.

war, each state wanted to take care of its own interests. Each one wanted its own government.

But there was a government over all the states. A **government** is the system by which laws are made and enforced. The first government of the United States was set up in 1781. At that time, all the states agreed on the **Articles of Confederation.** According to this agreement, the national government was to be made up of a congress with one house. This new Congress was much like the earlier Continental Congress. Each state had one vote in the Congress.

The Articles of Confederation gave Congress certain powers. Congress could set up post offices, charge postage, and coin or print money. Congress could trade with American Indian groups to the west. It also had the power to raise an army and make peace treaties.

Under the Articles of Confederation, the states agreed to work together. But each state also had its own government. These state governments remained stronger than the government of the nation as a whole. The Articles of Confederation did not give Congress

Farmers attacked the tax collectors during Shays's Rebellion.

some important powers. Congress could not make trade agreements that would go against any state laws. More important, Congress did not have the power to tax the states. It could only *ask* the states to pay their share of expenses. The state governments collected the money. Then they turned it over to Congress, if they chose to. Many states did not choose to pay. Congress found it difficult to pay the war debts and meet all the other national expenses.

There was an even bigger problem with the Articles of Confederation. Congress could not change any part of the Articles unless every state agreed. Since the states had different interests, they could not all agree on any changes. So Congress remained weak.

Many Americans came to feel that such a weak government could not hold the United States together. The states might all go their own ways. Then they would not be able to defend themselves against foreign nations.

Some Americans were afraid that there would be another revolution. After the war, times were very hard. Trade had not completely started up again. There was very little money to rebuild businesses and factories. Farmers could not sell their crops. People in all states were having trouble paying their taxes. The worst problem was in Massachusetts. The farmers in that state were very poor. The Massachusetts government often took a farmer's land as payment for taxes.

The farmers tried to stop this by legal means, but they could not. Then, in January of 1787, Daniel Shays took stronger action. He led a group of farmers in an attack on a government building where weapons were stored. But troops fired on the farmers. Daniel Shays and the farmers did not have weapons with which to defend themselves. They gave up the attack and fled. The windows of John Adams's house were broken during this uprising. But he understood the feelings of the farmers. Adams wrote to Thomas Jefferson that Shays's Rebellion was the act of a desperate people.

Many people were worried. They were afraid such things might happen again if they did not have a strong and fair government. Everything the colonies had fought for might be lost.

REVIEW

CHECK YOUR FACTS

1. What became important again once the Revolutionary War was over?
2. What agreement set up the first government of the United States?
3. The first national government (could/could not) make states pay taxes.
4. Why was it hard to change the first national government?
5. What event made people worry about the future of the United States?

THINK ABOUT IT

The first national government of the United States did not work well. What do you think was its greatest weakness? Give your reasons.

Lesson 2: Forming a New Government

FIND THE WORDS

Constitution   federal
compromise   ratify
antifederalist   right   federalist

In May 1787, 55 representatives chosen by their states met in Philadelphia. They came to discuss the problems of the Articles of Confederation. They soon decided that they would have to rewrite the Articles. For 4 months, they talked and argued about what the government of the United States should be like. When they were through, they had written the **Constitution** of the United States. This was a new plan of government for the new nation. George Washington was the president of the Constitutional Convention. James Madison probably influenced the outcome most.

The representatives at the Constitutional Convention faced one major problem. They had to give the new government enough power to do the necessary jobs. But they did not want to give it too much power. If the government had too much power, it might take away the people's freedom. The Convention did not want the new government to behave as the British government had before the American Revolution.

The representatives tried to solve this problem in several ways. One way was to carefully divide the powers of government. Some were given to the **federal,** or national, government. Others were given to the state governments. The federal government was given the powers to print money and make treaties. The federal government could also collect taxes directly from the people for certain things. State governments were allowed to pass laws about education, traffic, cities, and other things inside their borders. They could also collect taxes to pay for services they provided.

The representatives also had to make many compromises. There is **compromise** when people on both sides of an argument agree to give in a little. Then each side gets part of what it wants. For example, the large states wanted the number of votes in Congress to be based on population. The more people a state had, they felt, the more votes it should have. The small states did not agree. They wanted all states to have the same

George Washington was the president of the Constitutional Convention.

number of votes. Otherwise, they feared, the large states would have too much power over the small ones. The representatives decided that there would be two parts to Congress. One part of Congress would be based on population. In the other part of Congress, each state would have two votes.

There were other compromises. One solved a problem for the states that had slaves. These states wanted slaves to count as part of their population. In this way, they could have more votes in Congress. Yet they did not want slaves to count if there was a tax based on population. The compromise was to count only three out of every five slaves.

The Constitution was finally finished. Now it was up to the states to **ratify,** or approve, it. If nine states ratified the Constitu-

JOIN, or DIE.

Benjamin Franklin published this cartoon. The sections of the snake are the states.

tion, it would become law. Everywhere, people were talking about it. The people who were against the new Constitution were called **antifederalists.** They were afraid of a strong national government. They did not think enough powers were left to the states. Many people wanted the Constitution to spell out the rights of the people.

Rights are the privileges that belong to the people who live in a nation. Rights protect people from the power of the government.

The **federalists** supported the new Constitution. They believed that a strong national government was necessary. Then, they said, other nations would respect and trust the United States. They felt this would be good for trade and business. Also, they argued, the United States would be better able to defend itself. Federalists agreed that if the Constitution were ratified, they would back changes to protect the people's rights.

The federalists won. By June of 1788, nine states had accepted the Constitution. The Constitution would become the law of the land. Between 1788 and 1790, the other four states joined the Union.

REVIEW

WATCH YOUR WORDS

1. When people on opposing sides each give in a little, they reach a ___.
   Constitution   compromise   ratification

2. Nine states had to ___ the Constitution to make it law.
   oppose   compromise   ratify

3. The ___ government is the government of the nation.
   Constitution   federal   state

4. The ___ opposed the Constitution.
   antifederalists   federalists   ratifiers

5. The ___ favored the Constitution.
   antifederalists   federalists   compromisers

THINK ABOUT IT

Imagine you were a leader in the government of a large, rich state when the Constitution was proposed. How would you have felt about the Constitution? Why?

Lesson 3: The Constitution

FIND THE WORDS

legislative   executive   judicial
check   Congress
House of Representatives
elect   Senate   bill
President   veto
Supreme Court   justice
appoint   unconstitutional

The writers of the Constitution divided the powers of government between the federal government and the states. They also divided the powers of the federal government itself. The Constitution set up a government with three separate branches, or parts.

One branch makes the laws. This is the **legislative** branch.

The second branch carries out the laws. This is the **executive** branch of government.

The third branch settles questions about what the laws mean. This is the **judicial** branch.

Each branch has some—but not all—of the power needed to run the country. Each branch has some power to **check,** or limit, the other two. This keeps any one branch of the government from becoming too strong.

The legislative branch is called **Congress.** Congress is made up of two houses, or parts. The **House of Representatives** is the part that is closest to the people. The number of representatives a state has depends on its population. States with more people have more representatives than those with fewer people. Representatives are **elected,** or chosen, every 2 years by the people of their area. The other part of Congress is the **Senate.** There are two senators from each state. They are elected every 6 years by all their state's people.

Representatives and senators discuss proposals for new laws. These are called **bills.** For a bill to become a law, both parts of Congress must agree on it.

Through the laws it makes, Congress controls trade between states and with other nations. It has the right to print money. It decides how much money people must pay in taxes to the federal government. Congress also has the right to declare war. These are important activities in any national government.

The executive branch is headed by the **President.** The President is the leader of the whole nation. The President is elected by the people every 4 years. When the Constitution of the United States was written, no other nation elected its leaders. Those in power

OUR NATIONAL GOVERNMENT

LEGISLATIVE

THE CONGRESS

1. Suggests and passes the laws
2. Approves judges and heads of department chosen by the President
3. May accuse executive or judicial officials of wrongdoing
4. Approves treaties
5. Has the right to declare war

EXECUTIVE

THE PRESIDENT

1. Makes the laws of Congress work
2. Suggests new laws and may veto laws
3. Chooses judges and heads of government departments
4. Makes treaties with other nations
5. Is Commander in Chief of the Armed Forces

JUDICIAL

THE SUPREME COURT AND LOWER COURTS

1. Settles questions about the laws
2. May rule that the President or other official has acted illegally
3. Settles questions about treaties

did not think the people were wise enough to choose good leaders.

The President must sign bills before they can become law. The President directs the people who carry out the laws of the nation. Some of these people collect taxes. Some of them settle problems with other nations and make treaties with them. Others have duties such as giving licenses to radio and television stations. The President is also the commander in chief of the armed forces.

The President may suggest new bills to Congress. But Congress must approve them before they can become law. The President also has the power to **veto,** or stop, a bill passed by Congress. Presidents can veto bills they think are not good for the nation. Congress can try to pass such a bill again. After a veto, a bill can become law only if two-thirds of both houses of Congress approve.

The judicial branch includes courts in all parts of the nation. The highest court in the land is called the **Supreme Court.** The Supreme Court has nine members, called **justices.** They are not

Today, you can see the original documents that shaped American government.

elected. The President **appoints,** or chooses, them. The Senate must approve the President's choices. Justices of the Supreme Court may serve for as long as they live.

The Supreme Court can decide that a law passed by Congress or by a state is **unconstitutional.** Such a law does not fit in with the ideas and purposes of the Constitution. No one has to obey a law that the Supreme Court has called unconstitutional. The Supreme Court can also decide if an action of the President is unconstitutional.

REVIEW

WATCH YOUR WORDS

1. The President has the power to ___ bills.

   check   veto   appoint

2. Members of the Supreme Court are called ___.

   representatives   senators   justices

3. Congress is the ___ branch of the federal government.

   legislative   executive   judicial

4. The President heads the ___ branch.

   legislative   executive   judicial

5. The Supreme Court is the highest part of the ___ branch.

   legislative   executive   judicial

CHECK YOUR FACTS

6. Name the two houses of Congress.

7. What must happen before a bill can become law?

8. A bill can (never/sometimes) become law if the President vetoes it.

9. How are the members of the Supreme Court chosen?

10. What does it mean to say that a law is unconstitutional?

THINK ABOUT IT

Each branch of the Federal government has some power to check the other two. Do you think this is a good idea? Why, or why not?

162

Lesson 4: Defending Freedom

Built into the Constitution is a way of changing it. Such a change is called an **amendment.** Amendments are hard to make. Three-fourths of the states must ratify an amendment before it can become part of the Constitution.

In trying to get people to accept the Constitution, the federalists promised to make changes in it. These changes would describe the rights of the people. In 1791, 3 years after the Constitution was ratified, the first 10 amendments were added. These amendments make up the United States **Bill of Rights.** Since 1791, the Bill of Rights has been very important in the history of the United States.

Here are some of the main points of the Bill of Rights. Read them carefully. You can see in them what early Americans meant by the word *freedom.*

Amendment 1: Congress will make no law that (a) sets up a religion, helps one religion over another, or takes away a person's right to believe in a reli-gion; (b) takes away the freedom of newspapers to print the news or takes away a person's right to say what he or she thinks; (c) tries to stop people from getting together in a peaceful crowd and complaining about the government.

Amendment 2: The people's right to keep weapons cannot be taken away.

Amendment 3: In peacetime, no soldiers can be quartered in someone's house without the agreement of the owner. In wartime, laws must be passed if this is to be allowed.

Amendment 4: The government cannot search people's homes and property without a good reason. The courts must give permission for a search.

Amendment 5: People cannot be made to say anything against themselves in court. People cannot have their lives, freedom, or property taken away except according to the laws.

Amendment 6: People accused in court of committing a crime have the right to a public trial. They have the right to have a fair jury listen to the case against them. They have the right to know why they are

The Bill of Rights gave people the right to a trial by jury.

being tried. They have the right to have a lawyer defend them.

Amendment 7: People have the right to a jury in court cases involving disagreements about amounts of money over $20.

Amendment 8: **Bail,** money pledged to get out of jail while awaiting trial, should not be too great. **Fines,** money paid as punishment for crimes, should not be too large. Punishments for crimes cannot be cruel or strange.

Amendments 9 and 10: If a right is not mentioned in the Constitution, that does not mean the people do not have it. Any rights not given to the federal government in the Constitution belong to the states or to the people.

Many more amendments have been added to the Constitution since the Bill of Rights. These amendments have made it possible for the Constitution to meet the needs of a changing nation.

REVIEW

WATCH YOUR WORDS

1. A change in the Constitution is a(n) ___.
   bill   amendment   fine

2. A ___ is money paid as punishment for crimes.
   right   bail   fine

CHECK YOUR FACTS

3. What are the first 10 amendments called?

4. Which amendment gives people the right to speak freely?

5. Which amendments give people the right to trials by jury?

6. Which amendment prohibits bail and fines that are too large?

THINK ABOUT IT

Are there any rights that you think important that are not in the Bill of Rights? If so, what are they?

Lesson 5: The Early Years of the New Government

FIND THE WORDS

secretary   Cabinet   currency
credit   neutrality   political party
War Hawks   Monroe Doctrine

Once the Constitution was approved, the new government had to be set up. Members of Congress were elected from the states. Electors were chosen to vote for the President. It was no surprise that every one of them voted for George Washington of Virginia. He had led the nation in war. Now he was to lead it in peace. John Adams of Massachusetts was elected Vice President.

On April 30, 1789, President Washington took the oath of office in New York City. It was an exciting day. Cannons roared and church bells rang. A crowd shouted, "Long live George Washington!" The people were eager to see the President who had "the look and figure of a hero." The new President must have thought

George Washington was elected the nation's first President. An arch of laurel branches was made to welcome him to New York.

about the welcome as he settled down to work. He had to oversee the building of a government from a set of plans—the Constitution. The task was difficult. There was no example to follow. As one member of Congress said, "We are in a wilderness without a single footstep to guide us."

But George Washington had a clear idea of what he wanted to do. He wanted to win the respect of the people for the Presidency. He wanted to get people to trust the federal government. He wanted the nation to rebuild its business and trade. He wanted the United States to stay at peace with other nations.

The Cabinet

Congress soon set up departments to help the President. The first were the Department of State, the Department of the Treasury, and the Department of War. The heads of these departments were called **secretaries.** Together with the Attorney General and the Postmaster General, they met often with Washington. They talked about the problems of government and gave the President their advice. This group became known as the **Cabinet.** Since then, every President has had a Cabinet.

The members of the first Cabinet did not always agree with one another. Alexander Hamilton, the Secretary of the Treasury, wanted the nation to be ruled by rich people and government officials. He wanted a strong federal government that could help and protect trade and business. Thomas Jefferson, the Secretary of State, wanted the United States to be a nation of independent farmers. He wanted the federal government to stay small. He thought Hamilton would make America like Great Britain, with its ruling upper class. The ideas of both leaders were important to the nation.

WASHINGTON'S CABINET

Vice President	John Adams	1789, 1793
Secretary of State originally Department of Foreign Affairs established as Department of State September 15, 1789	John Jay Thomas Jefferson Edmund Randolph Timothy Pickering	1789 1790 1794 1795
Secretary of War established as Department of War August 7, 1789	Henry Knox Timothy Pickering James McHenry	1789 1795 1796
Secretary of the Treasury established September 2, 1789	Alexander Hamilton Oliver Wolcott, Jr.	1789 1795
Postmaster General established September 22, 1789; established as Post Office Department May 8, 1795	Samuel Osgood Timothy Pickering Joseph Habersham	1789 1791 1795
Attorney General established September 24, 1789	Edmund Randolph William Bradford Charles Lee	1789 1794 1795

Hamilton's Plans

Alexander Hamilton studied the nation's problems. He saw that the United States was deep in debt. The people, the states, and the nation owed money. But the **currency,** paper money issued by the government, was almost without value. Hamilton knew the United States must pay what it owed. If it did not, its currency would not be accepted. Business and trade would be hurt.

Alexander Hamilton believed he had to make people trust the credit of the government. **Credit** is the belief that someone who owes money will repay it. Hamilton wanted the national government to pay its own debts and the debts of the states as well. The Southern states were not happy with this

because their debts were small. The New England states supported the plan because they had large debts to pay.

Hamilton got what he wanted by compromise. The South, led by Jefferson, accepted Hamilton's plan. In return, the North, led by Hamilton, agreed to let the national capital be located in the South. The District of Columbia, between Maryland and Virginia, was the site chosen.

Next, Hamilton asked Congress to set up a national bank. The government would keep its money in this bank. The bank would control how much money other banks could lend. Some people were against the bank. They felt the government did not have the right to set up a bank. Hamilton argued

The First Bank of the United States was set up in Philadelphia.

Alexander Hamilton was the first Secretary of the Treasury. He asked Congress to set up a national bank.

that the Constitution said that Congress could do what was necessary to carry out its powers. Congress accepted Hamilton's idea. It voted for the First Bank of the United States. As trade became greater, people had more money in their pockets. More people trusted Hamilton's plans.

Foreign Affairs

The early days of the country were a dangerous time. The United States was a baby giant in the family of nations. There was often a difference between what the country wanted to do and what it could do. Soon after Washington took office, Great Britain and France went to war.

France had helped the United States defeat Britain in the Revolutionary War. Should the United States now help France? ·

Thomas Jefferson, the Secretary of State, wanted to help France. But President Washington and Alexander Hamilton agreed that the nation could not afford another war. In 1793, Washington issued a Proclamation of Neutrality. **Neutrality** is not taking sides in a war. Washington wanted the United States to stay out of problems between other nations. He repeated this idea in his famous Farewell Address in 1796.

Neutrality did not solve the problems the United States had with European nations. Both the French and the British attacked

George Washington was elected President again in 1792. This painting shows his second inauguration ceremony, at Independence Hall in Philadelphia.

American ships. The differences between Jefferson and Hamilton became greater. Jefferson did not want to allow British ships to trade with the United States. Hamilton and Washington knew that to stop British ships would destroy American trade.

Finally, Washington sent John Jay, the Chief Justice of the Supreme Court, to Britain to solve the problems. The United States and Britain signed the Jay Treaty. But in the treaty, Britain did not promise to leave American ships alone. As a result, many people, including Jefferson, were against the treaty. Jefferson resigned as Secretary of State because of it. The British did promise in the treaty to remove their troops from forts in the Northwest Territory. British troops had stayed there after the Revolutionary War had ended. The treaty also prevented, for a while, a war that could have destroyed the young nation.

Political Parties

The differences between Alexander Hamilton and Thomas Jefferson in the 1790s were not just arguments between two people. The first national political parties in the United States grew out of their conflict. A **political party** is a group of people that have similar ideas about how the government should be run. They join together and support candidates for public office. The followers of Hamilton became known as the Federalist

Party. They were not necessarily the same people as the federalists who had backed the Constitution in the 1780s.

Those who supported Thomas Jefferson were called the Republican Party. This group was later called the Democratic-Republican Party and, still later, the Democratic Party. The Democratic Party of today is descended from it. The present-day Republican Party has nothing to do with the Republicans of the 1790s. It is an entirely different group that was founded much later.

In 1796, George Washington said he would not run again for the Presidency. The Federalists picked Vice President John Adams as their candidate for President. Thomas Jefferson was the presidential candidate of the Republicans. Adams won and became the second President.

While John Adams was President, the United States had more problems with France. Alexander Hamilton wanted Adams to lead the nation into war with France. When Adams refused, Hamilton worked against his reelection. In this way, the Federalist Party was divided. As a result, the Republican candidate, Thomas Jefferson, was elected President in 1800. Hamilton's followers, the Federalists, were never again strong enough to elect a President.

The Nation Grows and Changes

While Jefferson was President, the United States continued to have problems with Britain and France. There were members of Congress who wanted the United States to go to war with Britain. They were called the **War Hawks.** War finally broke out in the year 1812, while James Madison was President.

James Monroe was President during the Era of Good Feelings. During these years from 1817 to 1825, the political parties came together. The United States showed that it was the most powerful nation in the Western Hemisphere. In 1823, President Monroe stated the **Monroe Doctrine.** He said the United States would not allow European nations to set up any more colonies in the Americas.

In 1828, Andrew Jackson of Tennessee was elected President. He was the first President to come from a state west of the Appalachian Mountains. The election of Jackson was a symbol of the growing power of the western part of the nation. Many Americans were moving west. Businesses were growing throughout the country. The United States had won its independence. It had set up a strong government under the Constitution. A time of great growth and change had begun.

War broke out between the United States and Britain in 1812. The first sea battle took place off New London, Connecticut.

REVIEW

WATCH YOUR WORDS

1. The heads of government departments were called ____.
   War Hawks   political parties   secretaries

2. A ____ is a group of people that run candidates for public office.
   cabinet   political party   currency

3. ____ is paper money issued by the government.
   Neutrality   Credit   Currency

4. ____ is the belief that someone who owes money will repay it.
   Neutrality   Credit   Doctrine

5. The heads of government departments form the ____.
   Cabinet   Secretariat   Doctrine

CHECK YOUR FACTS

6. When did George Washington become President?

7. What two members of George Washington's Cabinet had important differences?

8. With what two nations did the United States have trouble in its early years?

9. Name the first national political parties in the United States.

10. What was the Monroe Doctrine?

TRY SOMETHING NEW

Today, the President's Cabinet is much larger than it was under Washington. Find out how many and which government leaders are now Cabinet members. Use an encyclopedia or other source suggested by your teacher.

CHAPTER REVIEW

WATCH YOUR WORDS

1. The first government of the United States was created under the____.
   Constitution   Bill of Rights
   Articles of Confederation

2. The permanent government of the United States was created by the ____.
   Constitution   Bill of Rights
   Articles of Confederation

3. Under the Constitution, the branches of government____each other.
   veto   check   appoint

4. The____is the legislative branch.
   Supreme Court   President   Congress

5. Before a law is approved, it is a____.
   veto   check   bill

6. The President____ the justices of the Supreme Court.
   ratifies   appoints   fines

7. A change in the Constitution is a(n) ____.
   compromise   article   amendment

8. ____ is the money a person pledges to get out of jail while awaiting trial.
   Bail   Fine   Tax

9. ____is not taking sides in a war.
   Currency   Neutrality   Credit

10. The head of the executive branch is the____.
    Supreme Court   President   Congress

CHECK YOUR FACTS

11. What agreement did the states make in 1781?

12. What was the main problem the members of the Constitutional Convention faced?

13. What branch of government can decide that a law is unconstitutional?

14. What are the first 10 amendments to the Constitution called?

15. List the first three Presidents of the United States.

USE YOUR CHART

16. Look at the chart of our national government on page 161. What do the three branches have to do with laws?

17. Who approves judges and department heads appointed by the President?

18. What do the three branches have to do with treaties?

19. Which branch can declare war?

20. Who commands the armed forces?

THINK ABOUT IT

21. In the Congress of the Confederation, each state had one vote. Discuss what that meant.

22. Suppose you lived in a small, poor state when the Constitution was proposed. How might you have felt about it?

23. The Constitution made an elected President head of the American government. What kind of head did most governments in the world have at that time?

24. Why is it important that justices of the Supreme Court can serve as long as they live?

25. Do any parts of the Bill of Rights seem less important today?

CHAPTER 3 THE UNITED STATES EXPANDS

Lesson 1: The Westward Movement

FIND THE WORDS

**frontier   territory   pioneer
land speculator**

In North America, "the West" has meant many different things to many different people. What it has meant has depended on when a person lived.

To the early European explorers in North America, the West was the Atlantic Coast. As settlements grew, the West became the area where settlements ended and the woods began.

For about 100 years, only a few Europeans crossed the Appalachian Mountains. These mountains formed a barrier to settlement. They were very difficult to cross. At the time of the American Revolution, the Appalachians were the gate to the western frontier. A **frontier** is an unexplored or unsettled area.

$$\begin{array}{cc} 25 & 25 \\ +3 & +0 \\ \hline \overline{3} & \overline{2} \end{array}$$

173

Daniel Boone was a hunter, an explorer, and a soldier. He was the first White person to lead a group of settlers through the Appalachians. In the South, near Tennessee, there was a path through the mountains. It was called the Cumberland Gap. American Indians had used it for hundreds of years and had opened up trails around it. In 1775, Daniel Boone and about 30 woodcutters began clearing a road through the Cumberland Gap. They joined trails. They cut down trees and bushes. They rolled rocks out of the way. The route was 480 kilometers (300 miles) long. It was known as the "Wilderness Road."

Many hunters, trappers, and farmers began to move west along it.

By the end of the Revolutionary War, the United States stretched from the Atlantic Ocean to the Mississippi River. The United States did not then include Florida, which belonged to Spain.

In the 1780s, the government decided to make it easier for people to settle the Old Northwest. This frontier region extended west from the Appalachians to the Mississippi River. It stretched north from the Ohio River to the Great Lakes. Find the Old Northwest on the map on the facing page.

The government divided the land and offered it for sale at very

Many people traveled west in covered wagons. They faced a long, hard journey over poor roads and across rivers.

WHERE WE ARE IN TIME AND PLACE

WESTWARD GROWTH OF THE UNITED STATES

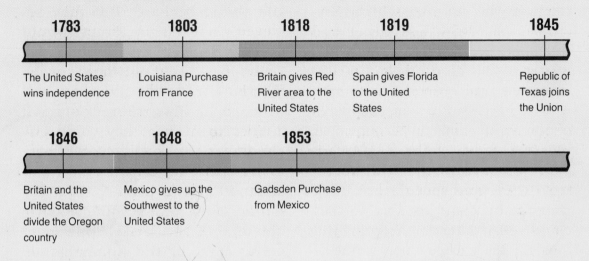

1783 The United States wins independence

1803 Louisiana Purchase from France

1818 Britain gives Red River area to the United States

1819 Spain gives Florida to the United States

1845 Republic of Texas joins the Union

1846 Britain and the United States divide the Oregon country

1848 Mexico gives up the Southwest to the United States

1853 Gadsden Purchase from Mexico

WESTWARD GROWTH OF THE UNITED STATES

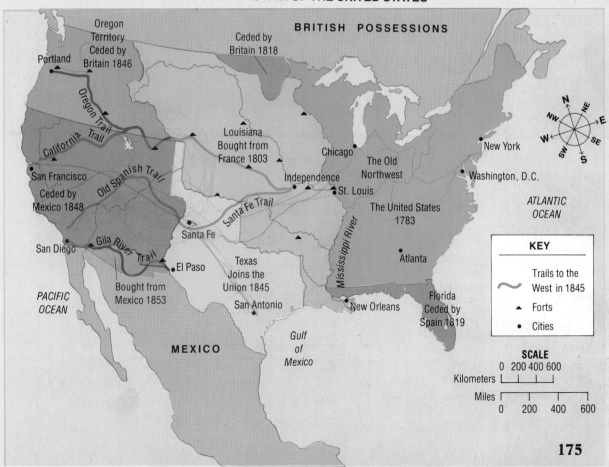

Oregon Territory Ceded by Britain 1846

Portland

BRITISH POSSESSIONS

Ceded by Britain 1818

Oregon Trail

California Trail

San Francisco
Ceded by Mexico 1848

Old Spanish Trail

Louisiana Bought from France 1803

Chicago

Independence

The Old Northwest

St. Louis

New York

Washington, D.C.

ATLANTIC OCEAN

Santa Fe Trail

San Diego

Gila River Trail

Santa Fe

El Paso

Texas Joins the Union 1845

Bought from Mexico 1853

San Antonio

The United States 1783

Mississippi River

Atlanta

Florida Ceded by Spain 1819

PACIFIC OCEAN

New Orleans

MEXICO

Gulf of Mexico

KEY

~ Trails to the West in 1845

▲ Forts

• Cities

SCALE

Kilometers 0 200 400 600

Miles 0 200 400 600

low prices. It passed laws about the rights of settlers. The Northwest Territory was then set up. A **territory** was an area with a government but with less power and independence than a state. When a part of this territory had 60,000 people, it could become a state.

The early settlers in each area of the West came to be known as **pioneers.** Some of the first Americans to move to the Old Northwest were **land speculators.** They came to buy land cheaply so they could sell it later for a profit. But most of the early settlers came to stay. Most were poor farmers. They wanted land on which to build a home and start a farm. These pioneers faced a long, hard trip over poor roads and across rivers. They faced dangers from the Miami, Sauk, and Fox. These American Indian peoples fought to keep the settlers away from their hunting lands. The pioneers knew life would be hard. But they believed that better times would come. Soon they would have neighbors. Towns would grow. There would be churches and schools. In time, they would sell their crops. Then they could buy the things they had gone without.

By 1820, the United States had about 10 million people. About 2½ million lived between the Appalachians and the Mississippi. New states west of the Appalachians had joined the Union. Kentucky became a state in 1792 and Tennessee in 1796. Mississippi, Alabama, Ohio, Indiana, and Illinois had become states by 1819. The western frontier was moving farther west.

REVIEW

WATCH YOUR WORDS

1. An unexplored or unsettled area is a ___.
   frontier   pioneer   territory

2. The early settlers in the West are called ___.
   frontiers   land speculators
   pioneers

3. A ___ has a government but is less independent than a state.
   nation   territory   frontier

CHECK YOUR FACTS

4. What was an important barrier to early settlement of the West?

5. What route did Daniel Boone help start?

6. What was the first state west of the Appalachians?

THINK ABOUT IT

Do you have any ancestors who were pioneers in the West? If so, what areas did they settle?

Lesson 2: Frontier Life

FIND THE WORD

porridge

The work on the frontier was shared by all. Men, women, and even children cleared the forest and turned it into farmland. They planted food, raised livestock, and hunted wild animals.

The frontier cabin was a sort of factory. There, raw materials were made into things that could be used. Wood from the forest was made into tools. Cotton, flax, or wool was spun into thread. The thread was then woven into cloth. The cloth was made into blankets and into shirts and other clothes. Hogs and cattle were butchered at home. The meat was salted and saved to be eaten later. Corn and other grains were made into breads, puddings, or porridges. A **porridge** is a souplike food made from grain or peas. Cream was churned into butter. Animal fat was made into soap and candles.

A woman who lived in the Old Northwest in the early 1800s told what it was like:

"We did most of our work in the summer kitchen. That was where we had the big brick oven. We used to fire it twice a week and do a sight o' baking all at once. We'd make a hot fire in the oven. Then, when the bricks were heated through, we'd scrape out

The early settlers often built homes of logs.

The frontier home was a sort of factory. This woman is making candles.

all the coals with a big iron scraper. We would dump the coals into the fireplace. Then we'd shove in the roast and fowls, the pies, and bread. At other times, we'd use the open fireplace.

"It was so easy, since we had no screens, to let the flies spoil everything. My mother just wouldn't have it so. We weren't allowed to bring apples into the house in summer. Apples attracted flies. If any of us dropped a speck of butter or cream on the floor, my mother would run for a cloth to wipe it up. At mealtime, someone stood and fanned to keep the flies away while the others ate.

"In warm weather, we washed outdoors. We used our well water.

We'd draw a barrel of water and put one shovel of ashes into it. It would just suds up like soft water, so white and clean. Our starch was of two kinds. It was made from a dough worked round and round until it was smooth. Or it was made from grated potato cooked to the right consistency.

"My mother used to spin. She made beautiful fine thread. I used to love to watch her at the spinning wheel. I can just close my eyes and see Ma standing over there spinning a thread as far as from here to the bed—say, twelve feet long.

"When I was eight years old, she wove me a plaid dress of which I was very proud. I remember the pattern. There were eight threads of brown, then one of red, one of blue, one of red, then brown again. It made the prettiest flannel. That dress lasted me for years."

Like the earlier settlers in the 1600s and 1700s, the western pioneers had to depend on their neighbors. Life on the frontier could be lonely as well as rough. People had to work together to do difficult jobs. Visiting was important to people who often lived 5 or 6 kilometers (3 or 4 miles) apart. A man from Ohio told how the pioneers worked and played together:

Life on the frontier could be lonely. Corn husking was an occasion for a social event.

"Houses and barns were raised by the collection of many neighbors together on one day. Men rolled up the logs in a clearing. They grubbed out the underbrush. Then they cut the logs for a house or barn. When such a gathering of men took place, the women also shared a job. There was quilting, sewing, or spinning of thread for some poor neighbor. This would bring together a mixed party. Usually, after supper there would be a dance or at least plays. These filled a good part of the night. The evening wound up with the young fellows seeing the girls home in the short hours or, if they went home early, sitting with them by the fire."

REVIEW

CHECK YOUR FACTS

1. Who did the work on the frontier?
2. How was the frontier cabin like a factory?
3. How did the pioneers make clothing? List three steps.
4. How did the pioneers save meat?
5. What were soap and candles made from?

THINK ABOUT IT

The lesson describes some things that pioneer neighbors did together. What other things can you think of?

Lesson 3: Across the Mississippi

Thomas Jefferson was elected the third President of the United States in 1800. He served two terms in office. Probably his greatest contribution as President was the Louisiana Purchase.

When Jefferson became President, France owned much of the land west of the Mississippi River. It also owned the port city of New Orleans. New Orleans was very important to American farmers living west of the Appalachians. They wanted to send their goods down the Mississippi and ship them from New Orleans. This was easier than sending them east over the mountain roads.

In 1803, Jefferson sent two representatives to France to try to buy New Orleans. To his surprise, the French ruler, Napoleon, offered to sell the whole Louisiana Territory. For $15 million, Jefferson bought a territory that doubled the size of the United States.

Look at the map on page 175. The Louisiana Territory stretched from the Mississippi to the Rockies.

The following year, President Jefferson sent a band of 42 people to explore Louisiana. They were led by Meriwether Lewis and William Clark. Lewis and Clark were to learn all about the land, climate, animals, and plants of the territory. They were to study the languages and ways of the American Indians of the area. They were to map the rivers and to go beyond Louisiana to the Pacific Ocean.

The daring explorers reached the Pacific a long year and a half later. A brave young Shoshone (shuh SHOH nee) woman named Sacajawea (SAK uh juh WEE uh) had guided them much of the way. Lewis and Clark made notes of all they saw and learned. They led the way for the millions of settlers who would follow.

TIME LINE: 1803–1830s

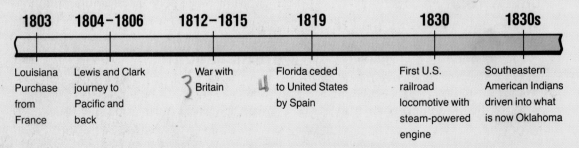

1803	1804–1806	1812–1815	1819	1830	1830s
Louisiana Purchase from France	Lewis and Clark journey to Pacific and back	War with Britain	Florida ceded to United States by Spain	First U.S. railroad locomotive with steam-powered engine	Southeastern American Indians driven into what is now Oklahoma

180

Lewis and Clark met many American Indians on their explorations.

In 1812, a war broke out between Britain and the United States. There were several reasons for this war. One reason was that the British were stopping and searching American ships. Another reason was that the British were causing trouble in American lands west of the Appalachians.

The war was short. Neither side won or lost. The Americans tried to invade Canada, which was

Sacajawea guided Lewis and Clark on their trip to the Pacific Ocean.

a British colony, but they were not successful. The British raided and burned Washington, DC, but they could not capture Baltimore. It was as a result of this battle that Francis Scott Key wrote "The Star-Spangled Banner."

The only big American victory was at New Orleans. The battle had no effect on the war. The peace treaty had already been signed. News from Europe was carried by ship. It did not reach America in time to stop the battle. But Andrew Jackson, the American general, became a popular hero. The fame and popularity he gained helped him win the Presidency years later.

Soon after the war, the border between Canada and the United States was set westward to the Rocky Mountains. The United States and Britain also agreed to share the Oregon country. In 1819, the United States bought Florida from Spain.

More and more Americans moved into the new lands. Thus, they came into contact with the American Indian peoples who had lived there for thousands of years. There were fierce battles as the American Indians tried to keep the settlers away. These battles were usually followed by treaties. In these treaties, the American Indian peoples would agree to give up some of their lands. In return, the United States government promised to protect their rights to their remaining lands.

Cotton was becoming an important crop in the South. Thousands of settlers crossed the Appalachians looking for good cotton lands. Several American Indian groups lived in the Southeast, the area between the Appalachians and the Mississippi. Most of these American Indians were farmers. Some, like the Cherokees (CHERH uh keez), had become used to European ways. They owned cotton lands and cattle. The Cherokees had developed their own system of writing for their language. They also had schools and a newspaper. These things did not make any difference to the American settlers who wanted their lands. In 1830, Congress passed a law ordering all American Indians to move west of the Mississippi. Congress promised them that the lands of the Great Plains would be theirs forever.

The Cherokees had their own system for writing their language. This sign is in English and Cherokee.

Congress ordered all American Indians to move west of the Mississippi. The Cherokees were forced to leave in the middle of winter. Their march west is known today as the "Trail of Tears."

So the American Indian peoples of the eastern United States were moved from their homes. Many were sent to dry, treeless places very different from the woodlands they knew. President Andrew Jackson sent the army to force out those who would not leave. The Cherokees were forced to make the long march west in the middle of winter. One-fourth of them died of hunger, cold, and sickness along the way. This march is known today as the "Trail of Tears."

REVIEW

CHECK YOUR FACTS

1. Who was President when the Louisiana Territory was bought?

2. What two men led the first expedition across the Louisiana Territory? What woman guided them?

3. With whom did the United States go to war in 1812?

4. How did the United States get Florida?

5. What American Indian people were forced west along the "Trail of Tears"?

TRY SOMETHING NEW

The Cherokees were one of five southeastern Indian groups known as the Five Civilized Nations. Find out the names of the other four. Where do most of their descendants live today?

Lesson 4: Oregon and the Mexican Lands

When the Far West was a frontier, its deserts, mountains, and rivers were explored by hardy fur trappers. Trappers often lived and worked along with American Indians. Many trappers caught beavers by the streams and rivers of the Oregon country. They sold the fur from beavers and other animals to trading companies. These companies then sent the furs to the East and to Europe. Jim Beckwourth, a Black man, was a famous mountaineer and trapper. He also became a chief of the Crow tribe.

By the 1830s and 1840s, the trappers' trails were being used by traders, missionaries, and farmers. **Missionaries** are people who travel to a new area to spread religion. News of Oregon's rich soil, forests, and rivers brought a new wave of settlers to the West.

These pioneers traveled in covered wagons known as **Conestogas** (KON uh STOH guz). These wagons moved in trains, or groups. Each wagon train had about 60 wagons. A wagon train was led by a captain called a wagonmaster.

Wagon trains usually left from Independence, Missouri. The trip west took about 6 months. There were many dangers. Sometimes, there were attacks by the American Indians of the Great Plains. But the everyday dangers were worse. The summer sun blazed

Jim Beckwourth was a mountaineer and trapper.

This wagon train has stopped so that the people can cook a meal.

down. The ovenlike heat dried out the wooden parts of the wagons. The spokes in the wheels would often break or fall out. Animals and people sometimes drowned crossing streams. Bad drinking water and spoiled food weakened the pioneers. As a result, deadly diseases sometimes swept through wagon trains.

By the middle 1840s, Americans in the Oregon country asked to join the United States. In 1846, Britain agreed to give up its claims to much of the area. Oregon became part of the United States because American pioneers had traveled there and built homes there.

South of Oregon, other Americans were settling a large stretch of land that belonged to Mexico. Much of this area is now called the American Southwest. Look at the map on page 175. Draw an imaginary line from San Antonio, Texas, through Santa Fe, New Mexico, to San Francisco, California. South of this line, Spanish-speaking missionaries, soldiers, ranchers, and farmers had explored and settled the land.

In 1821, the people of Mexico won their independence from

By the 1830s and 1840s, pioneers were using trappers' trails to go west. The Oregon Trail was one of these routes.

Spain. They welcomed American trade and settlement in their northern lands. The Santa Fe Trail became an important trade route. Long trains of pack mules carried goods between Santa Fe and Independence, Missouri. New England ships sailed around South America to trade in California.

Many Americans came to Texas. Some became ranchers. They copied the houses and ways of the Mexican ranchers. They rounded up the wild cattle and horses that roamed on the prairies. Others became owners of large cotton plantations.

By 1834, the Americans outnumbered the Mexicans in Texas. They felt they could no longer live under Mexican laws. In 1836, the Texans declared their independence from Mexico. For 9 years, Texas was an independent nation. It was called the Republic of Texas. It had its own constitution and president. Then, in 1845, Texas joined the United States as the 28th state.

The border between Texas and Mexico had not been settled, however. In 1846, Mexican and American soldiers shot at each other in the area under dispute. At the same time, many Americans were interested in gaining California and other lands in the Southwest. In 1846, the United States declared war on Mexico.

The war with Mexico lasted 2 years. After many battles, American soldiers captured Mexico City.

Ranchers rounded up longhorn cattle that roamed wild on the prairies.

Who was our 12th President? Any list will show you that Zachary Taylor was. But Davis Rice Atchison could also claim to have been our 12th President. Here is how.

James K. Polk was our 11th President. His term ended at midnight on Saturday, March 3, 1849. But, for religious reasons, Zachary Taylor did not want to be sworn in on a Sunday. So the country could have been without a President or Vice President for one day, Sunday, March 4, 1849.

But the law at the time filled the office. The law said that when the offices of President and Vice President are empty, the president pro tempore (for the time being) of the Senate becomes President. Atchison was president pro tempore of the Senate at that time. So Atchison was President of the United States for one day.

In 1848, Mexico and the United States signed a treaty. The Rio Grande became the border between Texas and Mexico. All of what are now the states of California, Nevada, and Utah became part of the United States. Most of Arizona and parts of New Mexico, Colorado, and Wyoming were also added by this agreement. Today, 48 of the 50 states border each other. This main part of the United States was almost complete in 1848. The last piece of it was added in 1853 when the Gadsden Purchase was bought from Mexico. The United States wanted this area of southern Arizona and New Mexico to build a railroad.

REVIEW

CHECK YOUR FACTS

1. What hardy group led the way west?
2. How did the pioneers travel across the country to Oregon?
3. Why did Britain give up much of its claim to the Oregon country?
4. What independent nation became part of the United States in 1845?
5. How did the United States gain the area south of Oregon and west of Texas?

THINK ABOUT IT

Was your state part of the Louisiana Purchase, of the Oregon country, or of the lands gained from Mexico? If not, how did it become part of the United States?

Lesson 5: The California Gold Rush

FIND THE WORD

forty-niner

"It was a clear, cold morning in January. I shall never forget that morning. As I was taking my usual walk, my eye was caught by a glimpse of something shining in the bottom of a ditch. There was about a foot of running water there. I reached my hand down and picked it up. It made my heart thump, for I felt certain it was gold. The piece was about half the size and the shape of a pea. Then I saw another piece in the water...."

The exact date was January 24, 1848. The place was a ditch near the Sacramento River in California. James Marshall, a Scottish carpenter, had made a very exciting discovery.

News of the gold spread quickly to all parts of the United States and the world. And a new wave of pioneers was to rush to the Far West.

Newspapers in the East were filled with stories about the rich

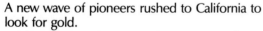

A new wave of pioneers rushed to California to look for gold.

189

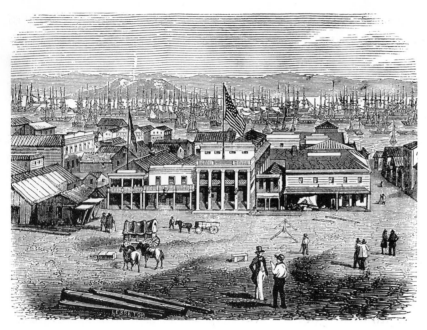
Ships lay deserted in San Francisco Bay during the gold rush.

gold deposits in California. Guidebooks told people what to take. They listed these supplies: a shotgun, horseshoes, pots and pans, a water barrel, a lantern, bars of lye soap, a rubber knapsack, a harmonica, a pick, and a pan.

Farmers left their fields. Ships lay deserted in San Francisco Bay as sailors ran into the hills to hunt for gold. Other people came overland. They traveled from the East, first by railroad and then by steamboat. They they crossed the Great Plains in wagons and on mules. Others, including some foreigners, came by sea.

In 1849, more than 80,000 hopeful newcomers arrived in Cal-

ifornia. They were called the **forty-niners.** They crowded into mining camps with names like Red Dog, Poker Flat, and Grub Gulch.

Life for the forty-niners was very different from the wonderful stories they had heard. A Philadelphia schoolteacher described it this way:

"We made $3.00 each today. This life has affected my health. Our diet consists of hard tack (a hard biscuit made of flour and water), flour we eat half cooked, and salt pork. Sometimes, we have some salmon which we buy from the Indians. Vegetables are not to be found. Our feet are wet all day while a hot sun shines down upon our heads. The very air parches the skin like the hot air of an oven.

"After our day of labor, we lie down in our clothes. We rob our feet of their boots to make a pillow out of them. Near morning, there is always a change in the temperature, and several blankets become necessary. The feet and hands of a newcomer become blistered and lame. Besides all these causes of sickness, the worries of so many men who leave their families to come to this land of gold, all work to the same result.

"We are quickly beginning to realize that our chances of making a fortune are about the same as those of drawing a prize in a lottery."

By the middle of the 1850s, many forty-niners had left. Most left poor. Some traded a bag of gold dust for a ticket home by ship. Some stayed to work as laborers for big mining companies. These businesses had heavy equipment for mining gold. Some stayed to farm the rich valleys of the area. Others stayed to work in the towns that had sprung up all over California.

San Francisco had become an important center of trade almost overnight. Thousands of people had come to the town during the gold rush. These people needed food, shelter, and supplies. More and more ships arrived with goods. The newcomers needed lawyers to arrange the sale of property. They needed banks. Soon, homes, churches, and schools were being built.

The gold rush was over. But it had opened up yet another part of the American West.

REVIEW

CHECK YOUR FACTS

1. In what year was gold discovered in California?

2. How did the gold seekers come to California? What were they called?

3. Life in the gold fields was (easy/hard).

4. How was mining done after the gold rush?

5. What town did the gold rush make important?

THINK ABOUT IT

Who do you think really became rich from the gold rush?

Lesson 6: Mexican-Americans in the West

FIND THE WORDS

mestizo   citizen

There were about 80,000 Mexican-Americans living in California and the Southwest in the 1850s. These Spanish-speaking people were the pioneers of what had been the frontier of northern Mexico. They founded and settled many of the western cities that have Spanish names today. Most of these people were **mestizos** (mess TEE zohz). These are people with Indian, Spanish, and sometimes Black ancestors.

The 1848 treaty with Mexico promised the Mexican-Americans "all the rights of citizens of the

San Antonio was an important city when Texas became a state in 1845. Today, more than half of its people are Mexican-Americans.

192

United States." A **citizen** is a person who is a member of a particular nation. What happened to these Mexican-American people, who were now living under a new government?

The Mexican-Americans were soon outnumbered in their own land. Before the gold rush, most of the people in California were Spanish-speaking. By 1850, there were 380,000 people in California. Now only about 15 out of every 100 were Spanish-speaking. The same thing happened in Texas and Arizona. As more and more English-speaking people came, the Mexican-Americans became a small part of the population. This meant that the Mexican-Americans now had less power. It was harder for them to protect their rights and property. Spanish-speaking Americans were not treated as well as English-speaking Americans in many ways.

Throughout these years, Mexican-Americans continued to press for their rights. A few were elected to positions in government. Many joined organizations to discuss problems they shared as Mexican-Americans. The Spanish-language newspapers encouraged people to vote. They told them to have pride in their language and to learn English, as well.

After 1910, there were political problems in Mexico and few jobs. Many jobs were open in the United States at that time. Many more Mexicans now moved into the part of the United States near Mexico. This new group reminded the older Mexican-Americans of their ties with Mexico. There were now more Mexican-Americans to work together for a better future.

REVIEW

WATCH YOUR WORDS

1. Most Mexican-Americans in the 1850s were____.
   Spaniards mestizos Texans
2. A ____ is a person who is a member of a particular nation.
   citizen mestizo foreigner

CHECK YOUR FACTS

3. Why did the Mexican-Americans become a small part of the population in the West?
4. When did more Mexicans begin to come to the United States?

THINK ABOUT IT

Besides the Mexicans, what other important group lived in the West before English-speaking settlers arrived?

Lesson 7: Hispanic-Americans Today

Have you ever seen this sign before? It is found in many stores and public places in the United States. Do you know what the sign means in English?

In English, *se habla español* (say AHB lah ES pah NYOHL) means

Se habla español

"Spanish is spoken here." This sign tells Spanish-speaking people that someone there can speak their language. Why do you suppose such signs are needed?

Today, there are about 15 million people of Spanish background in the United States. That is about 6 out of every 100 people in the nation. People of Spanish background are called **Hispanics.**

Hispanic-Americans share the Spanish language. They also share other parts of Spanish culture. But they are not all the same, just as other Americans are not all alike. Hispanic-Americans have different backgrounds and ways of living.

Most Hispanic people in the United States have come from countries settled by Spain more than 400 years ago.

As you know, Mexican-American families have been living in the West for hundreds of years. Many more Mexicans have arrived since the early days. Mexican-Americans today make up the largest Hispanic group in the United States.

Puerto Rican–Americans are the second-largest Hispanic group. Puerto Rico is an island southeast of Florida. It was taken by the United States from Spain during the Spanish-American War of 1898. All Puerto Ricans are citizens of the United States. Americans can easily travel between the mainland United States and Puerto Rico. They can do this just as easily as they can go from New York to California.

Many Cubans came to the United States in the 1960s and afterwards. They left Cuba after the

194

STATES WHERE MANY HISPANIC-AMERICANS LIVE

State	Number of Hispanic people in 1980
CALIFORNIA	4,500,000
TEXAS	3,000,000
NEW YORK	1,700,000
FLORIDA	900,000
ILLINOIS	600,000
NEW JERSEY	500,000
NEW MEXICO	500,000
ARIZONA	400,000
COLORADO	300,000
MICHIGAN	200,000

Cuban government became Communist in 1959. **Communism** is a system under which the government owns and runs all businesses. Many Cubans have settled in Florida. Most of them have become American citizens.

Look at the chart of states where many Hispanic-Americans live. Then look at the map of the United States on pages 8 and 9. Find these states on the map.

People of Mexican, Puerto Rican, and Cuban background are not the only Hispanic-Americans.

Hispanics have come to the United States from all the Spanish-speaking nations in Central and South America. Below is a list of them. Do you know anyone from these countries?

Argentina
Bolivia
Chile
Colombia
Costa Rica
Cuba
Dominican Republic
Ecuador
El Salvador
Guatemala
Honduras
Mexico
Nicaragua
Panama
Paraguay
Peru
Puerto Rico
   (United States)
Uruguay
Venezuela

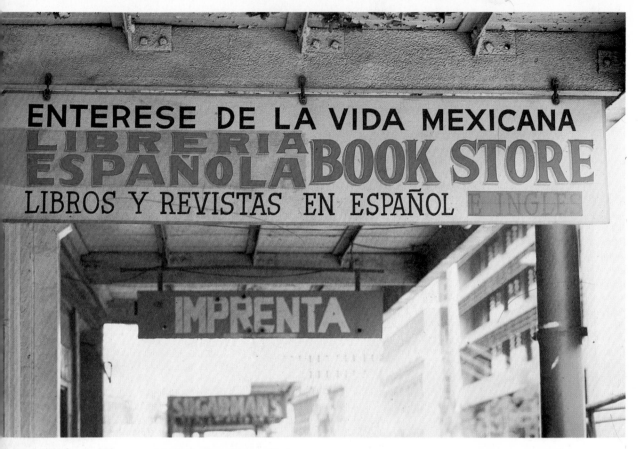

In places with many Hispanic-Americans, signs are in Spanish and English.

REVIEW

CHECK YOUR FACTS

1. What language do Hispanic-Americans share?

2. Hispanic-Americans (are/are not) all alike.

3. What is the largest Hispanic group in the United States?

4. Puerto Ricans (are/are not) American citizens.

5. What state has many Cubans?

THINK ABOUT IT

Does your state have many Hispanic-Americans? If so, to what group or groups do they belong?

CHAPTER REVIEW

WATCH YOUR WORDS

1. People who travel to a new area to spread religion are___.
   forty-niners pioneers missionaries

2. The people who came to California during the gold rush are called___.
   forty-niners pioneers Hispanics

3. The early settlers in the West are known as___.
   Conestogas pioneers missionaries

4. ___ are people who have a Spanish background.
   Conestogas Forty-niners Hispanics

5. The ___ bought cheaply and sold at a profit.
   Conestogas Communists
   land speculators

6. ___were large covered wagons.
   Conestogas Porridges Frontiers

7. A ___ is an unexplored or unsettled area.
   land speculator porridge frontier

8. Under___, the government owns and runs the businesses.
   land speculation Communism
   capitalism

9. ___ are people with both Indian and Spanish ancestors.
   Mestizos Citizens Hispanics

10. ___is a souplike food.
    Conestoga Porridge Pioneer

CHECK YOUR FACTS

11. What nation owned Florida at the end of the Revolutionary War?

12. Who was the third President of the United States?

13. With what European nation did the United States at first share the Oregon country?

14. With what two Spanish-speaking nations did the United States fight wars in the 19th century?

15. What is the largest group of Hispanic-Americans?

USE YOUR MAP

16. Look at the map on page 175. What was the western border of the United States in 1783?

17. When did the United States double in size?

18. In what town did the trails to the West begin?

19. What two trails split north of the Great Salt Lake?

20. When did the last part of the West become part of the United States?

THINK ABOUT IT

21. What did "the West" mean in 1607? In 1783? In 1803? In 1848?

22. If life on the frontier was so hard, why do you think people moved there?

23. When the American Indians were moved to the Great Plains, were they allowed to keep their lands there?

24. Why did the pioneers usually travel in groups?

25. Name some cities in the United States with Spanish names.

UNIT REVIEW

WATCH YOUR WORDS

Use the words below to fill in the blanks. Use each term only once.

amendments
ammunition
antifederalists
Articles of Confederation
Bill of Rights
bills
boycott

checked
Constitution
Continental Congress
executive
federal
federalists

independence
judicial
legislative
Loyalists
Parliament
quarter

ratified
revolution
taxes
treaty
unconstitu-
    tional
veto

In the 1770s, a(n) ___ began in British America. The quarrel started because the British ___ wanted to make the colonists pay ___ . The British also wanted to ___ troops in the colonists' homes. The colonists met together in the ___ and organized a(n) ___ of British goods. After the first battles, the Americans declared their ___ .

After years of fighting, a(n) ___ ended the war. The Americans had won even though they lacked supplies such as ___ . In addition, many American ___ had supported Britain.

At first, the new nation was governed under the ___ . Later, a new ___ for the ___ government was written. It was supported by the ___ and opposed by the ___ . All the states ___ it. The new government had ___ , ___ , and ___ branches. These branches ___ each other. For example, the Congress could pass ___ , but the President could ___ them. In addition, the Supreme Court could find laws ___ . Soon, 10 ___ known as the ___ were added to the Constitution to protect freedom.

CHECK YOUR FACTS

1. What two events in Boston helped lead to the Revolution?

2. Where did the first two battles of the Revolution take place?

3. Who commanded the Continental Army?

4. What early battle showed that the Americans could fight the British?

5. What battle led France to enter the Revolutionary War?

6. What battle brought the Revolutionary War to an end?

7. Who started the first Committee of Correspondence in Massachusetts?

8. Who wrote *Common Sense?*

9. What was the group called that governed the United States under the Articles of Confederation?

10. How did the members of the Constitutional Convention finally come to agreement?

11. How many amendments make up the Bill of Rights?

12. What group wanted the United States to fight Britain in the early 1800s?

13. Why has the meaning of "the West" changed?

14. Name the four natural borders of the Old Northwest.

15. What did land speculators do in the West?

16. Children (did/did not) work on the frontier.

17. Who guided Lewis and Clark?

18. How did many Americans travel to Oregon?

19. Why was California settled so quickly?

20. What group originally settled the area south of the Oregon country and west of the Louisiana Territory?

CLOSE THE MAP GAP

21. Draw a map that shows some of the major battle sites of the Revolutionary War. You might include Lexington, Concord, Bunker Hill, New York City, Trenton, Princeton, Philadelphia, Saratoga, Monmouth, Kaskaskia, Savannah, Camden, and Yorktown.

22. Draw a map that shows the westward expansion of the United States. Label each area with its name and the date it was added. Include the United States (1783), Louisiana Purchase (1803), British Cession (1818), Florida (1819), Texas (1845), Oregon Territory (1846), Mexican Cession (1848), and Gadsden Purchase (1853).

23. Draw a map that shows the states where many Hispanic-Americans live.

USE YOUR MAPS

24. Look at the map of the Revolutionary War on page 140. In what state is Bunker Hill? Saratoga? Valley Forge? Yorktown?

25. List the original 13 states.

26. Look at the map of westward growth on page 175. Name five important western trails.

27. Has the shape of Florida changed since 1819?

28. Has the shape of Texas changed since 1845?

THINK ABOUT IT

29. What part of British America remained loyal to Britain after 1776?

30. George Washington believed that it was more important to keep on fighting than to win particular battles. Do you think he was right or wrong? Why, or why not?

31. Some Revolutionary leaders fought in battle. Others worked for independence in other ways. What kinds of things did they do?

32. The United States has a single written Constitution. Britain has a constitution made up of many laws, traditions, and customs. List some advantages and disadvantages of each kind.

33. While the United States was expanding westward, another large North American nation was growing in a similar way. Can you guess what country that was?

TRY SOMETHING NEW

34. Draw a poster in which you try to get Americans in 1776 to fight Britain. Draw one in which you try to get them to stay loyal to Britain.

35. Draw a chart showing the parts of our federal government. Include the three branches, the President, the executive departments, the two houses of Congress, the Supreme Court, and the lower courts.

PUT IT ALL TOGETHER

36. Make a chart with the title "Westward Expansion of the United States." In the first column, list each part added (see question 22 under "Close the Map Gap" above). Then add columns for date added, previous owner, how added.

 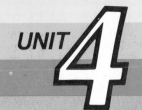

CHAPTER 1
DIVIDED STATES

Lesson 1: Black Slavery in the United States

FIND THE WORDS

master hold pass
abolitionist

In the years after 1619, the first Blacks were brought to the Southern colonies as indentured servants. They had to work for about 7 years to earn their freedom. But as time passed, the colonies passed laws about Blacks. Blacks soon were brought to the colonies as slaves.

Slaves could not earn their freedom by their work. They could be set free only by their **master,** the person who owned them. Slaves usually had to work their whole lives without any pay. Only

Slaves often had to use their free time to do their own chores. Families had little chance to rest or be together. Here, slaves enjoy a rare moment of relaxation near their homes.

a very few slaves were allowed to buy their freedom. They earned the money from work their masters let them do for other people.

Most of the Blacks sold in the colonies were captured in Africa. After their capture, they were packed into the holds of ships. A **hold** is the part of a ship below decks where goods are stored. There, the Africans were crowded very close together. On the voyage, many became sick and died. Others jumped overboard. They

Blacks were sold at auction to the buyer who offered the highest price.

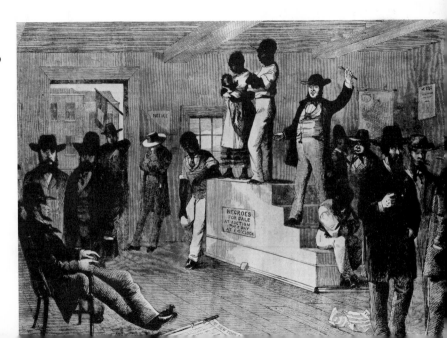

If slaves tried to escape, they were hunted down. This old picture shows runaway slaves going down a road in a large group. Do you think the picture is true to life?

drowned in the sea rather than be slaves. But most were chained down and could not escape.

In most parts of the United States in the early 1800s, Blacks had no rights at all. They did not have the right to vote. It was against the law for them to go to school with Whites. In some states, it was even against the law for them to learn to read and write. Slaves did not have the right to come and go as they pleased. To leave their master's land, they had to have a **pass.** This was a paper from their master giving written permission. Slaves were often separated from their families when they were sold. They had to work very long hours. If they did not do as they were told, they could be whipped. If they tried to escape, they were

hunted down. When caught, they could be punished harshly or even killed.

Until about 1800, there were slaves in almost every state in the United States. But slaves were not a big part of the Northern way of life. Northern factories hired workers. They did not use slaves. However, many Northern factories paid low wages. Often young children worked long hours. By 1850, all Northern states had made slavery illegal.

On the Southern plantations, however, most of the field workers were slaves. One out of every four families owned slaves. But out of the 5 million Southern Whites, only about 10,000 families owned most of the slaves. These people often had large plantations. They were very rich.

Here is a description of slavery on a Virginia plantation in 1778. It was written by a British soldier.

"The slaves are called up at daybreak. They barely have time to swallow a mouthful of hominy or hoe cake. They immediately go out to the fields, where they do hard labor without stopping until noon. Then they get barely an hour to eat hominy and salt pork. If their master is very kind, he may give them a little milk or rusty bacon twice a week. Or he may give his slaves an acre of ground, where they can grow their own food on Saturday afternoons. After their noon dinner, the slaves return to work in the fields until dark.

"At dark, their work is still not over. They must then strip tobacco or husk corn until late evening. They eat their last meager meal and then lie down to rest. They sleep on benches or on the ground in crowded miserable shacks.

"These poor creatures must submit to all manner of insult and injury without resisting. If they dare to defend themselves, the law directs the Negro's arm to be cut off."

The only power that the Blacks had came from their strength as individual women and men. They had to be smart and strong to stay alive. Being "smart," in this case, often meant playing dumb. They could pretend sickness or clumsiness. They would "accidentally" break tools. Some of them fought back and suffered for it.

But even in the early 1800s, there were many **abolitionists** (AB uh LISH un ists). These were people who wanted to abolish, or do away with, slavery. Particularly at first, there were some Southerners among them.

REVIEW

WATCH YOUR WORDS

1. The person who owned a slave was the____.
   abolitionist   master   hold
2. The____opposed slavery.
   abolitionists   masters   indentures

CHECK YOUR FACTS

3. Blacks (were/were not) always brought to the colonies as slaves.

4. Where did most of the slaves sold in the colonies come from?

5. Most Southern families (did/did not) own slaves.

THINK ABOUT IT

Crops are not grown in the winter. Find out what slaves did in the winter.

Lesson 2: Blacks Who Fought Slavery

FIND THE WORDS

racism   harpoon
Underground Railroad

Many Blacks in the United States were slaves. But there were also free Black men and women in both the North and South. All Black people in America had to fight against the idea of **racism.** According to this idea, White people are superior to Black people. In the past, many people believed this. They thought Blacks did not have the same talents or skills as Whites. Free Blacks, mainly in the North, had a chance to prove this idea false. Many of them were explorers, preachers, writers, artists, scientists, and inventors. Blacks in the South who were slaves proved it false as well. They had to have great strength of mind and spirit to endure slavery.

Several free Blacks became wealthy businesspeople during the 1700s and 1800s. Paul Cuffe of Massachusetts owned a fleet of ships and much land in New England. James Forten of Philadelphia was a sail manufacturer. He had 50 employees. John Jones was a rich Chicago businessperson. In Texas, a free Black owned one of the largest cattle ranches.

Black inventors were also important. Norbert Rillieux invented a new way of making sugar in the 1840s. Also in the 1840s, Lewis Temple invented a new **harpoon,** or spear, for whaling. This tool came to be used throughout the whaling industry.

In the 1840s, several Blacks returned to the United States from Europe with degrees in medicine. They set up medical practices in New York and Massachusetts and became well known. James McCune Smith was one such doctor.

The few Black people in the United States who were free, educated, and successful were very important. Some of them were among the first people to attack slavery. Benjamin Banneker was the first Black to receive a Presidential appointment. He was appointed to survey Washington, DC, by President Washington. Banneker wrote to Thomas Jefferson in the 1700s. He asked Jefferson how he could have written the Declaration of Independence and still own slaves. In 1827, the Reverend Samuel E. Cornish and John Russwurm set up the first Black newspaper. It was called *Freedom's Journal.*

Many slaves who had escaped also spoke and acted against slav-

Frederick Douglass was a very powerful abolitionist speaker.

After escaping from the South, Harriet Tubman guided other slaves to freedom. She never lost a "passenger" on the Underground Railroad.

ery. Among these were Frederick Douglass, Harriet Tubman, and Sojourner Truth.

Frederick Douglass became one of the most powerful abolitionist speakers of his time. In 1847, he set up his own newspaper, *The North Star.* During the Civil War, he urged Blacks to join the Union Army. Many did. After the Civil War, Douglass never stopped fighting. He continued to try to win equal rights for his people. He also fought for the rights of all people in the United States. In 1895, on the day he died, he spoke in favor of women's right to vote.

Harriet Tubman escaped from a slave farm in Maryland. She then returned to the South to lead other slaves to freedom in the North or in Canada. She risked her life to make 19 trips and free 300 slaves. The routes that escaped slaves followed to go north were called the **Underground Railroad.** "Stations" on the railroad

were places for escaped slaves to hide during the day. Harriet Tubman never lost a "passenger" on the Underground Railroad. During the Civil War, she served as a spy for the Union Army.

Sojourner Truth was a very important speaker against slavery and for women's rights. She often compared the situation of slaves to the situation of women. She saw many similarities and called attention to them.

At one women's rights meeting, men in the audience were shouting. They were making fun of the

The routes that escaped slaves used to travel north were called the Underground Railroad. In this picture, slaves arrive at a "station."

Sojourner Truth spoke against slavery and for women's rights. She compared the situation of slaves to the situation of women.

women who were speaking. At first, Sojourner Truth sat quietly. One male speaker after another got up and spoke against women's rights. It was becoming more and more difficult to continue the meeting. Then, Sojourner Truth stood up. She attacked the male speakers with powerful words. Here is part of what she said:

"That man over there says that women need to be helped into car-riages, and lifted over ditches, and to have the best place everywhere. Nobody ever helps me into car-riages, or over mud puddles, or gives me any best place!"

She raised herself to her full height of 6 feet. She spoke in a voice like rolling thunder:

"And ain't I a woman? Look at me, look at my arm! I have ploughed, and planted, and gath-ered into barns, and no man could head me! And ain't I a woman? I could work as much and eat as much as a man—when I could get it—and bear the lash as well! And ain't I a woman? I have borne 13 children, and seen most of them sold off to slavery. When I cried out with my mother's grief, none but Jesus heard me. And ain't I a woman?"

REVIEW

WATCH YOUR WORDS

1. ____ is the belief that Whites are su-perior to Blacks.
   Abolitionism   Racism   Slavery

2. Slaves escaped to the North on the ____ .
   Freedom Train   Trail of Tears
   Underground Railroad

CHECK YOUR FACTS

3. What idea did all Black people have to fight against?

4. What important work did Harriet Tubman do?

5. What two causes did Sojourner Truth fight for?

THINK ABOUT IT

6. What point do you think Sojourner Truth was making in her famous speech? Do you think she proved her point?

7. Is racism still a problem for Black Americans today? Give reasons for your answer.

Lesson 3: Slave or Free

FIND THE WORDS

tariff   fiber   cotton gin
secession

During the first half of the 1800s, the North and the South grew in different ways. In the North, cities became centers of wealth and manufacturing. There were many workers with different skills. In the South, there was little manufacturing. Most of the people were farmers. The wealth of the South came largely from plantation crops. These crops included tobacco, cotton, rice, and sugar cane. Slaves did much of the work on the plantations.

Meanwhile, the West was growing fast. Western farmers grew grain and corn and raised cattle and hogs. New businesses came to Western cities, such as Chicago and Cincinnati. These cities became centers where Western products were sold and shipped to the East. Many of the Western territories became new states.

As these changes took place, one question became more and more important. Who would control the federal government in Washington? Would Congress make laws mainly for the benefit of the North, with its banks, fac-

tories, and cities? Or would it make laws in favor of the South, with its plantations, slaves, and smaller population? New states were joining the Union. It became very important whether they would vote with the North or with the South in Congress.

Look at the chart on page 210. It shows some of the big differences between the North and the South in 1860.

The map on page 211 shows which states were "free" and which were "slave." Free states did not allow slavery. Slave states did.

The map also shows the territories. The territories could be either slave or free. It depended on what the people living there wanted. New territories that joined the Union as free states voted with the North. Those that joined as slave states voted with the South. The section that had the most votes in Congress would control the federal government. So the North and the South were divided over keeping a balance of free states and slave states.

There was another big problem dividing the North and the South. It was the **tariff**, or tax, placed on goods brought into the United States from Europe. Goods made

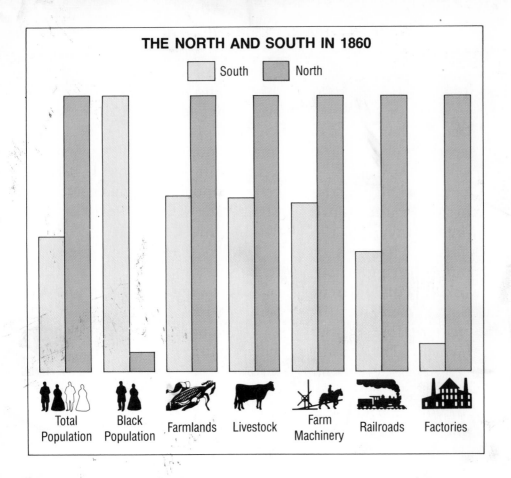

THE NORTH AND SOUTH IN 1860

South   North

Total Population   Black Population   Farmlands   Livestock   Farm Machinery   Railroads   Factories

in European factories were usually cheaper than those made in Northern factories. Northern factory owners did not want to have to compete with these cheaper European goods. The North wanted Congress to set a high tariff.

The South did not want a high tariff. Southerners did not manufacture many goods. Thus, they had to buy manufactured goods from outside the South. A high tariff just made these manufactured goods more expensive. It did not help the South. Also, the Eu-

ropeans did not only sell manufactured goods. They also bought Southern cotton, tobacco, and other crops. They paid higher prices for these things than the Northerners did. This trade with Europe was the main source of wealth in the South. A high American tariff tended to hurt such trade. Thus, it tended to hurt the South. The tariff was another major cause of conflict between the North and the South.

Slavery, however, was the main thing dividing the North and the

SLAVE AND FREE STATES IN 1861

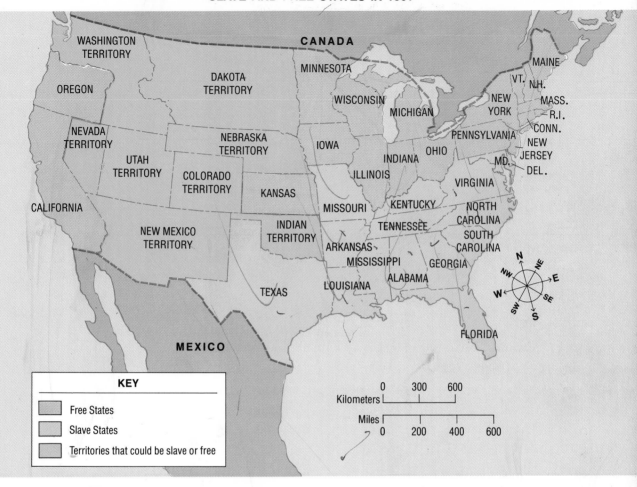

KEY
- Free States
- Slave States
- Territories that could be slave or free

South. In the late 1700s, some cotton was grown in the South. But the seeds had to be picked from the cotton **fiber,** or threads, by hand. This could not be done quickly enough for planters to make a real profit. At that time, slavery was becoming less important to the Southern economy. Then, in 1793, Eli Whitney invented the **cotton gin.** This machine cleaned the seeds from the cotton fibers 10 times faster than a human worker could. Cotton then became a great source of wealth. The number of slaves in the South increased. There were fewer than 1 million slaves in 1800. But there were over 3 million by 1850. Slaves were needed to raise the cotton. Their work was also important in growing tobacco and rice.

But in the North and elsewhere in the world, feelings about slavery had changed. Slavery was now

211

A cotton gin cleaned the seeds from cotton much faster than a person could. Here, slaves are using a cotton gin.

looked upon as wrong. It was seen as an injustice to those who were slaves. Britain freed the slaves in its colonies in 1833. In the United States, the movement to abolish slavery became very strong in the North. But the stronger the abolitionist movement grew, the more strongly White Southerners defended slavery.

Many important citizens and lawmakers in the North spoke out against slavery. William Lloyd Garrison founded a newspaper, *The Liberator*, in Boston. In it, he wrote articles attacking Congress for being so slow to take action against slavery. In 1852, Harriet Beecher Stowe wrote a book about slavery in the South. It was called

The stronger the abolitionist movement became, the more White Southerners defended slavery. In this picture, an 1860 abolitionist meeting is broken up.

TIME LINE: 1860–1877

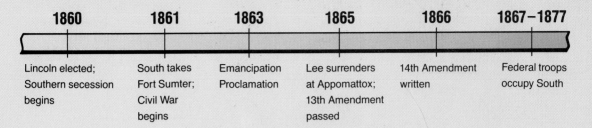

1860	1861	1863	1865	1866	1867–1877
Lincoln elected; Southern secession begins	South takes Fort Sumter; Civil War begins	Emancipation Proclamation	Lee surrenders at Appomattox; 13th Amendment passed	14th Amendment written	Federal troops occupy South

Uncle Tom's Cabin. It made many Northerners aware of the terrible things that often happened to slaves. Many people who read the book became angry.

With the Presidential election of 1860, the conflict between the North and the South grew worse. Abraham Lincoln, a member of Congress from Illinois, was nominated for President by the Republican Party. The Republicans were against slavery. The Democrats of the South were for it. Because the Democrats were divided, it was almost certain that the Republicans would win the election.

Many Southerners began to talk about **secession** (si SESH un). This meant they wanted to secede, or withdraw, from the United States. These Southerners said that the United States was created when the states agreed to form a new nation. Some Southerners believed that, just as they could join the Union, they could leave it.

On December 20, 1860, after Lincoln was elected President, South Carolina seceded. Within 4 months, six other states seceded. They were Georgia, Florida, Alabama, Mississippi, Texas, and Louisiana. Later, Virginia, Arkansas, North Carolina, and Tennessee joined them. These states formed a new nation called the Confederate States of America. They elected Jefferson Davis president of the Confederacy.

Lincoln took office in March 1861. In his first speech, he said he would not break the laws that protected slavery. But he also said

Abraham Lincoln was elected President of the United States in 1860.

Jefferson Davis was President of the Confederate States of America.

The Confederates captured Fort Sumter and raised their flag.

that he did not think the Confederate States could leave the Union. He said that the Confederacy had no legal right to destroy the government. The President, he said, had a legal duty to "preserve, protect, and defend" the government.

Lincoln said that he would keep control of all federal property in the South, especially forts. The Confederacy wanted Union sol-

diers to leave the forts. In Charleston, South Carolina, there was a federal fort called Fort Sumter. The Confederacy ordered the soldiers there to leave. The commander of the fort refused. The Confederates then fired cannons at the fort. This happened on April 12, 1861. It was the beginning of the Civil War. Southerners call this the War between the States.

REVIEW

WATCH YOUR WORDS

1. The ___ cleaned the seeds from cotton faster than workers could.
   fiber   cotton gin   tariff

2. A ___ is a tax on goods brought in from other nations.
   fiber   secession   tariff

CHECK YOUR FACTS

3. List three issues that divided the North and the South.

4. Who was elected President of the United States in 1860?

5. What nation did 11 Southern states form?

THINK ABOUT IT

Do you think the Civil War had to happen? If so, why? If not, how could it have been avoided?

Lesson 4: The American Civil War

The Civil War lasted from 1861 to 1865. It was the bloodiest war people in the United States had fought up to that time. On one side, the South, or the Confederacy, fought for Southern independence. These Southerners wanted to protect states' rights and the Southern way of life. On the other side, the North, or the Union, fought to preserve the federal union.

The North had many advantages. Three-fourths of the nation's wealth was produced in the North. Northern factories made everything the Union Army needed. There were 22 million people in the North. There were only 8 million in the South. The North had most of the nation's ships, banks, factories, and railroads.

The South did have some advantages. Most of the war would

In 1861, soldiers left for the war. Most thought it would soon be over.

be fought on Southern territory. Confederate soldiers would fight bravely to defend their homes. Union soldiers would have to fight in unfriendly and unfamiliar territory. Many of the nation's high-ranking army officers were from the South. That meant that the Confederate Army would have better generals. The South also had cotton. Many European nations needed that cotton to make cloth. Those nations might help the South in order to get cotton.

General Robert E. Lee was commander in chief of the Confederate armies. Lee was a great general. Both sides greatly respected him.

President Lincoln knew how important European trade was to the South. So the first war action he took was to order the Union Navy to blockade Southern ports. To **blockade** a port is to keep ships from entering or leaving it. Throughout the war, the South had a hard time getting supplies through the Union blockade.

On July 21, 1861, the first major battle took place between the Union Army and the Confederate Army. The Union Army had hoped to capture Richmond, Virginia, the capital of the Confederacy. They thought they could win the war quickly. But the Confederate Army met them at Bull Run, a small creek between Washington and Richmond. The Union Army was defeated in this first battle of Bull Run. The North began to realize that it would be a long war.

For 2 years, things went badly for the Union Army in the East. The Union soldiers were led by General George McClellan. He knew how to organize and train troops. But he was slow to attack.

The Emancipation Proclamation freed slaves living in areas still under Confederate rule. Here, freed slaves leave the plantations as troops pass by.

The Confederate armies were led by General Robert E. Lee and General Thomas "Stonewall" Jackson. These great generals won many battles. In the West, the Union Army did somewhat better under General Ulysses S. Grant.

In the North and in the South, many soldiers were **volunteers.** That meant that they joined the army of their own free will. The South also had a **draft.** That is a law that requires people to join the armed forces. The North did not start to draft soldiers until 1863. But the Northern draft law was different. Anyone who did not want to fight could avoid the draft by paying $300 to the government. This was unfair to poor people. They could not afford to pay so much money. At that time, many workers did not make that much in a whole year. Many riots broke out in New York and other cities in the North over the draft issue.

The abolitionists hoped that the war would free the slaves. They thought that free Blacks should be armed to fight with the North against the South. Blacks had fought bravely in the Revolution and in the War of 1812. But some White people did not know this. They thought that Blacks would not fight. Finally, President Lincoln allowed the Blacks to be armed. They proved once again to be brave soldiers. There were 186,000 Blacks who fought in the Union Army.

Lincoln believed that if he freed the slaves, many more Black soldiers would fight for the Union. Also, Lincoln did not want Europe to support the South. Many Europeans opposed slavery. Thus, if he freed the slaves, Europe would

At Gettysburg, there was a long, hard battle. Both sides lost thousands of soldiers.

sympathize with the North. So, on January 1, 1863, Lincoln issued the **Emancipation Proclamation** (i MAN suh PAY shun PROK luh MAY shun). This document freed only those slaves living in the parts of the South still under Confederate rule. The Thirteenth Amendment, passed in 1865, freed all the slaves in the United States.

By July 1863, Union forces, under General Grant, controlled the Mississippi River. Texas, Arkansas, and most of Louisiana were now separated from the rest of the Confederacy. In the East, the Union Army met the Confederate Army at Gettysburg, Pennsylvania, on July 1, 1863. General Meade

commanded the Union troops. The Confederates were under General Lee. There was a long, hard battle. Each side lost about 25,000 soldiers. But the Union Army had won. From that point on, the tide turned against the South.

In November 1863, Lincoln made a famous speech at the Gettysburg battlefield. It is called the Gettysburg Address. In it, Lincoln said that the soldiers buried there had given their lives so that "government of the people, by the people, for the people shall not perish from the earth."

The war continued for almost 2 more years after Gettysburg. In 1864, Lincoln made General Grant

had nothing under slavery, remained very poor as free people.

A Black scholar, W.E.B. DuBois, described the situation of Blacks after the war in this way:

"To white Americans, everything black seemed ugly. Everything Negroes did was thought wrong. If they fought for freedom, they were beasts. If they did not fight, they were cowards and born to be slaves. If they stayed on plantations, they loved slavery. If they ran away, they were lazy loafers. If they sang, they were silly. If they frowned or complained, they were trouble-makers.

"All hatred that the Northern and Southern whites had for each other during the war gradually focused on the blacks after the war. Blacks were looked on as the cause of the war. But they were really its victims.

"It was said that blacks were not smart enough to be educated. And it was said that free, educated black citizens and voters were an even worse problem. Equal education and job opportunities for blacks would lead to social equality. It was said that this would lead to a mixing of the white and black races. And this, it was said, would be the ruin of civilization."

President Lincoln felt sympathy for the South. He saw that the

W. E. B. DuBois was a Black scholar. He believed that Blacks should work together against prejudice and for equal rights.

South had suffered very much. He planned to provide money, food, and supplies for the **reconstruction,** or rebuilding, of the South. But 5 days after the surrender at Appomattox, Lincoln was killed. He was shot by an angry Southern White who blamed him for destroying the South. Andrew Johnson became President. Johnson wanted to carry out Lincoln's Reconstruction plan. However, Congress had its own plans.

In 1865, the federal government set up the **Freedmen's Bureau.** This agency was to help former slaves learn a new way of life. The bureau gave out goods and clothing. It set up schools in which

Black men, women, and children could learn to read and write.

Meanwhile, several Southern states passed laws called **Black Codes.** These laws kept Blacks from voting, serving on juries, and carrying guns. In some states, Blacks were allowed to work only as house servants or farmhands.

Congress did not like what was happening in the South. In 1867, federal troops were sent to run parts of the South. State elections were held in which Black men voted for the first time. Men who had been Confederate leaders during the war were not allowed to vote. No women—White or Black—were allowed to vote.

New state governments were elected. They were made up of Black men and of White Southern men who had not taken part in the war. Some Northerners who had come south after the war also took part in the new state governments. The White Southerners who could not vote resented these officeholders. They called the Northerners **carpetbaggers.** A carpetbag was an old-fashioned type of suitcase made of carpet cloth. The former Confederates had a name for the White Southern officeholders, too. They were called **scalawags** (SKAL uh wagz).

The Black officeholders had never had positions in the government before. They had little expe-rience to guide them. Often the carpetbaggers and the scalawags took advantage of them for this reason.

During the Reconstruction period, Congress sent to the states three important new amendments to the Constitution. These were the Thirteenth, Fourteenth, and Fifteenth Amendments. All were approved by the states.

The Thirteenth Amendment abolished slavery.

The Fourteenth Amendment made the Blacks citizens. It also said that all citizens must be treated equally under the law.

The Fifteenth Amendment said that no citizens could be stopped from voting because of their race or color.

In 1877, the last federal troops left the South. The South had suf-fered under Reconstruction. Many of the White Southerners resented the way they had been treated. Despite the new amendments, Black Southerners were gradually put down again. Laws were passed that provided for the **segregation,** or separation, of Southern society into two parts. For example, Whites and Blacks were to go to separate schools. But the schools for Blacks were not as good as the schools for Whites. Special tests and rules were set up to keep Blacks from voting.

The Freedmen's Bureau set up schools for Black people. Here, women learn how to make a living by sewing.

Under the laws of segregation, Whites and Blacks went to separate schools.

Booker T. Washington thought that the best way for Blacks to establish themselves was to learn skilled work. To help them do this, he set up the Tuskegee Institute for the education of Blacks.

In the North and the South, educated Blacks tried to stop segregation. They did this in many different ways.

Booker T. Washington believed that Blacks should try to gain skills and become good workers. He thought that when Blacks had money, businesses, and skills, equal rights would follow. Booker T. Washington was able to win support for his ideas from wealthy people. He set up the Tuskegee Institute in Alabama. At first, the institute trained people for practical jobs, such as bricklaying, shoemaking, and dairy farming. Later, George Washington Carver, a great Black scientist, worked and taught there. He developed hundreds of new products from peanuts, sweet potatoes, soybeans, and cotton.

Another Black leader, W.E.B. DuBois, had different ideas. He said that Blacks must learn to do more than lay bricks, make shoes, raise cows, and grow crops. He believed that Blacks had to stand up against laws that made segregation possible. These laws said that Blacks could not enjoy the same rights as other citizens. So these laws had to be changed.

REVIEW

WATCH YOUR WORDS

1. ____ were Northerners who came south after the Civil War.
   Carpetbaggers   Scalawags
   Freedmen

2. ____ were Southern Whites who took part in the Reconstruction governments.
   Carpetbaggers   Scalawags
   Freedmen

3. ____ separated Southern society into two parts.
   Reconstruction   Segregation
   Freedmen

CHECK YOUR FACTS

4. Why did many poor Whites resent the newly freed slaves?

5. What federal agency helped the former slaves?

THINK ABOUT IT

After the Civil War, some people wanted to divide the plantations among the former slaves. Do you think this was a good idea? Would it have been fair? Why, or why not?

CHAPTER REVIEW

WATCH YOUR WORDS

1. To leave the plantations, slaves had to have a ____.
   tariff   master   pass

2. A ____ is a spear used in whaling.
   blockade   harpoon   draft

3. ____ is the idea that states can leave the Union.
   Segregation   Secession   Reconstruction

4. A ____ requires people to serve in the armed forces.
   tariff   draft   secession

5. Immediately after the Civil War, the Southern states passed ____.
   tariffs   draft laws   Black Codes

6. ____ means rebuilding.
   Segregation   Reconstruction   Emancipation

CHECK YOUR FACTS

7. List three things the law did not allow slaves to do.

8. What name was given to the routes slaves used to escape?

9. Why did a Republican win the Presidential election of 1860?

10. Where did General Lee surrender to General Grant?

11. Which amendment abolished slavery?

USE YOUR MAPS AND CHARTS

12. Look at the chart on page 210. The South was a farming area. The North had many factories. Which section had more farmland and livestock?

13. Look at the map of slave and free states on page 211. Also look at the lesson. Which slave states did not join the Confederacy?

14. Which territory was set aside for American Indians?

THINK ABOUT IT

15. Why did the Northern states and Southern states disagree about the tariff?

16. Why did slavery end in the North long before the Civil War?

17. Did the Emancipation Proclamation immediately free anyone?

KNOW YOUR PEOPLE

Match the name with the clue.

18. Jefferson Davis   A. led the Union armies.

19. Frederick Douglass   B. issued the Emancipation Proclamation.

20. Ulysses S. Grant   C. founded Tuskegee Institute.

21. Robert E. Lee   D. led the Confederate armies.

22. Abraham Lincoln   E. was president of the Confederacy.

23. Harriet Tubman   F. published *The North Star*.

24. Booker T. Washington   G. led 300 slaves to freedom.

TRY SOMETHING NEW

25. Find out more about one of the leaders in the exercise above. Write a one-page report about that leader.

CHAPTER 2 INDUSTRY AND IMMIGRANTS

Lesson 1: The Industrial Revolution Begins

FIND THE WORDS

revolution   reaper   thresher
mass production   division of labor
interchangeable parts
assembly line   locomotive
process   ingenuity

A **revolution** is not always a war to change a government. It can be any great change in the way people think, work, or live. The earliest human beings hunted, fished, and gathered wild plants for their food. Then people learned to plant crops and raise animals. For thousands of years, most people herded flocks or raised food on farms.

Until the mid-1700s, most work was done with muscle. People and animals pulled, pushed, and carried heavy loads. Only a few other sources of power were used. Running water made water wheels go around. Rushing wind made the blades of windmills turn. This water and wind power ran machines that could grind grain into flour. Windmills also furnished power to pump water and saw wood.

Farm Machines

Then, in a single century, new machines changed the way most work was done. At first, power to move the machines was still furnished by a horse. Cyrus McCormick showed farmers his new invention in 1831. It was a horse-drawn reaper. A **reaper** is a machine that cuts down a crop and drops it in piles. A worker could cut 50 times more wheat with a reaper than by hand. Almost 50 years earlier, a Scottish inventor had invented a threshing machine. The **thresher** separated the seeds, or grains, of wheat from the rest of the plant. Using reapers and threshers, farmers could harvest much more wheat. So, much more wheat was planted and grown. Reapers and threshers were soon followed by corn planters, huskers, and other farm machines.

The Steam Engine

The Industrial Revolution was made possible by the power of steam. In Scotland, James Watt had invented a practical steam engine in 1769. Fuel was burned in a furnace. It heated water in a boiler. The heat turned the water to steam. Then the steam was condensed. Great pressure built up. Machine parts were moved by the force of the steam.

In the early 1800s, steam engines were improved. Soon they could furnish power for farm equipment, such as threshers. They could also drive factory machines. They could be used to raise coal out of mines. Steam engines could even provide power to move ships and railroad trains.

Home and Factory

For thousands of years, people made goods by hand. They worked in their homes or in small shops. Sometimes one person worked alone, using a few simple tools. Sometimes an assistant or other family members helped.

Suppose you had lived in those days. Suppose you wanted to make a wool shirt. First, you

Before the Industrial Revolution, people canned food by hand. How do you think this job is done today?

The steam engine changed the way work was done in textile mills. Machines driven by steam power could work much faster than people could.

would cut the wool off the sheep. You would wash and dry it. Next, you would dye the wool. Then, you would spin it into thread. You would weave the thread into cloth. Finally, you would use thread and cloth to sew a shirt. You would make the whole product, from beginning to end.

In the 1700s and 1800s, inventors found new ways to make things with machines. Now, one machine could do as much work as many different people. Using machines, people could work much faster. They could make many more goods. The age of mass production had arrived. **Mass production** is making a great many goods by using machines.

Machines changed more than the amount of work done and the speed. Machines also changed the work place and the way work was done. Before, business owners sometimes used workers who did the work in their own homes. Family members worked together there. Now, business owners were building factories to house their new machines. So workers started to work outside the home. They began to work with strangers in the factories. Some New England women went to work in cloth factories called textile (TEX tyl) mills.

In factories, work was divided up. Different workers did different jobs. This way of working is called the **division of labor**. Suppose a factory made wool shirts. One set of people would cut the wool and bring it to the factory. There, other people would wash and dry the wool. Still other people would dye it. Then spinners would use machines to spin it into thread. Finally, weavers would use other machines to weave it into cloth. Steam engines supplied the power to run the spinning and weaving machines.

The Assembly Line

In 1798, Eli Whitney built a factory to make guns. Whitney had already invented the cotton gin. Now he had another important idea. He wanted the parts from one gun to fit any other gun made in his factory. Before, each

With each worker doing a different job, more goods could be made in less time. Cash registers were among the products made this way.

Eli Whitney's gun factory changed the way goods were made. It was Whitney's idea to use interchangeable parts.

worker had made all the parts of a single gun. The parts for one gun would not fit any other gun. Now, each worker would make many copies of one part. The copies would be the same size and shape. That meant one part could change places with any other like it. So the copies were called **interchangeable** (IN tur CHAYN juh bul) **parts**. Workers making only one part needed less skill than workers making a whole gun.

Eli Whitney's idea spread. Today, because of Whitney, we have assembly lines. An **assembly line** in a factory is a line of workers and machines. Every worker or machine does a different thing to the product. No one person makes a whole product. Instead, each product is made by many people and machines, one step at a time. Interchangeable parts are used in products made on an assembly line.

Cities and Railroads

The growth of factories also led to the growth of towns and cities. Factory owners needed a supply of workers. They built their factories in places where workers could be found. Then, more workers moved to places where there were factory jobs. Going to work in a factory usually meant leaving a farm.

More people were traveling away from home to work. More products were coming out of factories. So better transportation was needed to move people and materials around. Before, sailors had needed wind to push a ship across the water. Other travelers had needed horses to pull a wagon over the land. The first railroads had horse-drawn cars. They were used to carry minerals from mines. Then, in 1830, the first steam railroad in the United States started to run. The railroad tracks were only 21 kilometers (13 miles) long. But something revolutionary had happened. A steam locomotive called *Tom Thumb* was moving under its own power! The word *locomotive* means "able to move from place to place." The **locomotive** of a train contains the engine. It can pull or push the other railroad cars.

Soon, workers were putting down thousands of miles of railroad tracks. Other workers were digging canals to connect large eastern rivers and lakes. By the 1840s, steamboats moved across the inland waterways. Steamboats and railroads carried raw materials from around the country to factories in the North.

There, workers processed the raw materials. To **process** something is to make it ready for sale or for use. Cotton was spun into thread and woven into cloth. Raw sugar was refined, or made pure.

Steam power drove the engines of early railroads. Trains carried raw materials to factories and took finished goods away. This train got stuck in the snow.

This drawing shows the progress made in travel and communication. How many signs of progress can you see?

Meat was cut up, cleaned, and packed. Then, the railroads and steamboats carried processed goods from the North to other parts of the United States. Steam transportation gave factories a much bigger market for their goods.

The Telegraph

As you can see, there were great changes in the ways people made and moved goods. There was also a great change in the way people sent messages. In 1844, Samuel Morse perfected the telegraph. The telegraph could send messages across many miles. These messages traveled over wires as electric signals. A newspaper reporter described the impact of this new invention. He was

in Washington, DC, getting a report of the Democratic National Convention in Baltimore. He wrote:

"Never before was anyone aware of what was happening in a distant city 40, 100, or 500 miles away. For example, it is now exactly 11 o'clock. The telegraph announces as follows: '11 o'clock—Senator Walker is *now* answering Mr. Butler on the adoption of the two-thirds rule.' It takes quite a mental effort to realize that this is a fact that *now is* and not one that *has been*. The telegraph is a most wonderful achievement."

By 1860, 80,000 kilometers (50,000 miles) of telegraph wires joined the different parts of the nation.

There were many other inventions in the first half of the 1800s. New ways of making steel were being used. Ways to mold rubber into firm shapes were found. New inventions ranged from the tricycle to the safety pin. A new kind of printing press came into use. It could print thousands of newspapers and books in a single hour.

The United States had a wealth of natural resources. The people had plenty of native cleverness, or **ingenuity** (IN juh NOO uh tee). The

FUN FACTS

Americans love ice cream. The United States manufactures enough frozen dessert each year to feed every American 23 quarts apiece! In the summer of 1790, George Washington spent $200 on ice cream. And in 1812, Dolley Madison served homemade ice cream at the White House.

Making ice cream was a long, hard job. Someone had to beat the cream, sugar, and flavorings by hand in a wooden pot. At the same time, the pot had to be jiggled up and down in a pan of ice and salt. Ice was hard to get in the days before refrigerators. And it took hours of work to make ice cream.

Nancy Johnson of New Jersey changed all that. In 1846, she invented the hand-cranked ice cream freezer. This freezer was a bucket with a paddle inside and a crank for a handle. The cream mixture went in a container in the middle.

Ice and salt were packed around the edges. Then one person could turn the crank that moved the paddle that beat the cream and shook the ice and salt around it.

Today, we can buy ice cream from pushcarts, grocery stores, and ice cream parlors. Over 500 different flavors have been invented. We can eat ice cream in cones, cups, sodas, sundaes, and banana splits. And we owe it all to the ingenious Nancy Johnson!

years before the Civil War brought new inventions and steam power. With new equipment, fewer farmers were needed to raise large crops. Some workers began to leave the farm for the factory. Around the factories, cities began to spread. People, goods, and messages were being moved faster than ever before. The pace of life had quickened. At home and on the job, people's way of life was changing. The Industrial Revolution had begun.

REVIEW

WATCH YOUR WORDS

1. A ___ cuts down a crop and drops it in piles.
   thresher   reaper   locomotive

2. A ___ separates the grains of wheat from the rest of the plant.
   thresher   telegraph   reaper

3. ___ are exact copies of one another.
   Threshers   Reapers
   Interchangeable parts

4. To ___ something is to prepare it for sale or use.
   telegraph   process   interchange

5. Each worker on a(n) ___ does a different job.
   thresher   reaper   assembly line

6. The ___ means that work is divided up among different people.
   revolution   mass production
   division of labor

7. Making many goods at once by using machines is ___.
   division of labor   mass production
   revolution

8. The engine of a train is in the ___.
   thresher   reaper   locomotive

9. Successful inventors have a lot of ___.
   ingenuity   process
   interchangeable parts

10. A ___ can be a great change in the way people live.
    process   division of labor
    revolution

CHECK YOUR FACTS

11. Who first had the idea of interchangeable parts?

12. Who invented the reaper? Who perfected the telegraph?

13. What new systems of transportation used the steam engine?

14. How was most work done before modern machines were invented?

15. Describe how work is done on an assembly line.

THINK ABOUT IT

16. Why did people begin to move from farms to cities? How did farm machines and factories help bring this move about?

17. Which invention mentioned in this lesson do you think was most important? Why?

18. What do you suppose the next great change in work will be?

Lesson 2: Industry after the Civil War

FIND THE WORDS

industry   manufacture
industrial   construction
entrepreneur   refine
patent   skyscraper

The word **industry** has three meanings. People can be praised for their industry. That means long, steady effort to get work done. People can work in a certain industry. The garment industry makes a certain kind of product. The tourist industry supplies services and promotes trade. A nation can also have a lot of industry. That means it has many large businesses that manufacture goods for sale. The word *manufacture* means "to make by hand." But to **manufacture** products is to make raw materials into finished goods by using machines.

A country that manufactures and sells many goods is called an **industrial** (in DUS tree ul) nation. The United States became an industrial nation in the years after the Civil War. Factories were

Steel supports raised elevated railroads over city streets. Tunnels were dug underground for subway trains.

being built everywhere. More and more of the nation's work was being done with machines. Using machines, people could produce many more goods and services. With machines, they could travel longer distances. They could send messages faster than ever before.

Energy was no longer supplied only by wind and water. Now, engines ran on steam. Before, people used surface sources for building materials. Mostly, they used wood. Now, they began to take fuels and building materials out of the ground. Minerals from the earth were the raw materials of a new industrial age.

Many construction workers were needed to build the Flatiron Building in New York. Work on the 20-story skyscraper was finished in 1902.

An Age of Steel

People used steam engines to drain water and lift coal out of mines. Coal is mostly carbon. Carbon is a better fuel than wood. It gives off much more heat when it is burned. Coal and iron are also used in making steel. The carbon makes the iron very hard and strong. The eastern United States had a lot of iron ore and coal. So steelmaking became an important industry. Soon, steel bridges replaced wooden bridges. These strong steel bridges could carry railroad tracks over wide rivers and valleys. Steel supports made it possible to build tracks high over city streets. Steel was also used to build factories, machines, and railroad cars.

When work moved from homes to factories, workers moved to cities from farms. The growth of Chicago shows how fast this movement took place. In 1860, Chicago had only 106,000 people. It had 20 times that many people 50 years later, in 1910. That meant over 2 million people were living in one place. They needed homes, schools, and stores. There was work in **construction** (kun STRUK shun), or building. There was work in manufacturing and trade. There was work providing services. There was a lot of money to be made.

Manufacturing and construction were at the heart of the new age. The most important new material was steel. Andrew Carnegie came to Pennsylvania from Scotland when he was a child. His first job was winding thread in a cotton factory. He made $1.20 a week. Later, he worked for the Pennsylvania Railroad. Since people often had to travel overnight, he introduced sleeping cars. Then, he started his own iron and steel business. He realized how important steel was going to be. By 1900, he owned a steel company, coal and iron mines, steamboats, and railroads. His factories were making one-fourth of the steel in the United States. His company was worth 500 million dollars. He was the richest steel manufacturer in the world.

American Entrepreneurs

A person like Carnegie is called an entrepreneur (AHN truh pruh NUR). An **entrepreneur** is someone who sees an opportunity and sets up a new business. Entrepreneurs have to be good managers. They have to be willing to take risks. The late 1800s were good years for entrepreneurs in the United States. With so much growth and change, it was a good time for businesses to start.

Railroads were one new business in which large fortunes could be made. Three rich and powerful railroad owners were Cornelius Vanderbilt, Collis P. Huntington, and Jay Gould.

Other new industries grew up around petroleum, or oil. In 1859, E. L. Drake drilled the first American oil well. Then the crude oil from the well had to be refined. To **refine** petroleum is to purify it. This is done by heating it to separate its substances. An industry was started to do this work.

At first, petroleum was used to make kerosene (KER uh SEEN). The kerosene was used as an oil for lamps. Then, in 1873, George Brayton of Boston built an engine that ran on kerosene. Later, petroleum was used to make gasoline. Not until 1889 did a German, Gottlieb Daimler (GOT leeb DYM lur), build the kind of gasoline engine we use now.

The Rockefeller fortune was made in petroleum. John D. Rockefeller began working when he was still a child. He earned $3.50 a week as a clerk in a grocery store. Then he started a business selling fruits and vegetables. With partners, he went into the oil-refining business when he was 24. His company was called Standard Oil. By 1911, this company produced, refined, and distributed most of the nation's petroleum. John D. Rockefeller lived to the ripe old age of 98. At the time he

Petroleum, or crude oil, gushed out of this oil well. Petroleum has to be refined before it is useful as fuel.

John D. Rockefeller started the Standard Oil Company. His company produced, refined, and sold most of the nation's petroleum.

died, he was the richest person in the United States.

With so much money being made, people needed banks. The Morgan family of Massachusetts made a fortune by investing money and making loans. J. P. Morgan built the family business into an empire of wealth. He controlled banks, steel, and railroads. His banks provided money to run factories and develop mines.

American Inventors

Inventors were also very important to the new age. In 1876, Alexander Graham Bell took out a patent on a new invention—the telephone. A **patent** is an official paper from the government. It gives the inventor all rights to the invention for a certain number of years. Using the telephone, people could speak to one another over long distances.

American inventors were full of new ideas. They were also good at figuring out practical ways to do things. In 1879, Thomas Alva Edison invented a long-lasting light bulb. Then he developed a new system to supply buildings with electric power and light. "Nothing that's good works by itself," he said. Edison also invented the record player. He invented the first practical movie camera and projector. He took out over 1300 patents on inventions during his life!

Elisha G. Otis invented the first safety elevator in 1853. The invention of elevators had important results. People no longer had to walk up and down stairs. That meant they could live and work in taller buildings. It was now possible to build very tall buildings by using a framework of steel. Such a building seemed to scrape against the sky. So it was called a **skyscraper.** The world's first skyscrapers were built in the United States. The first modern sky-

Thomas Alva Edison was one of the world's greatest inventors. He invented the electric light bulb, the movie camera, and the record player.

238

scraper went up in Chicago in 1883. Its steel framework supported both the floor and the walls. Then, beginning in 1887, electric elevators were used.

The Nation Grows

Now, cities could grow upward as well as spread out. That meant that people could live closer together than ever before. City people were not like independent farmers, living far apart. They were crowded together. Most had to depend on other people's businesses for jobs. People also had to rely on one another more. As cities grew larger, more services were introduced. Larger schools were needed. Hospitals were built. Some small shops expanded and became department stores. There were fire and police departments. There were also telegraph and telephone companies. There were power stations to produce, or

Telephone wires strung from posts carried people's words over long distances. As telephone companies grew, the lines of communication stretched farther.

generate, electricity. The 1880s brought the nation's first electric streetcar.

Manufacturing businesses also grew larger. Workers could make many more goods with machines. Large companies could buy more raw materials for less money. Also, it cost less per item to make many goods at one time. That meant large companies could sell their products at a lower price. Since the products were cheaper, more people could buy them. Then more trains and ships were needed to move products around.

Railroads brought distant parts of the country closer together. In 1860, the United States had 56,000 kilometers (35,000 miles) of railroad track. By 1900, almost six times as much track had been laid. This was more than in all of Europe. Now the United States had cities, factories, and railroads. It had communications and banking. It had steam engines and electric power. It had petroleum, coal, and steel. By 1900, the United States had become the largest industrial nation in the world!

REVIEW

WATCH YOUR WORDS

Fill in the blanks. Use the words in the list below.

1. A(n) ___ protects an inventor's rights to an invention.
2. A(n) ___ nation manufactures many goods.
3. One meaning of the word ___ is "hard work."
4. To ___ petroleum is to purify it.
5. A person who sets up a new business is a(n) ___.
   entrepreneur   industrial
   industry   patent   refine

CHECK YOUR FACTS

6. How did cities in the United States change after the Civil War?

7. What new fuels were used?
8. What material was important for building bridges, railroads, and skyscrapers? Why?
9. Who invented the telephone? The light bulb? The record player?
10. Why were the late 1800s good years for entrepreneurs?

THINK ABOUT IT

In the late 1800s, many factory and construction workers were needed in cities. Is this still true today?

TRY SOMETHING NEW

Find out three new things about one of the inventors or entrepreneurs in this lesson. Use an encyclopedia. Then write a one-page report.

Lesson 3: New Americans Arrive

FIND THE WORDS

immigrant   wave   famine
tenement

The United States was growing and developing very fast. In 1845, Texas joined the Union. By 1848, the nation had added on the whole West Coast. This meant there was much more land to farm. There were cities to build. There were railroad tracks to put down. There was work to be done in factories and mines.

The United States was still a young nation. The population in the mid-1800s was not large. But now the nation stretched from the Atlantic Coast to the Pacific Coast. American companies advertised in Europe for people to come to the United States. Many new Americans were needed to develop this vast land.

The United States has been called "a nation of immigrants." An **immigrant** is a person who leaves one country to settle in another. Except for American Indians, all Americans came from other parts of the world. In 1587, Sir Walter Raleigh sent settlers from England to North Carolina. They started a colony on Roanoke (ROH uh NOHK) Island. Their leader returned to England for supplies. When he came back 4 years later, the colonists had disappeared!

Now, immigrants have been coming to the United States for

IMMIGRATION 1840 to 1930

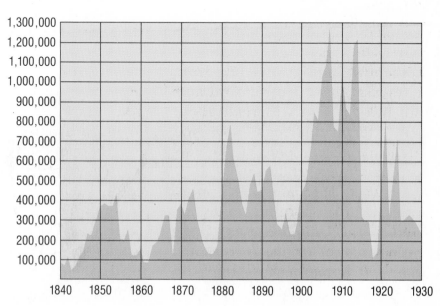

241

Immigrants brought their belongings with them to the United States. They came to America to start a new life.

400 years. Like the lost colonists of Roanoke, they faced dangers and hardships. They often risked their lives. They had to be very brave and determined. This is still true of immigrants coming to the United States today. Many of these new immigrants are from Southeast Asia, Central America, and Mexico. You will read about them later in this book. Now, you will learn about some of the earlier immigrants who came.

Between 1815 and 1915, more than 30 million immigrants arrived in the United States. These settlers came for many reasons. Some left home because they did not have enough food. Others left because of fighting in their land. Some wanted the freedom to say what they thought and to worship as they pleased.

Most immigrants came because they saw the United States as a land of opportunity. Some had heard stories about cheap land, high pay, and streets paved with gold. Here, they could work hard to make a better life. They could use their skills and their ingenuity. They could earn money. They could send their children to school. Then, they could work their way up in the world. They would be Americans.

In the 1600s and 1700s, most immigrants had been English.

There were also many Dutch, French, Germans, Scotch-Irish, Spanish, and Swedes. Then, in the 1800s, many more immigrants arrived. They came in two great waves. A **wave** of immigrants is a large group of people arriving around the same time. People from Europe seemed to move like an ocean wave toward America's shores.

The First Wave

The first great wave of immigrants arrived between 1815 and 1860. Five million people came then. Most came from Northern Europe. The greatest numbers came from Ireland and Germany.

The early Irish who came were poor. Families would save up to send their younger members to the United States. There, the young people would find jobs. Then they could send money home. With the money, the whole family could move to the new land. Then, in 1846, crops failed in Ireland, Holland, and Germany. In Ireland, the potato crops were ruined. Potatoes were the chief source of food. This terrible time was known as the potato famine. A **famine** is a serious shortage of food that lasts for a long time. During the potato famine in Ireland, many people starved. Half a million died of hunger and disease. Within 10 years, 1½ million

This picture was taken around 1900. It shows immigrants waiting in New York to enter the United States.

Irish people left for America.

The Irish immigrants landed in port cities on the East Coast. Most were farmers. But they could not afford to move to the country or buy farms. So they remained in cities like Boston, New York, and Philadelphia. There, they got the hardest jobs at the lowest pay. Irish men dug canals, built roads and railroads, and worked in coal mines. Irish women worked as servants or in textile mills.

Most Irish immigrants were Roman Catholics. They had moved to a country where most people were Protestants. The Protestants did not like or trust the Catholics. Many businesses would not even

COMING TO AMERICA.

RETURNING FOR A VISIT.

This old cartoon shows an Irish immigrant about to leave Dublin for New York. After a few years in America, he is rich enough for a trip back.

hire the Irish. Business owners put up signs that said: "No Irish need apply." In spite of these hardships, the Irish managed to succeed. Later, many made money in business. Others rose to high positions in education, politics, and law.

Millions of immigrants came from Germany to the United States. Most German immigrants were better off than the Irish. After the famine, many came for political reasons. Some of these had started a revolution to change their government. They left home because their revolution had failed. Most of the Germans had money enough to move to the Middle West and buy farms. Many others started businesses in cities such as Milwaukee, Chicago, and Detroit. The Germans were expert farmers and successful entrepreneurs. They brought many gifts to the United States. They even gave us the American hamburger!

Next came the Swedes, Norwegians, and Danes. They settled on the farmland and prairies of the Middle West. These people were hardy pioneers. Some lived in rough sod huts made of clumps of earth. To them, a log cabin seemed like a luxury. Many farmed. Some worked in the forests, cutting wood. The Danes helped to develop the dairy industry. Some of the Norwegians went all the way to the West Coast.

Many immigrants came to America from Germany. The German family in
this painting lived on a farm in the Middle West.

Many families from
Norway, Sweden, and
Denmark settled on
farms in the Middle
West. The pioneers in
this photograph lived in
Nebraska in a sod hut.

The Second Wave

The second great wave of immigrants came between 1890 and 1920. During those years, most immigrants came from Southern and Eastern Europe. Italians and Greeks began to arrive. So did Austrians, Hungarians, Russians, and Poles. All were coming in search of a better life. After 1900, as many as 15,000 immigrants would arrive in a single day!

Poor people in southern Italy had a very hard life. Some workers in Sicily made only 8 cents a day. People had to live in straw houses. Some even lived in caves and tombs. Different problems faced the Jews. They came from many parts of Europe. There, they were often treated badly because of their religious beliefs.

The new immigrants arrived in the United States with high hopes. Yet most faced many problems in the new land. Most had worked on farms. Now they were crowded together in cities. They moved into poor areas that earlier immigrants had left. There, they lived in overcrowded apartment buildings called **tenements**. Families often had to share one small, dark room. The living conditions were so bad that sickness spread. Many of the children died.

The second wave of immigrants had a very hard time. At first, most could not speak English. To other Americans, their clothes looked different. Their languages sounded strange. Some earlier immigrants resented them. They did not want new immigrants in their neighborhoods.

The new immigrants were far from home. They were tired after traveling such a long way. Often, they did not know where to go or where to stay. They did not know how to find jobs. Swindlers cheated many immigrants. They promised to find them jobs and places to live. Then, after taking the immigrants' savings, they would disappear.

The immigrants of the second wave learned painful lessons. The streets of America were not paved with gold. But they, too, succeeded by determination and hard work. The Poles realized their dream of owning land and homes. Many Jewish immigrants became great merchants, business leaders, and scientists. The Italians built subways and skyscrapers. They worked in factories and mines. They practiced crafts and opened shops and stores. Italians won success in business, banking, government, and the arts.

Not all immigrants came from Europe. Immigrants from Asia helped to open up and build the West. In the next lessons, you will learn about the Asian immigrants.

WHERE WE ARE IN TIME AND PLACE

PEAK IMMIGRATION YEARS: 1850–1920

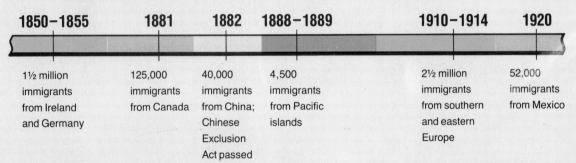

1850–1855	1881	1882	1888–1889	1910–1914	1920
1½ million immigrants from Ireland and Germany	125,000 immigrants from Canada	40,000 immigrants from China; Chinese Exclusion Act passed	4,500 immigrants from Pacific islands	2½ million immigrants from southern and eastern Europe	52,000 immigrants from Mexico

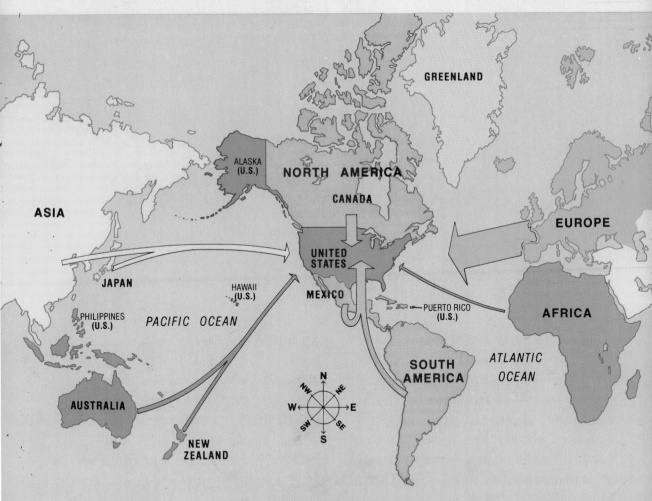

Factory work provided jobs for many immigrants. Many women and some children worked in textile mills.

This picture of a Chinese immigrant family is unusual. For many years, there were few Chinese women and children in the United States.

With the hard work and skills of the immigrants, United States farming and industry grew. For many years, immigrants were needed to help do the nation's work. Even when they were needed most, they were not always welcomed. Later, when there were fewer jobs, resentment against the immigrants grew. Some people said the immigrants had no skills. Others said immigrants worked for low wages and took away other workers' jobs.

Some people thought that the immigrants were making the United States different. They did not like or want people of different races, religions, and languages. In 1882, a law was passed to keep Chinese workers from entering the United States. Later laws greatly limited immigration from all of Asia and from Southern and Eastern Europe as well.

The Statue of Liberty was dedicated in New York harbor in 1886. This was 4 years after Chinese immigration was banned. The Statue of Liberty was a gift to the United States from the people of France. American school children collected pennies to raise the money to build the base. For this great statue, a Jewish poet, Emma Lazarus, wrote a poem. It ended:

"Give me your tired, your poor,
Your huddled masses yearning to
    breathe free,
The wretched refuse of your
    teeming shore;
Send these, the homeless,
    tempest-tost to me,
I lift my lamp beside the golden
    door!"

REVIEW

WATCH YOUR WORDS

Fill in the blanks. Use the words in the list below. You may use a word more than once.

Many Irish ___ left Ireland during the potato ___ . Many later ___ lived in ___, or crowded apartment buildings.

famine   tenements   immigrants

CHECK YOUR FACTS

Look at the Chart

1. In what 10-year period between 1850 and 1920 did immigration rise the highest?

2. In what 10-year period did immigration fall the most?

Look at the Map

3. Many immigrants came to the United States between 1850 and 1920. From what continents did they come?

Look at the Lesson

4. How many immigrants came to the United States between 1815 and 1915?

5. From what part of the world did most of the first wave of immigrants come?

6. From what parts of the world did most of the second wave of immigrants come?

7. Give three reasons why immigrants came to the United States.

8. What were some problems that immigrants faced? Name at least three.

TRY SOMETHING NEW

Try to find out when your ancestors first came to the United States. From what country or countries did they come?

Lesson 4: Chinese Come to the United States

FIND THE WORDS

sojourner   benevolent   enterprise
transcontinental   stereotype

Not all immigrants to the United States came from Europe. Immigrants also came from Asia. Most of them crossed the Pacific Ocean to the West Coast. The earliest Asian immigrants to arrive were the Chinese. Some people believe Chinese explorers may have discovered America before Columbus did.

In the Ch'ing Dynasty (1644–1911), a law forbade the Chinese to leave their land. Then, around the mid-1800s, European nations began to interfere in China's affairs. They wanted to control China's trade. The British attacked China's coast. They took over the port of Hong Kong. The Chinese government lost much of its power. Civil wars broke out. People's homes were burned. Many of the Chinese people were left hungry and poor.

Settlers and Sojourners

One of the first Chinese to leave for America during these years was Chum Ming. He was a young merchant. He landed in California in 1847. Then, in 1848,

Over Canton harbor in China fly many western nation's flags. The struggle to control China's rich trade brought war. Facing hunger at home, some Chinese left for America.

250

the California gold rush began. Chum Ming was one of the first to find gold. He sent the news back to China. Between 1848 and 1850, about 800 Chinese came. By 1860, 35,000 Chinese immigrants had arrived in America.

In the 1800s, whole families from Europe came to the United States. But in those days, not many women went to the "Wild West." Most of the early Chinese immigrants were men and boys. They came to the United States to work for pay. They wanted to send money home and to save money, too. Then they could go back to their families someday. Some early Chinese immigrants planned to return to China as soon as they could. They were called sojourners (soh JURN urs). A **sojourner** is someone who plans to live in a place only for a short time. Many Chinese came as settlers. They hoped to stay.

Immigrants with Enterprise

Chinese family members had a strong sense of duty and loyalty to each other. This made it very hard for sons and husbands to leave. But family and group loyalty helped the immigrants when they arrived in the United States. The Chinese already in the United States started self-help societies. They met new immigrants at the boat. They helped newcomers find homes and jobs. The self-help societies represented different districts in China. These societies formed the Chinese Benevolent (buh NEV uh lunt) Association. The word **benevolent** means "showing kindness and good will."

The Chinese immigrants were hard, steady workers. They were known for their industry and enterprise (EN tur PRYZ). Someone with **enterprise** uses new ideas and extra effort to reach a goal. Even so, many people were prejudiced against them. Special laws and rules were passed to drive them out of many businesses. So Chinese immigrants started greatly needed service industries. They opened laundries, stores, and restaurants. The restaurants served the best-prepared food in the old West.

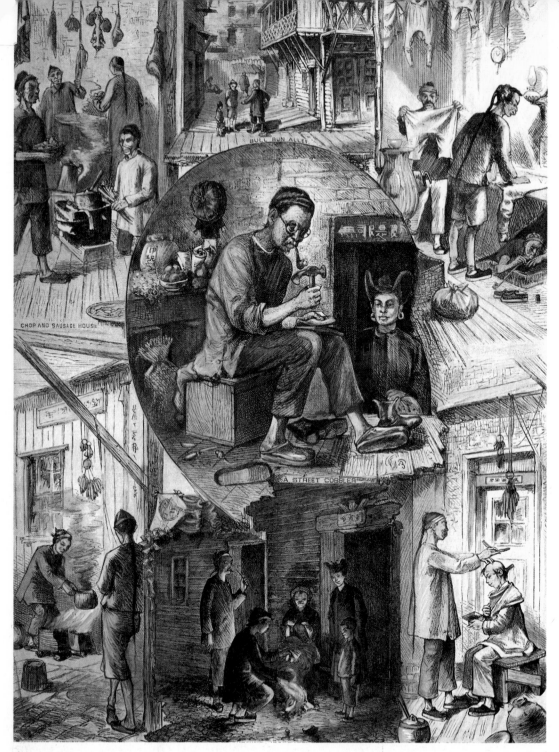

Views of life in the
Chinese community of
Virginia City, Nevada, in
1877

The Miners

At first, most Chinese immigrants worked for mining companies. In 1860, there were 83,000 miners in California. Of these miners, 24,000 were Chinese. The Chinese miners were good at teamwork. Some groups owned their own small mines. Many Chinese worked mining claims that other miners had given up. They used dams and pumps to drain water out of riverbeds.

The work of all the miners brought great wealth to California. In turn, California gold helped pay for the nation's growth. Later, Chinese immigrants mined gold, silver, and coal in other Western states.

The Railroad-Builders

Chinese immigrants also built much of the railroad linking the East and the West. This was the first railroad to cross the continent of North America. Thus, it was called a **transcontinental** (TRANS KON tuh NEN tul) railroad. Building it was a hard and dangerous job. One set of tracks was to start in Omaha, Nebraska, and go west. The other set of tracks was to start in Sacramento, California, and go east. Somewhere between these two towns, the tracks had to meet.

Chinese workers started in Sacramento in 1865. Irish workers started in Omaha. The Chinese laid tracks from California across

Chinese immigrants built the western part of the transcontinental railroad. They laid tracks over mountains and deserts. They performed many heroic feats.

the mountains to Utah. They worked from dawn to dark, 6 days a week. They brought their own food, tents, and supplies.

The Chinese railroad-builders carried out amazing feats. Sometimes, they cut roadways in solid rock at dizzying heights. Sometimes, they dug tunnels beneath great banks of snow. Some miners froze to death. Finally, in Utah, in 1869, the Irish and Chinese railroad-builders met. Immigrants to North America had connected the East Coast and West Coast!

Farm and Factory

Some of the Chinese in America decided to farm. In China, they had learned to drain swamps and irrigate dry land. In the valleys of California, they turned much poor land into good farmland. Some started small farms near California cities. Each morning, they sold flowers, fruits, and vegetables from door to door. The descendants of some of these growers raise million-dollar crops today.

Some Chinese immigrants developed new and better kinds of plants. Ah Bing developed the Bing cherry. Luey Gim Gong bred a new kind of orange. It ripened slowly and stayed juicy and sweet. Florida fruit growers began to raise and sell this kind of orange.

The Chinese also worked in factories. Some worked in woolen mills. Others made shoes or clothes. Some started their own shoe or garment factories.

American businesses needed many new workers to do all the work in the West. Some American business managers went all the way to China to hire the Chinese. But sometimes businesses used Chinese workers for other reasons. In 1875, Chinese workers were brought east to Massachusetts to work in a shoe factory. They were being used to replace employees who were on strike. This created very bad feelings among the workers the Chinese replaced.

Religion was very important to Chinese immigrants. Here are two Chinese houses of worship in San Francisco. One is a traditional Chinese temple, called a joss house. The other is a Chinese Methodist church.

Problems with Stereotypes

Some people distrusted the Chinese simply because they were different. The Chinese looked different from most other Americans. Their language sounded strange to Europeans. They wore different clothes and ate different foods. They also lived apart in special sections of American cities. Other Americans would call a Chinese community "Chinatown." The Chinese seemed very foreign and hard to understand.

Also, many people had strange ideas about the Chinese. Some sailors and traders said that the Chinese cared nothing for human life. Others blamed the Chinese because many of them were willing to work for low pay. They thought the Chinese were taking jobs away from other workers.

These ideas were stereotypes. A **stereotype** (STEH ree oh TYP) is a false idea about a group. It is a belief that everyone in that group is much the same.

The bad things people believed about the Chinese were not true. Many Chinese worked for low pay because they had no choice. They were thousands of miles from home. They had to work to live. Their pay was low because people took advantage of them. They lived in their own communities for companionship. Also, they faced discrimination elsewhere. They were safer among friends.

Chinese-Americans in the United States keep their ancient culture alive. Here, in New York City's Chinatown, young people celebrate the Chinese New Year.

In 1873, a depression hit the United States. A depression is a time when prices fall and companies go out of business. Many people lose their jobs. In 1873, some people in the West blamed the Chinese for the depression. They believed the Chinese were taking their jobs. Actually, this was not true. The Chinese had done much work that other workers were not willing to do. Even so, in some places, Chinese people were killed and their homes were burned.

Then, in 1882, Congress passed the Chinese Exclusion Act. The word *exclusion* (eks KLOO zhun) means "keeping out." This law said that no more Chinese workers could come to the United States. It also said that the Chinese in the United States could not become citizens. In many states, laws were passed saying that Chinese could marry only Chinese. But the Exclusion Act kept Chinese women out. Also, the men were often threatened and harassed. Many left. From 1890 to 1920, almost half the Chinese who lived in the United States left the country.

Success

Some Chinese stayed in the United States. Many managed to succeed. One of them, Yung Wing, was born in China in 1828. He came to the United States in 1847. In 1854, he graduated from Yale University. He was the first Chinese to graduate from an American college. He also became a citizen. Later, he represented the Chinese government. For 11 years, he brought other Chinese students to study in the United States.

By the time Yung Wing died in 1912, other Chinese were following his lead. Some entered professions, such as dentistry and law. Others started successful businesses. Joe Shoong built a small shop into a large chain of stores. Thomas Foon Chew turned a family business into a nationwide company.

The Chinese Exclusion Act was finally ended, or repealed, in 1943. Today, many people whose ancestors came from China are citizens of the United States.

REVIEW

WATCH YOUR WORDS

Match each word with its opposite.

1.	benevolent	A.	fact
2.	enterprise	B.	settler
3.	sojourner	C.	local
4.	stereotype	D.	unkind
5.	transcontinental	E.	laziness

KNOW YOUR PEOPLE

Match the name with the clue.

6.	Ah Bing	A.	bred a sweet, juicy orange.
7.	Chum Ming	B.	started a large chain of stores.
8.	Luey Gim Gong	C.	educated Chinese students in the United States.
9.	Joe Shoong	D.	found gold in California in 1848.
10.	Yung Wing	E.	developed a new kind of cherry.

CHECK YOUR FACTS

11. In the 1800s, why did Chinese immigrants come to the United States? Give three reasons.

12. What is the difference between a sojourner and a settler?

13. What did the Chinese self-help societies do?

14. What kinds of businesses did Chinese immigrants start?

15. Why did so many Chinese leave the United States after 1882?

THINK ABOUT IT

16. Why were most of the early Chinese immigrants men?

17. Why do you think business managers wanted Chinese workers in the Wild West?

18. Chinese workers were often paid less than other workers. What kinds of problems did this cause?

19. What is the difference between a fact and a stereotype?

20. What do you think was the most important work the early Chinese immigrants did? Why?

TRY SOMETHING NEW

Some big cities have a Chinese community called Chinatown. What can you find out about Chinatown in New York, Boston, Los Angeles, or San Francisco?

Lesson 5: Japanese and Filipinos Arrive

FIND THE WORDS

discrimination alien melting pot

In 1898, the United States took possession of two island groups in the Pacific Ocean. These were the islands of Hawaii and the Philippines (FIL uh peenz). These islands were in the same ocean as Japan. Each island group was to give the United States new citizens.

The Japanese

It was around the middle of the 1800s that foreigners began to buy land in Hawaii. Planters came from Europe and the United States. They started plantations to grow sugar cane. Workers came to these plantations first from China and later from Japan. By 1896, there were over 20,000 Japanese people in Hawaii. They were the largest culture group there.

FROM ASIA TO THE WEST COAST

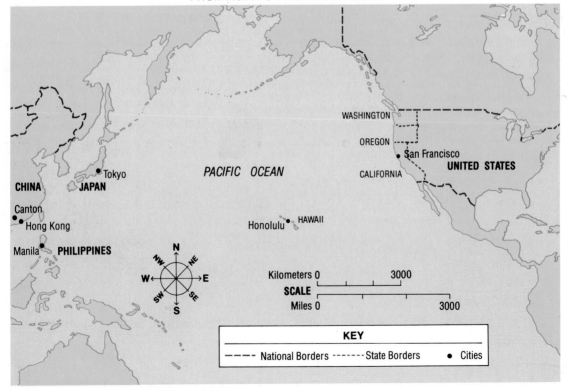

Right: The port of Honolulu, Hawaii, had only a few small houses in 1821. By the 1850s, foreign planters were buying up Hawaiian land.

Below: There were many more buildings in Honolulu in 1875. Soon, thousands of people came to Hawaii from Japan. They worked on plantations growing sugar cane.

By the late 1880s, Japanese immigrants had started to come to the United States. Most came after the Chinese Exclusion Act was passed. In those years, many Chinese immigrants went back to China. The Japanese immigrants took their place. They did many jobs that the Chinese had once done. Some Japanese workers canned fish or fruit. Others worked on farms or in mines. From 1901 to 1910, nearly 130,000 Japanese arrived. The year in which the most Japanese immigrants came was 1907. In 1907, 27,000 men and 3000 women came from Japan to the United States.

But feelings against the Japanese were strong. In 1906, there were 93 Japanese children in school in San Francisco. City leaders decided to put these students in a separate school for Asians. The Japanese government protested this insult. President Theodore Roosevelt then stepped in. He got the schools in San Francisco to take the Japanese students back. But he also worked out an agreement with the Japanese government. This was called the Gentleman's Agreement of 1907–1908. This agreement stopped Japanese immigration to the United States.

However, this agreement did not stop discrimination against the Japanese. To *discriminate* (dis KRIM uh NAYT) is to treat some

This Japanese family keeps its traditions but also tries out new ways. In California, Asian men wore boots instead of sandals to work in mines.

The Japanese knew how to use and preserve the resources of their land. Immigrants brought these skills to California, where they grew rice, vegetables, and fruit.

people less well than others. Thus, **discrimination** (dis KRIM uh NAY shun) means treatment that is unequal or unfair.

In 1913, California passed the Alien Land Law. This law said that aliens could not own California farmland. An **alien** (AY lee un) is simply someone who came from another country. A foreigner who becomes a citizen ceases to be an alien. But Japanese people were not allowed to become American citizens then. So the Alien Land Law stopped them from buying California farmland.

Even so, many Japanese immigrants managed to get land. Sometimes they rented land. Sometimes they bought swampland. They drained this swampland and grew good crops on it.

The Japanese planted crops that needed human labor. They did not plant the kinds of crops that were harvested with machines. Soon, Japanese farmers were growing strawberries, celery, peppers, cabbages, and artichokes. The Japanese farmers were the first to successfully grow rice on the West Coast.

One very successful Japanese farmer was George Ushijima (OO shi JEE muh). He was a hard worker who saved his money. In 1898, he bought land at the mouth of the San Joaquin (san WAH keen) River. He and other Japanese drained this land and turned it into good farmland. As time passed, George Ushijima bought more and more land. He planted potatoes in his fields. By 1920, he

260

Most Japanese immigrants to the United States were men. Many were skilled in crafts. This picture shows a Japanese carpenter at work.

owned or rented 13,000 acres of farmland. When he died in 1926, he was rich. People called him "the potato king."

In 1924, the United States Congress passed a new immigration law. As a result, no more Chinese or Japanese immigrants could en-

In the 1920s, Filipinos farmed in Hawaii and on the United States mainland. Today, farmers in the Philippines use modern farm machines.

ter the country. At this time, most Japanese in the United States were men.

The Filipinos

In 1898, the United States went to war with Spain. Because of this war, Spain gave up the Philippine Islands to the United States. These islands are in the Pacific Ocean, south of Japan. The people of these islands are called Filipinos (FIL uh PEE nohz).

When the United States took over the Philippine Islands, some Filipinos resisted. They were led by Emilio Aguinaldo (a MEE lee oh AHG ee NAHL doh). For 3 years, these Filipinos fought a war against the United States. The United States won the war. But before the fighting ended, a million Filipinos died.

The Gentleman's Agreement of 1907–1908 kept Japanese workers out of the United States. At that time, sugar planters in Hawaii began hiring Filipinos. By the early 1920s, there were over 25,000 Filipinos in Hawaii.

In the 1920s, there was also a lot of work to be done on California farms. The 1924 immigration law kept out most Asians. But the Philippines were then owned by the United States. By 1930, over 100,000 Filipinos had immigrated to Hawaii and the United States mainland.

The Filipinos on the West Coast were treated much as the Chinese and Japanese had been. Their work was needed. But in bad times, they were blamed for taking other workers' jobs away. Laws in some states limited what Filipinos were allowed to do. Laws like that do not exist today.

Today, the Philippines is an independent nation. Now, many Filipinos are immigrating to the United States once more.

The Melting Pot

People have called the United States a melting pot. A **melting pot** is a place where immigrants from many different cultures come together to live. People in a melting pot become more alike. But they do not become all the same. Each group has different customs and beliefs. Each person has different talents and skills. New immigrants add their strengths to the melting pot. Today, Asian immigrants are coming to the United States again.

The Industrial Revolution brought immigrants to America a century ago. They built cities and railroads. They worked on farms, in factories, and in mines. They gave their industry, enterprise, and ingenuity to America. They helped the United States to grow.

Today, the immigration laws of the United States have changed. Now the nation welcomes immigrants from all over the world. But now the nation is seeking people with special talents and skills. Now many immigrants are doctors, scientists, business managers, and engineers.

REVIEW

WATCH YOUR WORDS

1. What does *discrimination* mean? Give an example.
2. A foreign-born person who becomes a citizen (is/is not) an alien.
3. People in a melting pot become (more alike/the same).

CHECK YOUR FACTS

4. Where are Japan, Hawaii, and the Philippines?

5. Name three jobs the Japanese did in the 1880s on the West Coast.
6. What was the Alien Land Law?
7. How did Japanese farmers get land? What crops did they grow?
8. In the 1920s, why did California farmers hire Filipinos instead of Japanese?

THINK ABOUT IT

Suppose you went to live in a country where people did not speak English. What kind of work could you do?

CHAPTER REVIEW

WATCH YOUR WORDS

Match each word with the phrase that fits it best.

1. alien
2. construction
3. discrimination
4. industrial
5. patented
6. processed
7. refine
8. stereotype

A. purify
B. prepared for sale or use
C. manufacturing many goods
D. noncitizen
E. false idea about a group
F. registered by the inventor
G. unequal treatment
H. the business of building

CHECK YOUR FACTS

9. How did the Industrial Revolution change people's work? Name three ways.
10. How did steamboats and railroads serve factories?
11. How were coal and petroleum used?
12. What did people build with steel?
13. How did cities change after the Civil War? Name five ways.
14. Give three reasons why immigrants came to the United States.
15. Name three hardships that many immigrants faced after they came.
16. Which immigrants built the transcontinental railroad?
17. Name three things that Chinese and Japanese immigrants had in common.
18. Why has the United States been called "a nation of immigrants" and "a melting pot"?

GET THE DATE STRAIGHT

Match the date or time with the event.

19. 1815–1860
20. 1882
21. 1898
22. 1890–1920
23. 1901–1910
24. 1907–1908
25. 1924

A. the Chinese Exclusion Act
B. Gentleman's Agreement with Japan
C. immigrants from Northern Europe
D. immigrants from Southern Europe
E. over 100,000 immigrants from Japan
F. law stopping Chinese and Japanese immigration
G. U.S. got Hawaii and the Philippines

USE YOUR CHART

26. Look at the chart of immigration on page 241. In how many 10-year periods did immigration rise above 700,000?
27. During what 10-year period did immigration first rise above 500,000?
28. During what 20-year period did the most immigrants arrive?
29. In what period after 1880 did immigration fall to the lowest point?

THINK ABOUT IT

30. Why was the railroad important to a large nation like the United States?
31. What changes did the telegraph and telephone bring?
32. Why does an industrial nation need banks?
33. Which of the inventions below do you think was most important? Why?
steam engine   telegraph
electric light bulb

CHAPTER 3
THE LAST FRONTIER

Lesson 1: The Great Plains Are Settled

FIND THE WORDS

sod   locust   longhorn

From 1865 to 1900, the land west of the Mississippi was settled. Before the Civil War, few people wanted to live on the Great Plains. The area between the Mississippi River and the Rocky Mountains was called the "Great American Desert." Settlers just wanted to get across it on their way to California and Oregon. But after the Civil War, people began moving onto the Great Plains to stay.

In 1862, the Homestead Act helped open up the Great Plains. This law gave free land to settlers. All they had to do was live on the land and work it for 5 years. Many farmers quickly claimed their land. With it, they claimed a

There were not enough trees on the Great Plains to provide wood for houses. So settlers built houses made of sod.

very hard life. There were few trees on the Great Plains to provide wood. Thus, they built houses made of prairie sod. **Sod** is soil held tightly together by the roots of grass. The settlers lived through bitter winters and blazing-hot summers. They had to struggle to plant their fields. The prairie sod was very tough. Sometimes, farmers would have to chop the sod with an ax before they could plow the soil underneath. And then grass fires, locusts, or hail could wipe out a year's work in a few days. **Locusts** are swarming insects that often eat crops.

Farming on the Great Plains was best done by big machines. These machines could easily turn over the tough sod. However, many farmers could not afford such machines. Without them, they could barely raise enough crops to stay out of debt. Little by little, the small farms were combined into larger ones. Some "sodbusters," as ranchers called the farmers, gladly sold out. They moved to the cities to find better-paying work. But farming was established on the Great Plains. Before long, much of the area was planted in wheat and corn.

In the Southwest, cattle ranching became important in the 1870s. Tough, half-wild cattle called **longhorns** were a main source of beef for markets in the East. These cattle could be turned

265

At the end of a cattle drive, cowhands herded the longhorns into boxcars. The cattle were then shipped east.

There were many Black cowhands in the West. One of them was Nat Love.

loose to feed on the millions of acres of unclaimed grassland. Ranchers did not have to pay for feed. They did not even have to build shelters for the cattle. Every spring, the cowhands would round up the animals. Then they would start the long drive north to the railroad towns in Kansas. The cowhands took their time. If the drive moved slowly enough, the cattle often gained weight on the way to market. Then they could be sold for more money in Kansas. Finally, the cattle were herded onto trains and shipped east to stockyards in Chicago, Kansas City, or Omaha. After spending most of their pay, the cowhands headed for home. They were soon ready to do it again the next year.

The days of the cattle drives did not last long. By the 1880s, this way of life had almost disappeared. The invention of barbed wire was the most important reason. With barbed wire, farmers could build fences to keep cattle out of their fields. Before long, even old cattle trails were blocked by fences. The open range was mostly closed. Cattle raising changed. Ranchers, too, used barbed wire—to fence their cattle in. Penned in small areas, the cattle could be fattened with grain from farms. Ranching was more expensive than in early days. It became a big business. This helped to make life in the West more settled.

Towns and cities grew up. They attracted more and more people. In 1850, there were only half a million people living west of the Mississippi. In 1890, there were almost 9 million.

The people who settled the Great Plains were different from each other in some important ways. But they also had some things in common. Although many were immigrants, they came to share a common language—American English. They shared many beliefs about what was good and right. They shared beliefs about the land. For example, they agreed that the land should belong to someone. They believed that it should be used for something.

There were people living in the West who did not share many of these beliefs. These were the native peoples of the Great Plains. The Plains peoples were among the last of the American Indians to lose their freedom and their old ways.

The last parts of the United States were also added as the Great Plains were being settled. In 1867, the United States government bought Alaska from Russia. Hawaii was added to the nation in 1898. It would be many years before Alaska and Hawaii became states. But the present-day borders of the United States were finally complete.

REVIEW

WATCH YOUR WORDS

1. ___ is soil held tightly together by the roots of grass.
   Fiber Longhorn Sod
2. The tough, half-wild cattle of the Southwest were called___.
   scalawags longhorns locusts

CHECK YOUR FACTS

3. When were the Great Plains of North America settled?

4. What law helped open the Great Plains to settlers?
5. Why did the Great Plains farmers often build sod houses?
6. When did the United States get Alaska and Hawaii?

TRY SOMETHING NEW

Pretend you are a cowhand on a cattle drive. Write a diary that covers 5 days on the trail. Tell things that happen. Say what life on the trail is like.

Lesson 2: American Indians of the Plains

FIND THE WORDS

buffalo   bison   carcass

Between the Mississippi River and the Rocky Mountains lived many different groups of American Indians. The Comanches (kuh MAN cheez) lived in northern Texas. The Kiowas (KY oh wayz) and Southern Cheyenne (shy AN) lived in Kansas and eastern Colorado. The Pawnee (paw NEE), Crow, Northern Cheyenne, and several Sioux (SOO) groups lived in Nebraska, the Dakotas, Wyoming, and Montana. These were only some of the American Indian peoples living on the Great Plains.

The Plains peoples depended on the buffalo to live. A **buffalo** is a large animal related to ordinary cattle. Its proper name is **bison** (BY sun). In earlier times, the American Indians hunted buffaloes on foot. They did not yet have horses. Spanish explorers first brought horses to North America. Some horses escaped and became wild. As the years passed, herds of wild horses grew and wandered over the grasslands. By the early 1700s, the Plains peoples had learned to capture and ride them.

From then on, hunting was easier. The vast buffalo herds had to move in order to eat. They also moved south or north during certain parts of the year. With horses, the Plains peoples could follow them. They could stay close to the animals that provided almost everything they needed.

Zona Thunderhawk is a Sioux teacher at the Standing Rock Reservation in North Dakota. Here she describes how the Sioux used buffaloes:

"Our braves hunted the buffalo because it had plenty of meat. They never killed for sport. The men shot the buffalo and brought it to camp. Then it was mostly up to the women to do what they had to do. The older women taught the younger ones to prepare everything for the year.

"First, we skinned the buffalo. We staked out the hide and dried it on the ground. We then removed all the meat off the bones. Some we ate fresh. But most of it we dried to eat in the winter. We even used the muscles—the muscles of the leg that people throw away today. We cut them into long strips and dried them. And

At first, American Indians hunted buffaloes on foot. Here, two Indians, disguised in wolfskins, move in for the kill.

even the windpipe, we cut and dried that, too. Because we never knew when we might be without food in the wintertime. We always prepared for the long winter months.

"When the hides were dry, we sewed them together to make into tents. We boiled the muscles and hoofs and spread the slimy stuff on the tents. This hardened and kept the rain out of the teepee. Our clothing was made from hides as well. For thread we used sinew (SIN yoo), the stringy part of the buffalo's muscles. Sinew was also used for rope and bowstrings.

"We used the tail of the animal. We put it in the pot until all the meat was cooked off the bones. The little bones we used as playthings. There are holes in them. We laced them and gave them to the children to play with. The horns of the beast were carved into spoons, chisels, and other tools. Other bones were cut into pieces and boiled. We made a kind of bone grease out of this. This lard was then stored in a pouch made from the buffalo's stomach.

"We scraped all the fur from the hide. The longest hair from the front of the buffalo was saved for mattresses. Tanned buffalo skins were sewed and stuffed with the fur. It made a soft mattress.

Plains Indians lived in teepees, or tents made of dried buffalo hides.

"We used everything. I mean everything. When we ate, if there was grease on our hands or on our lips, we wiped it off and put it on our hair. It oiled our hair. It made our hair grow thick and long.

"But the buffalo was hard to catch. Our chief would go up on the high hills to fast and pray for food for his people. Our chief was guided by mighty spirits. He always put the widows and fatherless children first. They ate first. Braves and their families got their share later."

The railroads dealt the first blow to the culture of the Plains people. Railroad workers needed food. Hunters like Buffalo Bill Cody were hired to shoot buffaloes to feed the workers. After the railroads were built, settlers came to the Great Plains in great numbers. They wanted protection from the American Indian peoples. The Army quickly saw that killing buffaloes was one way to control the Plains peoples. So settlers were encouraged to shoot buffaloes. Passengers shot the animals from train windows just for sport. Millions of buffaloes were killed for their hides or their tongues. The tongues were shipped back to restaurants in the East. The **carcasses**

The Army saw that it could control the Plains peoples by killing buffaloes. So the Army encouraged settlers to shoot the animals. There were special trains just for buffalo "hunters."

(KAHR kuh sez), or dead bodies, were left rotting on the Great Plains.

In the early 1800s, there were about 60 million buffaloes. Sometimes, a single herd would stretch from horizon to horizon. About 100 years later, only a few were left, in a national park. The American Indians of the Great Plains found themselves without the animals that supported their culture. Soon, they would also be without their land.

REVIEW

WATCH YOUR WORDS

1. The Plains peoples depended on the ____.
   railroad   beaver   buffalo
2. *Buffalo* is another word for____.
   carcass   bison   sinew

CHECK YOUR FACTS

3. How did the Plains peoples get their horses?

4. The American Indians (did/did not) kill the buffalo for sport.
5. How much of the buffalo did the Plains peoples use?
6. What groups killed many buffaloes?

THINK ABOUT IT

Why were the American Indian cultures destroyed when the buffalo was destroyed?

Lesson 3: Whose Land?

Not all the Plains peoples were friendly with one another. For example, the Sioux were given that name by one of their neighbors. *Sioux* comes from a word meaning "snake in the grass" or "enemy." The Sioux call themselves Dakotas. *Dakota* means "allies" or "friends."

The Plains peoples often fought over the right to hunt in, plant on, or travel across a certain territory. Each tribe tried to protect some areas of land for its members. But all the members of a tribe had equal rights to the land. The idea of *owning* the land was completely strange to these people. For many people in Europe and the United States, land was something to own. It was owned just as one owns a tool or a house. Land belonged to the person who bought it or claimed it. The owners could do whatever they wanted with it. No one could come onto their property without their permission.

This difference in values caused many misunderstandings. Often, settlers would offer to buy some

Not all the Plains peoples were friendly with one another. The title of this painting is *When Sioux and Blackfeet Meet.*

The Plains peoples made treaties with the United States government. This painting shows the Pawnee at a treaty council.

land from American Indians. They would give gifts, usually blankets, guns, coffee, or whiskey. The American Indians thought they were allowing the settlers to use the land. The settlers thought they were buying it. Too late, the American Indians discovered that they could no longer move freely on the land. They began to realize what the idea of land ownership meant.

Some American Indians would "sell" land used by other tribes. They thought that no individual person could sell or even give land away. They thought that no other American Indian had to honor such a sale. Settlers did not understand this. They became angry when other American Indians con-

tinued to use the land. They went to courts and to the Army to get support.

Until the 1880s, many fierce battles were fought between the U.S. Army and the Plains peoples. These battles were followed by treaties with the United States government. In these treaties, the Plains people agreed to stop fighting. They also agreed to give up some of their lands. In return, the government promised to protect the rights of the American Indians to their remaining lands.

These treaties were broken again and again by settlers. The settlers were backed up by the United States government and the Army. The American Indians fought hard. But without food or freedom to hunt, the Plains peoples could not resist for long.

In 1877, some Nez Perce (NEZ PURS) people under Chief Joseph tried to escape from the Army into Canada. Chief Joseph had a handful of warriors and several hundred women, children, and old men. Finally, after they journeyed almost 1600 kilometers (1000 miles), the Army trapped them.

When Chief Joseph surrendered, he said this:

"I am tired of fighting. Our chiefs are killed. The old men are all dead. It is cold and we have no blankets. The little children are freezing to death. My people, some of them, have run away to the hills and have no blankets, no food. No one knows where they are—perhaps freezing to death. I want to have time to look for my children and see how many of

Chief Joseph tried to escape to Canada with a band of his people. But the Army stopped him.

them I can find. Maybe I shall find them among the dead. Hear me, my chiefs! I am tired. My heart is sick and sad. From where the sun now stands, I will fight no more forever."

American Indians in different parts of the country had been fighting with settlers for 300 years. With the settling of the Great Plains, the struggle was almost over.

REVIEW

CHECK YOUR FACTS

1. The Plains peoples (often/seldom) fought each other.
2. At first, the American Indians of the Great Plains (did/did not) understand the principle of land ownership.
3. What group fought the American Indians?
4. What followed the battles with the American Indians?
5. Who usually broke the agreements about the American Indians' lands?

THINK ABOUT IT

Did the area you live in once belong to an American Indian people? Who were they? If you don't know, look up your state in the encyclopedia.

Lesson 4: American Indian Reservations

FIND THE WORD

reservation

As the United States grew, American Indians steadily lost their lands. Settlers pushed west, starting farms and founding towns. The United States government felt it had to protect the settlers. It also tried to see that they got the lands they wanted. To do these things, the government had to deal with the American Indians. Until 1871, Congress treated American Indian tribes as independent nations. After 1871, Congress said the American Indians were no longer independent. But they were not made American citizens either. It was not until 1924 that they became citizens and were given the right to vote.

Making jewelry is an ancient Navaho Indian craft. Navaho children learn this craft today.

American Indian children like to learn about their people's past.

In 1824, the government established the Bureau of Indian Affairs (BIA). The BIA was set up to manage the **reservations.** These were areas of land set aside for American Indians. The BIA sent agents to the reservations. They were supposed to see that the American Indians had enough food, warm clothing, and other necessities. The American Indians needed such help because reservation land was often poor and hard to farm. The American Indians could no longer hunt for food, and now they could not grow good crops. They had to rely on White traders for food and other goods. Often these traders cheated the American Indians.

Some agents from the BIA cheated them, too.

The government set up schools on the reservations. In the schools, American Indian children were often not allowed to use their own language. They were taught to read and write only in English. They studied the same subjects that other children in the United States did. The schools wanted to make the American Indians more like other people in the United States. They wanted them to live as most Americans did. Then, it was thought, American Indians would fit in. They would not be unhappy. They would not be a "problem" anymore. In fact, this

The reservation land is better for raising sheep than other animals. Children do most of the herding.

idea lay behind most of the government programs and laws. Here is an example:

In 1887, the government passed a law to divide up land that was owned by whole tribes. Smaller pieces of this land would be owned by individual American Indians, instead. The government hoped this would make American Indians want to become farmers. Then they would be more like

Navaho Indian children learn about their culture in school. They also study history, geography, English, and arithmetic.

other Americans. But many American Indians did not want to be farmers. They wanted to hunt and gather their food, as they had done in the past. Besides, owning land individually and plowing up the earth went against their beliefs. Confused and bitter, many American Indians sold their little plots of land. When the money was gone, they had nothing. Within 30 years, American Indians lost or sold about 90 million acres. This was about two-thirds of the land they had owned.

In 1934, the government again allowed whole tribes to own reservation lands. In some cases, it gave groups loans to buy back reservation land that had been sold. It tried to improve education and medical care. It also allowed American Indians to practice more of their old ways.

AMERICAN INDIANS TODAY

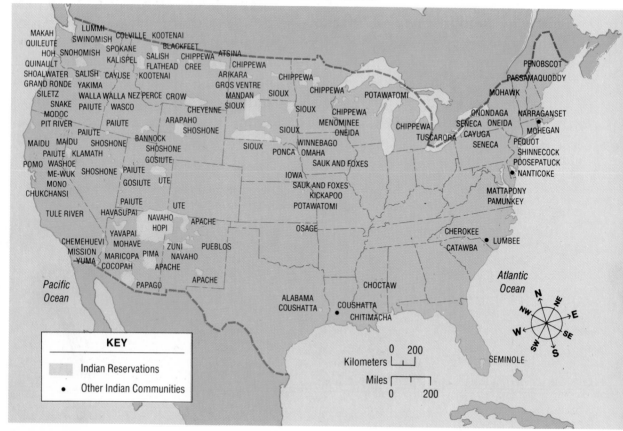

Today, there are about 275 reservations in the United States. Many American Indians still live on reservations. There, much of their way of life is like that of other people in the United States. But the old cultures are still alive. They are being passed on to the young with pride. Children are learning their people's tribal songs and dances. They study ancient arts and crafts. And they, in turn, will pass this culture on to their children.

Still, life for most American Indians on reservations is not as good as it should be. Many people are poor and cannot get good jobs. They do not have good medical care. And many, even though they do go to school, do not have good educations.

One of the most important things you can learn about American Indians is this: Any statement that begins "All American Indians are" is probably false. It is almost impossible to make true general statements about American Indians. There are too many cultural groups. There are too many differences among the groups. For example, there are nearly 100 different American Indian languages and religions.

Today, there are about 1.4 million American Indians in the United States. Separate communities can be found in almost every part of the country.

REVIEW

CHECK YOUR FACTS

Look at the Lesson

1. How did Congress treat the American Indian tribes until 1871?
2. When did American Indians become citizens of the United States?
3. What government agency was set up to manage reservations?
4. What was the goal behind the government's school and land policy toward the American Indians?
5. Where do many American Indians live today?

6. About how many reservations are there today?

Look at the Map

7. Is there an American Indian reservation in Texas?
8. What American Indian groups live in North Carolina?

THINK ABOUT IT

Do you think the government was right or wrong in trying to make American Indians like other Americans? Give reasons for your answer.

Lesson 5: Contributions of the American Indians

FIND THE WORDS

quinine   malaria

American Indians have made many contributions to North America and to the world.

The settlers in Jamestown and Plymouth might have starved to death without the help of American Indians.

The settlers learned about corn from the American Indians. Today, corn is one of the most important crops in the United States.

The native peoples of North America introduced settlers to corn, beans, squash, melons, pumpkins, and other fruits and vegetables. From the native peoples of Central and South America came sweet potatoes, white potatoes, peanuts, tomatoes, chocolate, and many more farm products.

Try to imagine what your life would be like without even some of these things. Corn, potatoes, and beans are very important foods. Today, millions of people throughout the world depend on these basic foods.

American Indians influenced the early settlers in other ways, too. While the American states were still colonies, the Iroquois tribes had an advanced form of government. It was called the Iroquois Confederacy, or the Six Nations. There were representatives from all the tribes. They took part in decisions that affected more than one tribe. In 1754, Benjamin Franklin wrote to colonists who were thinking of forming a union. "It would be strange," he said, "if Six Indian Nations can have a union like this and we can't. They have made it work. We need such a union. . . ."

American Indians invented the canoe. This family is using a modern canoe.

American Indians have also made contributions to medicine. For hundreds of years, they have used plant roots and herbs as medicines. Many of these medicines came to be used by European settlers. Willow bark is a good example. It was used for hundreds of years by several tribes. What we know as aspirin is made from an ingredient the American Indians got from willow bark. At least 59 drugs have come from wild plants that American Indians used as medicines. One of these drugs is **quinine** (KWY nyn). Made from the bark of a tree, it is used to treat **malaria** (muh LAIR ee uh). That is a disease spread by mosquitoes.

The rubber ball came from South American Indians. North American Indians invented lacrosse, a popular sport.

We now use many other things the American Indians invented. We also often use the native names for them. For example, we use the canoe, kayak (KY yak), hammock, and toboggan. We also use parkas, snowshoes, rubber, pipes, and cigars—all from the American Indians.

The English language is full of American Indian words. Many animals are called by their native names. Chipmunks, skunks, moose, opossums, and raccoons are just a few such animals. Many tree names, such as hickory, catalpa,

You might think that popcorn is a modern invention. But American Indians were popping corn long before Columbus came to America. As a matter of fact, ears of popcorn are the oldest corn found in America. These ears are over 5000 years old.

Some Indians believed that a little demon lived inside each kernel of corn. When the kernel was heated, the demon escaped with a big "pop." We now know that water inside the kernel makes it pop.

and pecan, are also American Indian. Words as different as *pow-wow*, *hurricane*, and *totem* have their roots in American Indian languages.

States, towns, lakes, and rivers all over the United States have American Indian names. There are many of these names and they are very familiar. As a result, we tend to forget where they came from. Ohio, Chicago, Kansas, Miami, Milwaukee, Mississippi, Omaha, Peoria, Seattle, Tallahassee, Tucson, Tulsa, and Wichita are American Indian names. So are Canada and Mexico.

We can find American Indian contributions in almost every part of American life. These contributions have not stopped. There are still many things all Americans can learn from American Indians. Today, some American Indian values are especially important for all Americans. Among these is the American Indians' deep love and respect for the land.

REVIEW

CHECK YOUR FACTS

1. What three American Indian foods do millions of people in the world now depend on?
2. Name the American Indian group that had a very advanced form of government.
3. What important medicine for malaria was first used by American Indians?
4. Name a sport invented by American Indians.
5. Where did the names Canada and Mexico come from?

THINK ABOUT IT

Get a map of your state. Make a list of towns, rivers, mountains, and other features that have American Indian names.

CHAPTER REVIEW

WATCH YOUR WORDS

1. A bison and a ___ are the same thing.
   locust   longhorn   buffalo

2. ___ are swarming insects that eat crops.
   Locusts   Carcasses   Bison

3. ___ are a kind of cattle.
   Locusts   Longhorns   Carcasses

4. ___ is soil held tightly together by the roots of grasses.
   Sod   Fiber   Bison

5. A ___ is a dead body.
   sod   carcass   locust

CHECK YOUR FACTS

6. What was the land between the Mississippi River and the Rocky Mountains called before the Civil War?

7. What did the Homestead Act do?

8. Why was it hard to plant fields on the Great Plains?

9. What gradually happened to the size of farms on the Great Plains?

10. What invention helped end the cattle drives?

11. At first, how did the Plains peoples hunt the buffaloes?

12. Why was the killing of buffaloes encouraged after the settlers came?

13. How did the American Indians and the newcomers differ in their use of buffaloes?

14. What was the attitude of the American Indians toward the land?

15. In general, the treaties between the government and the American Indians were (kept/broken).

16. When did the government set up the Bureau of Indian Affairs?

17. What language was usually used in the schools on the reservations?

18. About how many American Indian languages are there?

19. Who helped the settlers at Jamestown and Plymouth survive?

USE YOUR MAP

20. Look at the map on page 278. It shows where most American Indian peoples live. In what part of the nation are most reservations located?

21. What part of the United States seems to have the fewest American Indian groups today?

22. What American Indian group is scattered all the way from Michigan to Montana?

THINK ABOUT IT

23. How did the interests of the ranchers and farmers conflict at first on the Great Plains?

24. The Spanish brought horses to North America. How would using horses have changed the lives of the American Indians?

25. Why did the Plains peoples not live in one place and plant crops?

26. Why did the government not make the settlers obey the treaties with the American Indians? Do you think the treaties should have been enforced?

27. How might American history have been different if all treaties with American Indians had been honored?

28. Should American Indians today live on reservations or move elsewhere? Give reasons for your answer.

29. Why has it been hard for the American Indians to unite?

30. Why is it important for the cultures of the American Indians to survive?

WATCH YOUR WORDS

Use the words below to fill in the blanks. Use each term only once.

abolitionists
assembly lines
blockade
buffalo
carpetbaggers
civilians
cotton gin
draft

fibers
Freedmen's Bureau
immigrants
interchangeable parts
master
pass
racism
reaper

Reconstruction
scalawags
secession
segregation
tariff
tenements
Underground Railroad
volunteers

Slavery was a very harsh system. Slaves even had to get a(n) ___ from their ___ to leave the plantation. Slavery was opposed by the ___ . The idea of ___ helped support slavery. Some slaves escaped north on the ___.

The slave system had been dying in the South. However, Eli Whitney invented a(n) ___ that separated the cotton ___ from the seeds. The South and North began to have conflict over slavery and the ___ on imported goods. After Lincoln was elected President, Southern ___ took place. Eleven Southern states withdrew from the Union.

One of the first things President Lincoln did was have the Union Navy ___ Southern ports. Many soldiers joined the army as ___. But there was also a(n) ___ law that required people to join. Not only soldiers but also many ___ suffered from the war.

After the Civil War, a new federal agency, the ___ , was set up to help former slaves. A(n) ___ period began. Federal troops were sent to run parts of the South. Some Northerners came south to help run the government. They were called ___. White Southerners in the government were called ___ . After Reconstruction ended, the Southern states passed ___ laws.

Even before the Civil War, the Industrial Revolution began. Eli Whitney was the first to use ___. This made factories with ___ possible. There were many new inventions, such as the ___ for cutting grain. Many ___ came from other nations to work in the United States. Some lived in crowded ___ in the cities. At the same time, the American Indians were being pushed off the Great Plains. The great herds of ___ were killed, on which their way of life depended.

CHECK YOUR FACTS

1. At first, Blacks in the colonies (were/were not) slaves.

2. Until about 1800, there (were/were not) slaves in most states.

3. What Black abolitionist helped slaves escape on the Underground Railroad?

4. Before the Civil War, the South had (many/few) factories.

5. Who invented the cotton gin?

6. In what year did the Civil War begin? In what year did it end?

7. What battle was the turning point in the Civil War?

8. When did the last federal troops leave the South after Reconstruction?

9. Who invented the reaper?

10. List some changes that helped lead to the growth of industry in the United States.

11. Where did most of the first wave of immigrants come from?

12. Most German immigrants settled in the (East/Midwest).

13. In the 1920s, Congress passed laws that (increased/decreased) immigration to the United States.

14. The (Chinese/Japanese) worked on the first railroad to cross the nation.

15. In what two areas did most Japanese and Filipinos live?

16. The Great Plains had (many/few) trees.

USE YOUR MAPS AND CHARTS

17. Look at the chart of the North and the South in 1860 on page 210. What did the South have more of than the North?

18. Look at the map of slave and free states on page 211. What area then belonged to American Indians?

19. Look at the time line for the years 1860–1877 on page 213. Did federal troops immediately occupy the South after the war?

20. Look at the chart on immigration on page 241. In about what year *before* the Civil War was the rate of immigration the highest?

THINK ABOUT IT

21. Do you think the fast growth in industry after the Civil War was related to the Northern victory? Give reasons for your answer.

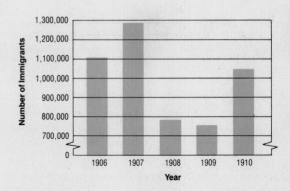

22. In what ways was the Civil War a turning point in American history?

TRY SOMETHING NEW

23. The graph shows the number of immigrants entering the United States from 1906 through 1910. Use it to answer the questions below.

    a. In which year did the most immigrants come to the United States?
    b. In which year did the fewest immigrants come?
    c. About how many immigrants arrived in 1906?
    d. In how many years from 1906 through 1910 did more than a million immigrants arrive?

24. Find out what Asian groups are coming to the United States today.

PUT IT ALL TOGETHER

25. Draw a map of the United States during the Civil War. Label the following and show them in different colors: the Confederacy, the Union, the slave states remaining in the Union.

26. Make a time line on immigration to the United States. Use Chapter 2 to find important dates.

THE UNITED STATES IN THE
MODERN WORLD

UNIT 5

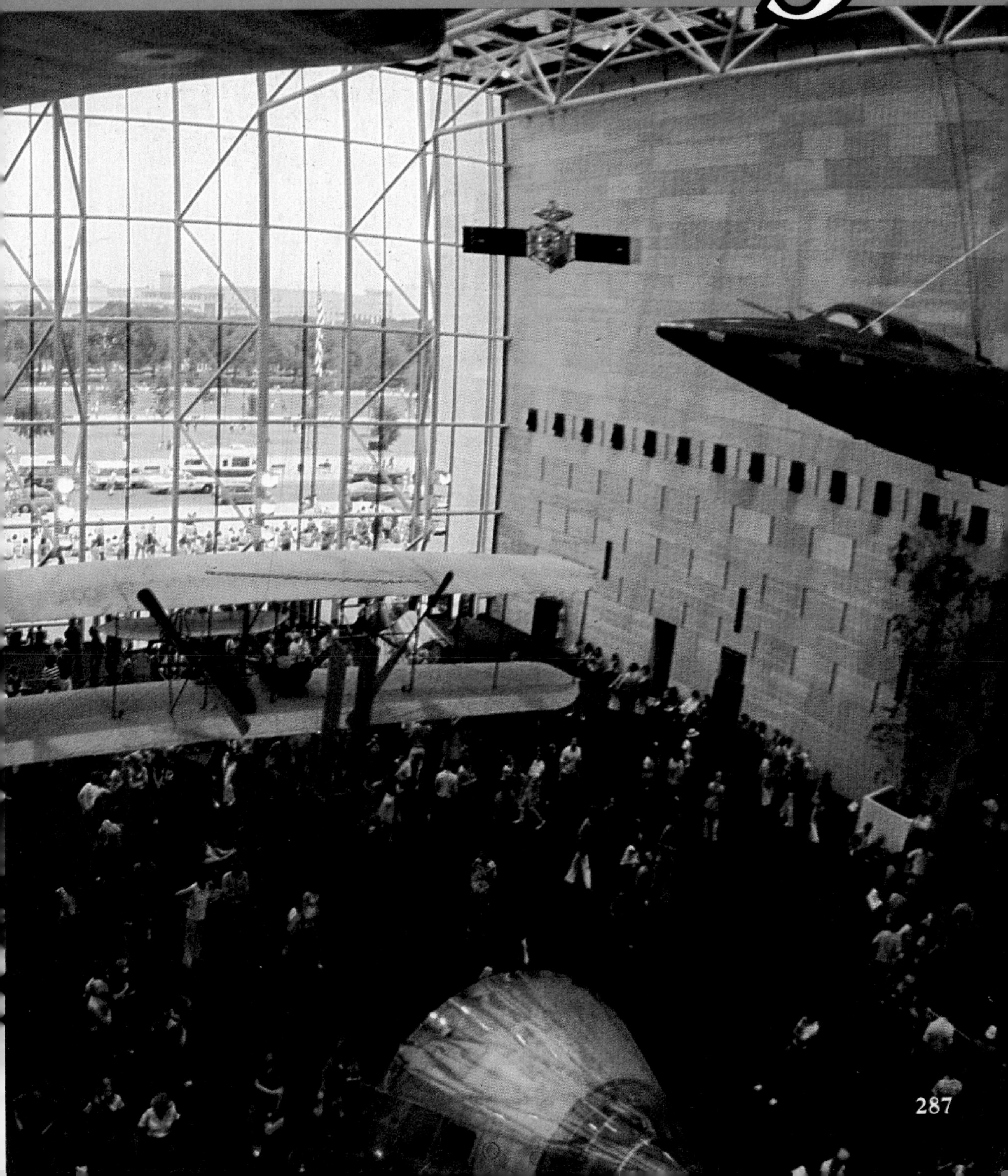

1 THE EARLY TWENTIETH CENTURY

Lesson 1: The United States in 1900

FIND THE WORDS

migration   subway   congestion   reformer

In 1900, the United States was a rapidly growing nation. Industry and business were expanding. The cities were getting bigger. Huge numbers of immigrants were coming into the cities from abroad. Many people were also leaving the farms. In particular, many Black people left farms in the South.

They were seeking a better life in cities in the North.

This movement of people from one place to another is **migration** (my GRAY shun). City governments had to spend large sums of money to provide services for all these new people. At that time, people needed to live near where they worked. There were few ways to travel long distances to work. Besides, few people could afford a long trip every day. So people had to live in the center of the city.

Builders had to construct higher buildings to house everyone. High buildings were also put up for business offices. Construction became an important industry.

As the cities grew larger and more crowded, new means of transportation came to be used. The horse-and-buggy days were ending. Now, in the early 1900s, factories were making cars. City streets soon became crowded with traffic. The streets had to be paved as more people rode on buses and trolley cars. Bridges and tunnels were built to carry the streets across rivers. Tracks for trains were also built in tunnels underneath some cities. These underground railroads were called **subways.** As crowds of people, cars, and buses filled the streets, a new problem arose. This crowding of vehicles and people on city streets is called **congestion** (kun JES chun).

In the early 1900s, there were few laws in the United States telling people how to run businesses. Because of this, there were many abuses. Children often worked long hours in factories. They had to work to help support their families. Sometimes, big companies drove smaller companies out of business by cutting prices. Sometimes, large companies sold spoiled food to stores that sold it to the poor. What is more, many people were not treated justly. Women were not allowed to vote. Blacks, American Indians, and other minority groups were not treated as full citizens. Some people in the United States protested against these conditions. These protesters were called reformers. A **reformer** is someone who tries to change things for the better.

REVIEW

WATCH YOUR WORDS

1. The crowding of streets with vehicles and people is called____.
   migration   construction   congestion
2. ____ is the movement of people from one place to another.
   Migration   Reform   Congestion
3. People who try to change things for the better are____.
   migrants   reformers   minorities

CHECK YOUR FACTS

4. Many new people came to the cities around 1900. Where did they come from?
5. What did migration force city governments to do?

THINK ABOUT IT

Today, do most people still live in the centers of large cities? If not, where do they live?

Lesson 2: Reformers in the United States

FIND THE WORDS

muckrakers   Progressives

There are many advantages to living in an industrial nation. An industrial nation produces more goods. The goods can be sold at a lower price. In an industrial society, many people can buy things that once only the rich could afford to buy.

But the growth of industry in the United States brought some problems, as well. There were people who wrote about the problems and about other things they thought were wrong. They wanted to bring wrongdoing to public attention. They were called **muckrakers** (MUK RAY kurz).

One of the muckrakers was Ida Tarbell. She was concerned that

Ida Tarbell was a reformer. She wanted to bring wrongdoing to public attention. In the early 1900s, reporters who exposed wrongdoing were called muckrakers.

some businesses and industries were becoming too big. She feared that big business would be able to control society and take advantage of people. Ida Tarbell wrote a book about this problem. The book told about the Standard Oil Company. Standard Oil had become so big that it forced many other oil companies out of business. The company was then able to make people pay whatever price it asked for its oil. Ida Tarbell's book also explained how the oil company used other businesses to make itself even larger. Standard Oil was run by John D. Rockefeller.

Another muckraker was Lincoln Steffens. He wrote a series of magazine articles that became known as "The Shame of the Cities." In the series, Steffens wrote about how politicians helped big business take unfair advantage of smaller businesses. He also described how politicians were cheating the people in order to help industries grow and prosper.

Other muckrakers wrote about different kinds of unfair conditions. While the rich built palaces, other citizens had barely enough to eat. Factory workers were at

This cartoon shows huge companies called trusts dominating the United States Senate. At the time, senators were elected by state legislatures. And state legislators could be influenced by rich companies in their state.

their jobs 12 hours a day, 6 or 7 days a week. They seldom earned more than 15 cents an hour. Some children began working when they were 8 or 10 years old. Here is a description of the unfortunate conditions at one factory that used child labor:

"I shall never forget my first visit to a glass factory at night. It was a big wooden structure, so loosely built that it had no protection from draft. It was surrounded by a high fence with rows of barbed wire stretched across the tops. The foreman of the factory explained to me the reason for the fence. 'It keeps the young imps inside once we got 'em for the night

shift,' he said. The young imps were, of course, the boys employed. There were about 40, at least 10 of whom were less than 12 years of age."

Poor people on farms lived no better. In the South, Blacks and Whites had to rent land in order to farm. Often, most of their crops went to the landlord as payment for use of the land. These farmers did not have enough money left to pay for good food and housing.

Muckrakers were responsible for making the nation aware of many bad conditions. Thanks to them, people in the United States learned that meat and medicines were often unhealthful.

In the early 1900s, a group of people started a movement to correct some of these injustices. These people were known as **Progressives.** The Progressives did not want to destroy American business. They understood that big business is important because it produces much wealth. But the Progressives wanted to make sure that everyone was treated fairly by the law. They wanted ordinary people to have a voice in government. They also wanted to make sure that everyone had a chance to earn a good living.

The Progressives were able to bring about important reforms. In part, this was because a President of the United States, Theodore Roosevelt, came to support many of their views. Roosevelt understood some of the problems of the poor. He tried to fight injustice. He wanted to make the government work for all the people.

Roosevelt's program became known as the Square Deal. Under his leadership, the government acted to stop many harmful business practices. It tried to improve some of the poor living conditions of that time.

In 1906, Roosevelt and the Progressives in Congress were able to get the Meat Inspection Act passed. Under this law, the government could inspect all meat transported between states. It could stop any bad meat from being shipped. In the same year, the Pure Food and Drug Act was passed. It kept businesses from manufacturing, transporting, or selling medicines and foods that might be harmful to people. Roosevelt was also concerned about saving natural resources. He ordered that 60 million hectares

As President, Theodore Roosevelt helped the Progressives bring about important reforms.

(150 million acres) of government forest land be set aside. It could not be sold to private businesses or individuals. These lands were to be used as national parks and forest preserves.

Another leader of the Progressives was Florence Kelley. Florence Kelley was a leader of the National Consumers League. She brought public attention to the hardships and unhealthful conditions of child labor. She worked to help women receive pay equal to that of men. Kelley also worked against businesses that had dangerous or unsanitary working conditions. Today, many people are still fighting for some of the things Florence Kelley wanted. These people especially want women to receive equal pay for equal work.

FUN FACTS

The first subway in America was built in New York City in 1866. The tunnel was 312 feet long and 9 feet wide. The subway had one train that moved on metal tracks. A big fan at one end of the tunnel pushed the train to the other end of the tunnel. Then the fan was run backwards. It then sucked the train back.

Alfred Beach was the builder. He did not have permission from the city to build a subway. So he built it in secret in just 58 nights. City officials were very displeased. So the project was eventually closed and forgotten about.

In 1912, a crew was digging a tunnel for another subway under New York. Suddenly they went through the tunnel of Beach's subway. There sat the train, still waiting for passengers after half a century.

REVIEW

CHECK YOUR FACTS

1. What leading muckraker wrote about the Standard Oil Company?
2. What muckraker wrote a series of articles about the influence of big business on politicians?
3. What group of people tried to correct the injustices?
4. What President favored reforms?
5. What group did Florence Kelley lead?

THINK ABOUT IT

Have all the things the Progressives fought for been won? If not, which problems that they were concerned with still remain?

Lesson 3: World War I

FIND THE WORDS

alliance   assassinate
Central Powers   Allied Powers
neutral   U-boats   armistice

Americans did not pay much attention to Europe during the early 1900s. Many Americans were surprised when war broke out in Europe on July 28, 1914.

At this time, five nations dominated Europe. They were Great Britain, France, Germany, Austria-Hungary, and Russia.

Two other nations, the Ottoman Empire and Italy, were also important. But they were less powerful. All these nations were rivals in many ways. They competed not just in Europe but all over the world. Britain and France had huge empires, with land on almost every continent. Russia had huge amounts of land in Europe and Asia, but no colonies. Germany and Italy had only a few colonies. Yet all these nations thought they needed colonies. They were very afraid of any other

EUROPE BEFORE WORLD WAR I

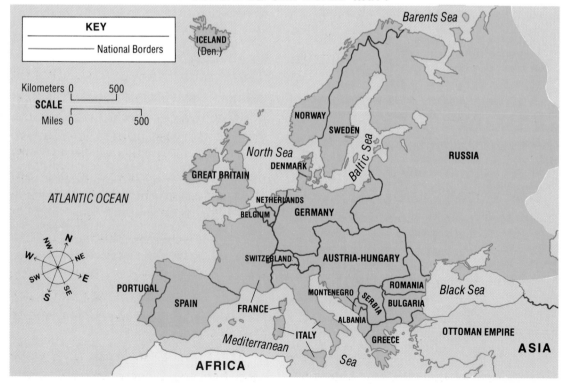

nation's gaining power where they were already powerful.

The powerful nations of Europe feared each other. Each nation was afraid that two or more powerful nations might gang up on it in war. As a result, these nations formed alliances. An **alliance** (uh LY uns) is an agreement that nations make with each other. The partners in such an agreement are called *allies* (AL EYEZ). In effect, nations that are allies will fight for each other. They say, "For protection, we will stick together. An attack on one of us is like an attack on all of us." There were two great alliances in Europe. On one side were Britain, France, and Russia. On the other were Germany, Austria-Hungary, and Italy.

Then, in June 1914, the son of the emperor of Austria-Hungary was **assassinated** (uh SAS uh NAY tid), or killed. The killer was a Serbian. The Austro-Hungarian government blamed the small nation of Serbia for the murder. On July 28, 1914, it declared war on Serbia and sent an army into that nation. Germany supported Austria-Hungary. Within a week, Russia, France, and Great Britain had entered the war against Germany and Austria-Hungary. Germany and Austria-Hungary were later joined by the Ottoman Empire and Bulgaria. They were known as the **Central Powers.** Italy changed

REMEMBER! THE FLAG OF LIBERTY SUPPORT IT!

BUY U.S.Government Bonds 3rd. LIBERTY LOAN

The United States entered the war in 1917. The government sold bonds to help pay for the war. This poster was aimed at immigrants.

sides and supported Russia, France, and Britain. These nations were known as the **Allied Powers.** They were also joined by Japan.

At first, the United States was **neutral.** That meant it did not take sides in the war. President Woodrow Wilson had been elected in 1912. He urged Americans to be "neutral in fact as well as in name." However, this was not easy. The United States had long had close ties with Britain and France.

The fighting in Western Europe soon became trench warfare. Long lines of trenches and barbed wire faced each other all across France. From these trenches, large numbers of soldiers attacked each other. They were trying to gain small pieces of land. Poison gas, airplanes, and tanks were used in war for the first time. Hundreds of thousands of soldiers died.

The submarine, another new weapon, helped bring the United States into the war. German submarines, called **U-boats,** began to sink all ships sailing to Britain or France. In May 1915, the ocean liner *Lusitania* was sunk by a U-boat. More than a thousand people died, including many Americans. The United States government protested. As a result, the German government ordered the U-boats to stop attacking passenger liners.

In February 1917, almost 2 years later, the German government announced that the U-boats would again attack all ships around Britain. The Germans had decided that it was more important to sink those ships than it was to keep the United States out of the war. As a result, the United States broke off relations with Germany. In March, the United States government learned that the Germans were trying to get Mexico into an alliance. The Germans promised to help the Mexicans get back the land they lost to the United States in 1848. All Mexico had to do was enter the war on Germany's side if the United States declared war on Germany. Americans were shocked and angry.

Finally, in April, President Wilson asked Congress to declare war on Germany. This was done on April 6, 1917.

The United States entered the war at a time when the Allied Powers needed help. U-boats were sinking many Allied ships. Allied armies made unsuccessful attacks on the German trenches. The czar (ZAHR), or emperor, of Russia was overthrown. The new government in Russia took Russia out of the war. This freed German troops to fight in France.

But the United States soon brought new strength to the Allied armies. About 1.4 million American soldiers fought in Europe. In 1918, the Americans helped stop the German armies when they attacked in the spring. In the summer, the Allies launched many successful attacks in which Americans fought bravely. Finally, the Central Powers could fight no more. Early in November, Austria-Hungary surrendered and the German government fell. The war ended when an **armistice** (AHR muh STIS), or agreement to stop fighting, was signed. This took place on November 11, 1918.

President Wilson wanted to use "14 Points" as a basis for peace. He also wanted to set up a League of Nations.

During the war, President Wilson had wanted "14 Points" as a basis for peace. He called for open treaties instead of secret treaties. He also called for freedom of the seas and a limit on the weapons nations could have. He wanted European culture groups to have their own nations. And he wanted to set up a League of Nations. Wilson's points were fair to all nations. But the nations that won the war did not want to be fair. They wanted to punish the nations that lost. As a result, the Treaty of Versailles (vur SY) that ended the war was very harsh. Germany was forced to admit guilt for the war. It had to pay money to the Allied Powers. The United States Senate rejected the treaty. As a result, the United States made a separate peace with the Central Powers.

REVIEW

WATCH YOUR WORDS

1. The United States fought on the side of the ___.
   neutrals   Central Powers
   Allied Powers

2. To ___ someone is to kill for political reasons.
   neutralize   assassinate   ally

3. An ___ is an agreement to stop fighting.
   armistice   assassination   alliance

4. A(n) ___ is an agreement nations make to protect each other.
   armistice   power   alliance

5. The ___ helped bring the United States into World War I.
   armistice   assassination   U-boat

CHECK YOUR FACTS

6. What were the two groups of nations that fought in World War I called?

7. Who was President of the United States during World War I?

8. Name three new weapons used in World War I.

9. What did Wilson want as the basis for peace?

10. What treaty ended the war?

THINK ABOUT IT

Did the United States have good reasons for entering World War I? Why, or why not?

Lesson 4: The Vote for Women

FIND THE WORDS

suffrage   suffragist

Before World War I, many efforts to correct bad conditions and injustices in the United States had succeeded. Laws had been passed to limit the power of big business. New laws protected children from being used as cheap labor. Women had worked hard for these laws. There were other reforms in law and in government.

The Declaration of Independence had stated that all men were created equal. But half the nation's citizens were women. They were still not treated equally. Until 1920, most women did not have the right to vote. In the nineteenth and twentieth centuries, women in the United States fought for reforms. They demanded the equal rights that had long been denied them.

During the 1800s and early 1900s, the role of women was the subject of much heated discussion. People had been taught to believe

Until 1920, most women did not have the right to vote. These women are demonstrating to get the vote.

PRESIDENT WILSON SAYS: "This is the time to support Woman Suffrage."

that a woman's place was in the home. Girls were often told that they were too weak in mind and body to go to college.

But many women proved that these beliefs were wrong. A determined few did go to college. Some women went on to become doctors, lawyers, scientists, and business managers. Women continued to do many things that some people believed only men could do. Maria Mitchell discovered Mitchell's Comet in 1847. She was later professor of astronomy at Vassar College. In 1849, Dr. Elizabeth Blackwell graduated from medical school at the head of her class. She was the first woman in the United States to earn a medical degree. In 1879, Mary Baker Eddy founded the Church of Christ, Scientist. She also started her own newspaper, the *Christian Science Monitor.* In 1926, Gertrude Ederle (A dur lee) swam the English Channel. She broke all the earlier records set by men. And, in 1932, Amelia Earhart became the first woman to fly a plane across the Atlantic alone. She was also the first person to fly alone from Honolulu to California.

There was a shortage of workers during World War I. For the first time, many women had the chance to work outside the home. During wartime, women were hired for jobs that were usually done by men. They worked in factories making tools, weapons, and explosives. They made airplane and automobile parts. They refined petroleum and metals. They ran farms. They worked on the railroads. They did everything that was necessary to support the war effort at home.

More women than ever before were taking those jobs that were open to them. Many became secretaries and clerks. Some held jobs as bank tellers, nurses, and teachers. But after the war, women lost the better-paying factory jobs. High-level jobs in all areas were also reserved for men. Women were not even considered for such jobs. Many people believed that men should earn money and women should raise families.

Women sometimes disagreed with each other about whether or not women should hold jobs. But most women did agree that they should have the right to vote. For a long time, women had been fighting for suffrage. **Suffrage** means the right to vote. People who fight for the right to vote are called **suffragists.**

The suffrage movement had started in 1848 in Seneca Falls, New York. There, Elizabeth Cady Stanton and Lucretia Mott held the first Women's Rights Convention. At Seneca Falls, women

Susan B. Anthony devoted her life to the women's suffrage movement. The Nineteenth Amendment was named the "Anthony Amendment" in her honor.

declared that all men and women are created equal. Later, in 1872, Susan B. Anthony, the suffragist leader, was arrested for voting in the presidential election. Susan B. Anthony led the struggle for the vote until she died in 1906.

By the early 1900s, the women's suffrage movement had grown larger. Women began to win limited voting rights in some states. But at that time, almost all men and even many women were opposed to women's suffrage. Over the years, the suffragists won much more support. The efforts of Susan B. Anthony, Elizabeth Cady Stanton, Julia Ward Howe, and Carrie Chapman Catt were succeeding.

Millions of women who worked in the United States wanted better jobs. They wanted higher wages and better working conditions. These women believed that the vote would give them the power to bring about these changes. They also realized that, with the right to vote, they could help correct some other injustices. For example, during the 1800s, married women were not allowed to own property in most states. Even those who worked did not really own their earnings. Under the law, everything a woman had belonged to her husband. One of the causes of the American Revolution was the colonists' complaint about taxation without representation. Yet, 125 years later, working women had to pay taxes without being represented in the nation's lawmaking bodies.

Some women, such as Alice Paul, told people about their cause by leading marches and demonstrations. Often the women who took part in these events were laughed at and insulted. Some were beaten and jailed. But they did not stop fighting for their rights. Other women worked through the political system. Carrie Chapman Catt organized women to work in local political districts. She had 2 million women working in a national campaign. All this effort finally paid off. Also, many people realized that women had helped win the war. So in 1920, the Constitution was changed. The Nineteenth Amendment gave women across the nation the full right to vote in elections.

Winning the right to vote brought women closer to the American ideal of equality for all. But it did not solve all their problems. It did not change the attitudes of many people. Many still believed that women and men were not equal. Women could vote. But few women were elected to office. Many opportunities, such as important jobs, were still denied to women.

Pictured are Carrie Chapman Catt, Julia Ward Howe, and Alice Paul. They were early suffragist leaders.

REVIEW

CHECK YOUR FACTS

1. Who was the first American woman to earn a medical degree?
2. What jobs did women hold during World War I? List five kinds.
3. When and where did the women's suffrage movement begin in the United States?
4. Who was Susan B. Anthony?
5. What amendment to the Constitution gave women the right to vote?

THINK ABOUT IT

How old do you have to be to vote today? How long have people this age had the right to vote?

CHAPTER REVIEW

WATCH YOUR WORDS

1. Systems of trains that run through cities in tunnels are called____.
   U-boats   muckrakers   subways
2. The ____ wrote about bad things done by big business.
   migrants   muckrakers   suffragists
3. A____was a German submarine.
   U-boat   suffrage   subway
4. ____is the right to vote.
   Armistice   Suffrage   Migration
5. Many people, cars, and buses cause ____on city streets.
   suffrage   migration   congestion

CHECK YOUR FACTS

6. In 1900, what two groups were moving into the cities?
7. Name two leading muckrakers.
8. Name an important reform group of the early 1900s.
9. What President helped bring about many important reforms?
10. Who was President of the United States during World War I?
11. Name the two groups that fought one another in World War I.
12. What did the U-boats do?
13. On what day was the armistice signed to end World War I?
14. What did Carrie Chapman Catt do?
15. With what amendment and in what year did American women win the right to vote?

THINK ABOUT IT

16. Think of an invention that made tall buildings possible. What is it?
17. Are there any people like the muckrakers today? If so, who are they?
18. What might have happened if the United States had not entered World War I?
19. Why do you think women got factory jobs during World War I? Why do you think they lost the jobs later?

TRY SOMETHING NEW

20. Find out more about one of these leaders: Susan B. Anthony, Elizabeth Cady Stanton, Lucretia Mott, Julia Ward Howe, Alice Paul, Carrie Chapman Catt. Use an encyclopedia and other library books. Then write a one-page report.

2 THE UNITED STATES IN A CHANGING WORLD

Lesson 1: The Twenties

FIND THE WORDS

suburb   advertising   Prohibition

The 10 years between 1919 and 1929 were thought of as good years for the United States. Many people were making money. Business was booming. It seemed that the day would soon come when every American citizen could live in comfort.

New products were being manufactured. Radios offered exciting home entertainment. Refrigerators were introduced that used electric motors instead of blocks of ice to cool food. People bought electric vacuum cleaners and washing machines. Many of these new products made housework much easier.

Henry Ford started manufacturing cars on an assembly line. The assembly line made it possible to build more cars at a faster rate. Each worker put on one part as cars moved down the line. Ford lowered prices until many more people in the United States could afford to buy a car. More cars meant more jobs for workers. More cars meant that more and better roads were needed. Dirt roads were paved with concrete and asphalt. Motels were built to give travelers a place to sleep along the roads. Families could now easily travel long distances to visit each other. People no longer had to live near their work. Many people moved from the city to the suburbs. A **suburb** is a community near a city where people who work in the city live.

In the 1920s, advertising became an important new business. **Advertising** is telling people about products or services. Businesses advertised on signs, in newspapers and magazines, and on radio. Through advertising, businesses tried to get people to buy their products. Advertising suggested that the more people bought, the happier they would be.

It did seem as though people were happy in the 1920s. These years have been called the Roaring Twenties or the Jazz Age. In 1919, the Eighteenth Amendment to the Constitution had been approved. This amendment made it illegal to make or sell alcoholic beverages. This was known as **Prohibition** (PROH uh BISH un). But some people drank alcoholic beverages anyway. They broke the law. Gangsters got rich supplying them with alcohol. There were also some dishonest people in the federal government when Warren G. Harding was President. When their wrongdoing was found out, some important government leaders went to jail.

Many of the changes of the

Left: Amelia Earhart flew across the Atlantic as a passenger in 1928. In 1935, she became the first pilot to fly solo from Honolulu to California. *Below:* George Herman ("Babe") Ruth hit 60 home runs in 1927, setting a season record. Babe Ruth was the most famous sports hero of his time.

1920s were reflected in entertainment. Going to the picture show became very popular. In turn, the movies helped spread new ways of acting and dressing. During the 1920s, Harlem in New York City became a center for Black artists, musicians, and writers. Harlem jazz clubs became popular and famous throughout the nation. Duke Ellington and Count Basie were two of the greatest jazz musicians.

Things were changing very fast in the 1920s. Some Americans wanted things to stay the same. They reacted to change by attacking new people and ideas. Many had bad feelings about foreigners. So the government placed limits on immigration in 1921 and 1924.

The good times of the 1920s did not reach most of the people in the United States. In some industries, such as coal mining, workers often did not have jobs. Farmers' earnings did not rise. Most factory workers continued to be underpaid. Many women worked long hours for low wages in laundries and textile mills. Very few people in the United States were truly well-off.

The twenties were also a time of heroes who often seemed larger than life. Gertrude Ederle swam the English Channel. Amelia Earhart was a brave aviator and one of the pioneers of flight. Baseball player Babe Ruth was the most famous sports figure of the age. The greatest hero was Charles A. Lindbergh. In 1927, this young aviator became the first pilot to fly across the Atlantic alone.

REVIEW

WATCH YOUR WORDS

1. The law against drinking alcohol was known as____ .
   suffrage   amendment   Prohibition
2. ____ is telling people about products and services.
   Advertising   Entertainment   Prohibition

CHECK YOUR FACTS

3. List four new products that were manufactured during the 1920s.
4. Who started manufacturing cars on an assembly line?
5. What area of New York City became an important center for Blacks in the arts?

THINK ABOUT IT

What was life like for most working people in the 1920s?

TRY SOMETHING NEW

Find out more about one of these people: Count Basie, Amelia Earhart, Gertrude Ederle, Duke Ellington, Charles A. Lindbergh, Babe Ruth. Use an encyclopedia and other library books. Then write a one-page report.

Lesson 2: The Great Depression and the New Deal

FIND THE WORDS

Great Depression   stock
drought   bonus   erosion
session

In 1929, the booming good times of the twenties quickly came to an end. The period that followed was known as the **Great Depression.** A depression is a time when many businesses fail. Many workers do not have jobs. The Great Depression lasted for 10 years. It was one of the most difficult periods in American history.

There were many reasons for the Great Depression. During the 1920s, many people bought stocks. **Stocks** are shares in a company. The prices of stocks kept going up. Many people thought this would continue forever. They put all their money into stocks. Then, in October 1929, the prices of stocks began to fall. Many people who had bought stocks on credit could not pay for them. They sold stocks at lower and lower prices. Whole fortunes were wiped out.

Business owners became frightened. Factories began to produce

During the Great Depression, many workers lost their jobs. Work was hard to find. Bread lines set up by charities kept many people from starving.

fewer goods. Stores ordered fewer goods. Workers had to be laid off. As people lost their jobs, they bought fewer goods. This made prices drop and caused more factories to close. People had to take their savings out of the banks in order to live. Many banks then had to close. They soon had no money left.

These were terrible times for the nation. To make matters worse, in the early 1930s there was a terrible drought (DROWT) in the Great Plains. A **drought** is a period of little or no rainfall. During a long drought, land and crops are ruined. In the 1930s, dust storms destroyed land, machinery, and homes. These storms also killed farm animals. Thousands of people had to leave their farms and go to the cities to look for work. But there was no work.

Franklin D. Roosevelt promised a "New Deal" to solve the nation's problems.

At first, the federal government did little to help people. President Herbert Hoover and others believed that people should solve their own problems. At the time, many veterans were asking for the government to pay them a **bonus.** This was an extra payment that would be a reward for fighting in World War I. Many poor veterans came to Washington and formed a "Bonus Army." Some camped out near the Capitol. After a time, President Hoover ordered the Army to remove the veterans. Troops forced the unarmed men to leave and burned their camp. To many, this was a sign of the government's lack of concern for the people's suffering.

In 1932, Franklin D. Roosevelt was elected President of the United States. He promised a "New Deal" to cure the nation's problems. Roosevelt brought many advisers to Washington to find ways to help. These advisers were often called the "Brain Trust." Congress soon passed laws to help banks, industry, farmers, workers, and the unemployed. The Tennessee Valley Authority (TVA) was set up. This government company built dams to control floods and provide electricity. As a result, the TVA improved a vast area in several states.

In 1935, Roosevelt began the second part of the New Deal. More help was given to the unemployed and to farmers. The right of workers to join labor unions was protected. Housing was built for the poor. The Social Security Act set up a system of pensions for retired people. Money was taken out of working people's salaries. It was used to make monthly payments to older people when they stopped work. Another program protected natural resources, especially soil. At the time, there was very bad erosion in the United States. **Soil erosion** is the washing away or blowing away of the soil.

President Roosevelt did not succeed at everything he tried. The Supreme Court declared some of his program unconstitutional.

In 1937, Roosevelt tried to add extra judges to the Supreme Court. These judges supported his programs. But his plan was defeated. A special **session,** or meeting, of Congress that same year refused to pass the laws he wanted. In 1938, the President campaigned against opponents in his own party. Most of them were reelected anyway.

The New Deal did succeed in helping millions of people who were suffering because of the Great Depression. Because of the New Deal, the role of the federal government in the economy and society grew. However, the American economy did not fully recover from the Great Depression until World War II began.

REVIEW

WATCH YOUR WORDS

1. ___ is the washing away or blowing away of soil.
   Drought   Erosion   Depression

2. A ___ is a share in a company.
   stock   bonus   session

3. A ___ is an extra payment given as a reward.
   stock   bonus   session

4. A(n) ___ is a period of little or no rainfall.
   drought   erosion   depression

5. A meeting of Congress is called a(n) ___.
   depression   erosion   session

CHECK YOUR FACTS

6. What were the bad times after the 1920s called?

7. When did the prices of stocks begin to fall?

8. What happened on the Great Plains in the 1930s?

9. What was President Franklin Roosevelt's program called?

10. When did the American economy fully recover from the bad times?

THINK ABOUT IT

Suppose you were President when a depression started. Make a list of things you could do to help.

Lesson 3: World War II

FIND THE WORDS

dictator   Axis
concentration camp
isolationism
Allies   atomic bomb

The Great Depression that hit the United States in the 1930s was worldwide. Nations everywhere felt its effects. The Depression years caused great changes, especially in Germany.

After World War I, a democratic government had been set up in Germany for the first time. But the Treaty of Versailles that ended the war had taken land and resources from Germany. It had made the Germans pay more money than they could afford to the winning nations.

During the 1920s and 1930s, the German government could not solve the people's problems. The Great Depression was especially bad there. The German people became angry and resentful.

Adolf Hitler became a powerful leader in Germany. He told the

EUROPE BETWEEN THE WORLD WARS

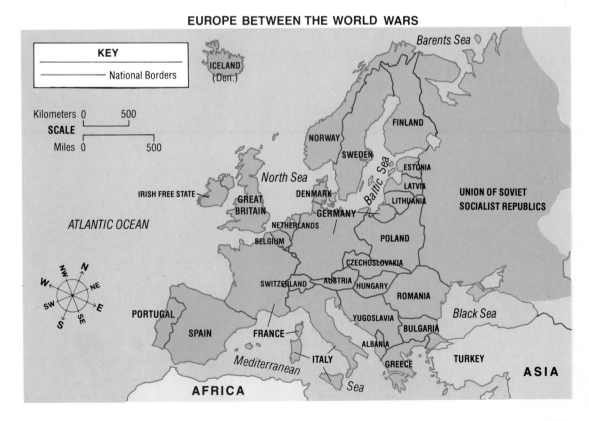

KEY
—— National Borders

Kilometers 0   500
SCALE
Miles 0   500

Barents Sea
ICELAND (Den.)
ATLANTIC OCEAN
IRISH FREE STATE
GREAT BRITAIN
North Sea
NORWAY
SWEDEN
FINLAND
Baltic Sea
ESTONIA
LATVIA
LITHUANIA
UNION OF SOVIET SOCIALIST REPUBLICS
DENMARK
NETHERLANDS
GERMANY
BELGIUM
POLAND
CZECHOSLOVAKIA
SWITZERLAND
AUSTRIA
HUNGARY
ROMANIA
PORTUGAL
SPAIN
FRANCE
YUGOSLAVIA
BULGARIA
Black Sea
ALBANIA
ITALY
GREECE
TURKEY
Mediterranean Sea
AFRICA
ASIA

Germans that they were better than any other people in the world. He said Germany's problems were caused by the Treaty of Versailles and by Jewish people. Hitler said that the solution was to get more land and to get rid of the Jews. Some Germans were so unhappy and in such a bad situation that they believed what Hitler said.

Hitler was the head of the Nazi (NAHT see) Party. Hitler and the Nazis were able to take over the German government. Hitler became a dictator. A **dictator** is a ruler who has complete power over a government. In Germany, Hitler and the Nazis controlled everything. The Germans lost the rights they had gained under their democratic government. Hitler began building an army. He began preparing for war.

In Italy, another dictator, Ben-ito Mussolini, had seized power. Mussolini was the leader of the Fascist (FASH ist) Party. Conditions in Italy were also bad. The Italian people thought that the Treaty of Versailles did not give them enough land. So Italy decided to take over lands in Africa.

Hitler and Mussolini joined forces. They began to attack other European nations. They began to take over other nations' land. Their partnership was called the **Axis.** Japan later joined the Axis.

On September 1, 1939, the German army marched into Poland. World War II had begun. Britain and France declared war on Germany. But Germany was better prepared for war than the other nations were. Between 1939 and 1941, Germany conquered most of Europe. The German army took over Poland, Norway, Czechoslovakia, Denmark, the Netherlands,

Adolf Hitler became a powerful leader in Germany. He used huge rallies to stir up the patriotism of the German people.

Benito Mussolini seized power in Italy. He joined forces with Hitler to attack other European nations.

Belgium, and France. Great Britain stood alone against the Nazis. Soon the Germans started bombing British cities.

Throughout Europe, Hitler had special prisons built for the Jews and others he was trying to destroy. These prisons were called **concentration camps.** Millions of people died in them. By the time the war ended, the Nazis had murdered 6 million Jews. Hitler also had several million other people who opposed him killed.

At first, the United States wanted to stay out of the war. Many people felt that the nation should worry only about itself. They thought it should not get involved with the problems of other nations. Such a policy was called **isolationism** (EYE suh LAY shuh NIZ um). But by that time, isolationism was no longer practical. American businesses were trading with other nations. Thus, the United States was affected by events in those nations.

During the 1930s, the Japanese were trying to build an empire in Asia. Japan, too, was becoming an industrial nation. The Japanese needed raw materials and markets for their goods. They wanted to control lands in southeast Asia. These lands had rich resources such as petroleum. They also grew many foods Japan needed. Japan went to war against China in

Thousands of Japanese-Americans joined the United States armed forces in World War II. These soldiers are being honored for bravery.

1931. By the late 1930s, Japan controlled all the coastal provinces of China.

But the United States did not want Japan to control China and southeast Asia. The United States wanted those areas to remain open to American trade. The Japanese would not have allowed that. Relations between Japan and the United States became worse.

On December 7, 1941, the Japanese made a surprise attack against the United States Navy base at Pearl Harbor in Hawaii. Thousands of Americans were killed or wounded. Many American ships were destroyed. The next day, the United States declared war on Japan.

The United States then joined forces with Britain and the Soviet Union to fight Germany and Italy. This group was called the **Allies.**

311

On December 7, 1941, Japan attacked Pearl Harbor in Hawaii. Many American ships were destroyed.

The bravery of Soviet soldiers impressed many Americans. Here, United States soldiers and Soviet soldiers meet after the defeat of Germany.

Once again, war reached around the world. Now it was truly a world war.

The United States and the Soviet Union had not been friendly for some time. The problems went back to the time of World War I. The Soviet Union had become Communist after a revolution in 1917. Many Americans did not like the Communists.

During the war, the bravery of Soviet soldiers changed many Americans' ideas about the Soviet Union. When the Germans attacked the Soviet Union in June 1941, the Soviets were nearly defeated. They retreated as far east as Moscow before they finally stopped the Germans. Millions of Soviet citizens died. But the Germans could not get the Soviet Union to give up. This made Americans think less about Com-

munism and more about courage. Many Americans hoped that, after the war, the United States could remain friendly with the Soviet Union.

On May 8, 1945, the war ended in Europe. Germany finally surrendered. The Allies had already defeated Italy. Now they were preparing to invade Japan. The new President of the United States was Harry Truman. Truman wanted the war to end quickly. That way, he thought, fewer American troops would die. By this time, the United States had built the most powerful weapon the world had ever seen. This weapon was the **atomic bomb**. It used the power of the splitting atom. Truman decided to use this weapon against Japan.

On August 6, 1945, the United States dropped the atomic bomb on the Japanese city of Hiroshima (HIR uh SHEE muh). Over 100,000 people were killed immediately. Three days later, a second bomb destroyed the city of Nagasaki (NAH guh SAH kee). Japan surrendered, and World War II was over.

Soon after the war began, the Allies started to plan for peace when the war would be over. In 1941, President Roosevelt and British Prime Minister Winston Churchill signed the Atlantic Charter. They wanted to protect weak nations from stronger ones.

They wanted to prevent the use of force and to ensure peace. In 1943, the United States, Britain, China, and the Soviet Union called for an international organization for peace. Planning for the new organization was done over the next 2 years. Finally, in 1945, the Charter of the United Nations was signed at San Francisco. The United Nations has worked since then for peace and cooperation among all nations. The headquarters of the United Nations is in New York City.

REVIEW

WATCH YOUR WORDS

1. Hitler had the Jews put into____.
   isolation   the Axis
   concentration camps

2. ____ is the policy of staying out of other nations' affairs.
   Isolationism   Nazism   Fascism

3. A ____ is a person who controls everything in a nation.
   dictator   Nazi   Fascist

4. In World War II, the United States fought on the side of the____.
   Allies   Axis   dictators

5. Germany, Italy, and Japan formed the____.
   Allies   Axis   isolationists

CHECK YOUR FACTS

6. Right after World War I, the government of Germany (was/was not) democratic.

7. What group did Adolf Hitler lead?

8. What nation stood alone for a time against the Axis?

9. What happened at Pearl Harbor on December 7, 1941?

10. During World War II, the United States fought (with/against) the Soviet Union.

GET THE DATE STRAIGHT

Match the event with the date.

11. World War II began.
12. Pearl Harbor was attacked.
13. The war ended in Europe.
14. Hiroshima was bombed.

A. May 8, 1945
B. September 1, 1939
C. August 6, 1945
D. December 7, 1941

THINK ABOUT IT

How might history have been different if the Axis had won World War II?

Lesson 4: The War at Home

FIND THE WORDS

ration   integration
relocation camp   Nisei

During World War II, almost everyone in the United States contributed to winning the war.

While millions of men were

Many American women supported the war effort by working in factories on the home front.

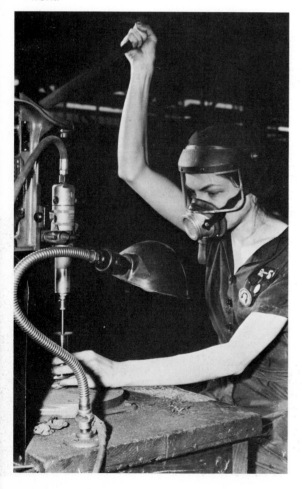

fighting overseas, women stepped into important jobs in industry at home. This had also happened during World War I. Again, women proved that they could do the work as well as men. Some women became welders. Others drove trucks, worked in construction, and did thousands of other jobs. Women also joined the armed forces in great numbers. There were thousands of women in the Army and the Army Air Corps. After the war ended, the soldiers came back to their jobs. Again, many women lost their wartime jobs. But American industry was changing. Women still worked in some jobs that were filled only by men before. During the war, women had been needed as workers. After the war, many women wanted to keep on working outside the home.

During World War II, factories stopped producing ordinary goods so that they could manufacture war materials. Automobile manufacturers began building airplane engines, tanks, and army trucks. Textile manufacturers were developing new materials, such as nylon. Americans were learning to do without many things they had been used to having. The government told people that they must use less of goods such as meat, butter, and gasoline. Such goods were **rationed** (RASH und). That meant that the amount a person could buy was limited. The government gave out ration coupons. These had to be used along with money to buy things. Each person had only so many coupons. When they were used up, people had to do without the rationed goods.

The United States gave the other Allies many weapons and supplies to use in fighting Germany and Japan. In 1944, the United States built over 60,000 planes and 45,000 tanks. Many Americans went overseas to fight in the war. Over a million of them were killed or wounded.

During World War II, many of the soldiers who fought and died for their country were Black. Yet Black people still did not have all the rights and freedoms that other Americans had. Even in the Army, Black soldiers had to live in separate barracks and fight in separate units. After the war, President Harry Truman ordered the **integration** of the armed forces. That meant that there would no longer be segregation, or separation by race, in the armed forces.

Many Black Americans served their nation in the armed forces in World War II. After the war, the armed forces were integrated.

The United States government sent thousands of Japanese-Americans to relocation camps.

Because of the war with Japan, some people in the United States began to distrust Japanese-Americans. People suspected the Japanese-Americans of spying for the Japanese government. In 1942, the government removed thousands of Japanese-Americans from their homes on the West Coast. They were placed in special prison camps called **relocation camps.** These relocation camps were located far from the West Coast. Men, women, and children were imprisoned in these camps. The treatment of the Japanese-Americans was harsh and unfair. Yet they continued to be loyal and good American citizens. The people born in the United States of Japanese parents were called **Nisei** (NEE SAY). About 8000 Nisei joined the armed forces and fought bravely for their country.

American scientists were also working for the war effort. They developed the atomic bomb in 1945. This powerful weapon began a new age in the history of the world.

REVIEW

WATCH YOUR WORDS

1. The Nisei were put into____.
   concentration camps
   relocation camps   isolation
2. To ____ goods is to limit the amount people can buy.
   ration   relocate   integrate
3. President Truman ordered the ____ of the armed forces.
   segregation   relocation
   integration

CHECK YOUR FACTS

4. Who did many jobs at home while the soldiers were fighting overseas?
5. Name two groups that were not treated equally during the war.

THINK ABOUT IT

How can war help citizens who are discriminated against to improve their situation?

Lesson 5: The Cold War

FIND THE WORDS

cold war   economy   socialism
capitalism   free enterprise

By the end of World War II, the Soviet Union and the United States had become rivals. They did not agree about what should happen in certain countries. The Soviet Union wanted Communist governments in Poland and other Eastern European nations. The United States wanted democratic governments there. But the Soviet Union had its army in Eastern Europe. The American army was in Western Europe. So the Soviets helped Communists take over the governments in Eastern European countries. Soon, Poland, Hungary, Bulgaria, Romania, and Albania had Communist governments. Later, Yugoslavia and Czechoslovakia fell under Communist rule.

Meanwhile, in Asia, a civil war was going on. The Soviet Union and the United States took sides in this war. This war was fought in China between Chinese Communists and Chinese Nationalists. The Soviet Union supported the Communists. They were led by Mao Tse-tung (MOW tzay DUNG). The United States supported the Nationalists. Chiang Kai-shek (JYANG KY SHEK) was leader of that side. Chiang's government was weak. It did not have the support of most Chinese. Partly for this reason, the United States began withdrawing its support of the Nationalists in 1948. In 1949, the Communists won. The Nationalists withdrew to Taiwan (TY WAHN). This is a large island off the coast of China. There, the Nationalists set up a separate Chinese government. For many years, the United States did not recognize the Communist government of China. It dealt only with Taiwan.

By 1949, the Soviet Union had developed an atomic bomb. The United States was no longer the only nation in the world with this weapon. Both nations realized that if they fought each other now, they could destroy much of the world. They began to wage a new kind of war—a war without fighting. It was called the **cold war.**

The United States and the Communist nations disagreed about what kind of economy was best. An **economy** is the way in which people produce and distribute goods and services.

The Communists believed in an economy controlled by the government. This kind of economy is called **socialism.** In a socialist

WHERE WE ARE IN TIME AND PLACE

THE COLD WAR IN EUROPE

1944–1947	1945	1946	1946–1949	1948	1948–1949
Communist governments are set up in Eastern Europe	World War II ends; United Nations Organization is set up	Cold war begins	Communist revolt in Greece	Communists come to power in Czechoslovakia	Soviets blockade Berlin

1949	1955	1956	1961	1963	1968
The Soviet Union gets the atomic bomb; North Atlantic Treaty Organization is formed; West Germany is set up	Soviets withdraw from Austria; Allied occupation of West Germany ends; Communists form Warsaw Pact	Soviets crush revolt in Hungary	Communists begin building Berlin Wall	The United States and the Soviet Union set up "Hot Line" and agree to ban most testing of nuclear weapons	Communist troops invade Czechoslovakia

EUROPE AFTER WORLD WAR II

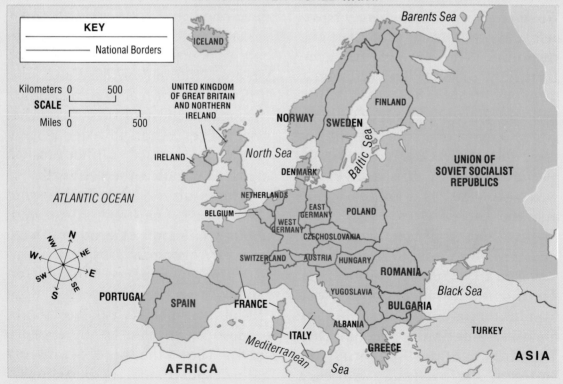

KEY
— National Borders

SCALE
Kilometers 0 — 500
Miles 0 — 500

ICELAND

Barents Sea

UNITED KINGDOM OF GREAT BRITAIN AND NORTHERN IRELAND

IRELAND

NORWAY

SWEDEN

FINLAND

North Sea

Baltic Sea

DENMARK

UNION OF SOVIET SOCIALIST REPUBLICS

ATLANTIC OCEAN

NETHERLANDS

BELGIUM

WEST GERMANY

EAST GERMANY

POLAND

CZECHOSLOVAKIA

SWITZERLAND

AUSTRIA

HUNGARY

ROMANIA

YUGOSLAVIA

PORTUGAL

SPAIN

FRANCE

ITALY

ALBANIA

BULGARIA

GREECE

Black Sea

TURKEY

Mediterranean Sea

AFRICA

ASIA

economy, the government decides what will be produced and who will get the products.

Most Americans believed in an economy run by private individuals and businesses. This kind of economy is called **capitalism** or **free enterprise.** In a capitalist economy, business leaders decide what to produce. People decide what they want to buy.

The Communists wanted to destroy capitalism. They said it was a bad system. They said it did not treat workers fairly. Most Americans disagreed. They believed that socialism gave the government too much power. Communist governments denied their people many rights and freedoms.

In the 1950s, the United States became involved in conflicts in different parts of the world. One of these conflicts was the Korean War. After World War II, Korea was split into two parts. The part north of 38° north latitude became North Korea. It had most of the factories. The part south of 38° north latitude became South Korea. It had most of the good farmland. Then, in 1950, the Korean War began. Communist North Korea attacked South Korea. United Nations troops, mostly from the United States, were sent to help South Korea. China and the Soviet Union supported the Communists in North Korea. At first, the North

John F. Kennedy was sworn in as President of the United States on January 20, 1961.

Koreans drove the United Nations troops into a small corner of South Korea. Then the North Koreans were pushed back toward China. As the United Nations forces neared China, Chinese troops entered the war. The United Nations forces again retreated south. Finally, in 1953, there was an armistice. It drew a border between the two Koreas close to the boundary of 1950.

There was also a civil war in Cuba. There, the Communists were led by Fidel Castro. Castro gained control of Cuba in 1959.

John F. Kennedy was elected President in 1960. In 1961, he started the Alliance for Progress to combat poverty in Latin America. It was poverty that made many people support Communism. In

John Kennedy announced the blockade of Cuba.

Union began to build missile bases in Cuba. The United States protested and began a blockade of Cuba. The Soviet Union backed down and withdrew the missiles. The world had come very close to nuclear war. Some people in the United States and elsewhere began to oppose the cold war.

The missile crisis had another result. The United States and the Soviet Union opened up a "Hot Line" in 1963. If another crisis arose, leaders of the two nations could talk to one another at once. That way, they could keep a war from happening by accident. Also in 1963, the two nations agreed to ban most testing of nuclear weapons. Many other nations also joined in this agreement.

1961, the United States supported an invasion of Cuba by anti-Communists at the Bay of Pigs. This attack failed, and Castro became stronger. In 1962, the Soviet

REVIEW

WATCH YOUR WORDS

1. Capitalism is also called____.
   free enterprise   socialism   economics

2. Socialism is a kind of____.
   free enterprise   nationalism   economy

3. The ____ is the struggle between the Soviet Union and the United States that began after World War II.
   free enterprise   economy   cold war

CHECK YOUR FACTS

4. What parts of Europe and Asia did the Communists take over shortly after World War II?

5. Over what nation did the Soviet Union and the United States almost fight a war in 1962?

6. What is the difference between capitalism and socialism?

THINK ABOUT IT

Why was it hard for Korea to be split into two parts?

Lesson 6: Equal Rights

American citizens often pledge allegiance to their country. When they do this, they speak of a nation that believes in "liberty and justice for all." These are the values that the United States stands for. These values have been called the American Dream.

Some citizens do not feel that they share fully in the American Dream. These people suffer from discrimination. This means that they are not given the same opportunities as other people.

Blacks in the United States have always been victims of discrimination. For years, some of the states had laws that said Blacks had to attend separate schools from Whites. When Blacks rode on public buses, they had to sit in the back. As you learned before, this is called segregation.

In the North, there were few laws establishing segregation, but it existed all the same. In many parts of the nation, Blacks were kept from voting in elections. Blacks were also discriminated against in employment. It was hard for them to get good jobs.

During the 1950s and 1960s, Black leaders fought against the segregation laws in the South. Their struggle was known as the civil rights movement. In 1954, they succeeded in getting the Supreme Court of the United States to declare segregation in public schools illegal.

In 1955, a Black woman, Rosa Parks, refused to give up her seat on a bus in Montgomery, Alabama. She was arrested. Some people became determined to do something. They started a movement to end segregation in public transportation. Blacks in Montgomery began a boycott of the city buses. They did this to protest

Rosa Parks and Dr. Martin Luther King, Jr., fought to win civil rights for Blacks.

Representative Robert Garcia, whose ancestors came from Puerto Rico, was elected to Congress from the Bronx, New York.

March Fong Eu, a Chinese-American, was elected Secretary of State in California.

having to sit in the back. A boycott is a refusal to use goods or services until a change is made. The bus boycott was led by Dr. Martin Luther King, Jr., a Black minister. A year after the boycott started, the bus company gave in. The buses were losing money. So Blacks were allowed to sit anywhere they chose. Dr. King became a leader of protests against segregation throughout the South. He was honored for his efforts with the Nobel Prize for Peace in 1964.

In 1964 and 1965, Congress passed civil rights laws. These laws made discrimination illegal in jobs, education, voting, and public facilities.

Over the next years, Blacks made more progress. Some were elected to high public office.

There are other groups in the United States who faced discrimination. They, too, have struggled to win equality. American Indians asked the government to pay for land it had taken away from them years before. Mexican-Americans worked in the Southwest to make schools use both Spanish and English in classrooms.

There were also many injustices in the way women were treated in the United States. They were often denied jobs just because they were women. Even when women did the same jobs as men, they were usually paid less. Often, women were not given promotions. Unmarried women could not get loans from banks even if they had high-paying jobs. This was not true for unmarried men.

Representative Shirley Chisholm of New York was the first Black woman elected to Congress.

Daniel Inouye, a Japanese-American, is a United States senator from Hawaii.

Many women and men felt that this unequal treatment was wrong. They began to work together to oppose discrimination. They won major improvements for women in education, jobs, credit, and other fields. People were also concerned with protecting the family. They wanted to safeguard and strengthen the rights of women who worked at home.

There have been many changes in social conditions in the United States. There will probably be still more reforms in the future. Americans believe in justice for all.

REVIEW

CHECK YOUR FACTS

1. What is discrimination?

2. There (was/was not) racial segregation in the North.

3. In what year did the Supreme Court declare segregation in the public schools illegal?

4. Name an important leader of the civil rights movement.

5. How did Blacks in Montgomery, Alabama, get the bus companies to end segregation?

TRY SOMETHING NEW

Find out more about the American Indians. How did they lose their lands? What promises did the government make and break? Find facts in an encyclopedia. Then make a report to the class.

Lesson 7: Conflict and Compromise

FIND THE WORDS

escalate   embargo

The Soviet Union and the United States became more friendly after the Cuban missile crisis of 1962. However, the American struggle against Communism continued. In 1961, President Kennedy began to increase the American role in Vietnam. Communists in North and South Vietnam were fighting the anti-Communist government of South Vietnam. The Soviet Union and China supported the Communists. The United States backed the government of South Vietnam.

In 1964, American warships became involved in fighting with the North Vietnamese in the Gulf of Tonkin. Congress passed a resolution backing the actions of President Lyndon Johnson. In 1965, President Johnson began to **escalate,** or greatly increase, American involvement in the war. American planes started to bomb North Vietnam. About 500,000 American troops were eventually sent to fight in Vietnam.

Many Americans began to oppose the role of the United States in the war. To many, the leaders of South Vietnam seemed little better than the Communists. Huge antiwar demonstrations were held.

A turning point came early in 1968. It was the time of the Asian New Year, called Tet. The Communists started a whole series of attacks. This was known as the Tet offensive. The Communists showed great power and will to fight. Even more Americans began to oppose the war. President Johnson stopped the American bombing of North Vietnam. Peace talks between the United States and North Vietnam began.

After President Richard Nixon took office in 1969, he began to withdraw troops from Vietnam very slowly. Huge antiwar demonstrations continued in the United States.

In 1970, President Nixon sent American troops across the South Vietnamese border into Cambodia. The Communists had been hiding troops and supplies there. Many Americans protested against this widening of the war. Four students were killed in an antiwar demonstration at Kent State University in Ohio. This increased protests even more. In 1971, it became clear that the war had also spread to neighboring Laos.

In 1972, the North Vietnamese began a major attack. President

Nixon ordered the bombing of North Vietnam to start again. The ports of North Vietnam were also mined and blockaded. But the withdrawal of American troops continued. Peace talks seemed to be succeeding. So the bombing of North Vietnam was stopped. But when no final agreement was reached, the heaviest bombing of the war was done. Finally, in January 1973, a peace agreement was signed. American prisoners of war were released. All American troops were withdrawn from Vietnam.

Despite the peace agreement, fighting continued between the Communists and the South Vietnamese for 2 years. In 1975, the South Vietnamese government fell. Vietnam was soon united into one Communist nation. Cambodia and Laos came under Communist rule.

In spite of the Vietnam War, the United States became more friendly with the Soviet Union. A 1967 treaty allowed each nation to set up offices in the other. One treaty banned the use of arms in outer space (1967). Another banned the use of nuclear arms on the seabed (1972). A 1969 treaty sought to stop the spread of nuclear weapons. In 1972 and 1973, President Nixon exchanged visits with the Soviet leader. A number of agreements were signed, including one to limit nuclear weapons. President Nixon also visited China

In the Vietnam War, civilians suffered the most. Heavy bombing and fighting forced many people to leave their homes.

in 1972. This visit improved relations between the United States and China. In 1974, President Gerald Ford also visited the Soviet Union and China. In 1979, under President Jimmy Carter, the United States set up diplomatic relations with China.

Since World War II, the United States has also been involved in the conflict between the Arabs and the Israelis (iz RAY leez). This conflict has taken place in the Middle East. In 1948, the United States supported the founding of the Jewish state of Israel in Palestine. After the Six-Day War in 1967, the United States supplied weapons to Israel. The United States also supported Israel in the Yom Kippur War of 1973. As a result, Arab nations put an **embargo,** or ban, on oil sales to the United States. Beginning in 1973, the American government helped bring about agreements between Israel and Egypt and Syria. With President Carter's help, Israel and Egypt signed a peace treaty in 1979. However, this did not solve the problem of the Arabs of Palestine. In 1948, they had lost their country. Many also lost their homes.

After Jimmy Carter became President in 1977, he insisted that all nations respect their people's human rights. This caused some nations to become less friendly with the United States.

A revolution in Iran created many problems for President Carter. Many Iranians were angry because the United States had supported their former ruler, the shah. In 1979, a group of Iranians seized some Americans and held them as hostages. It was more than a year before their release.

In the mid-1970s, the influence of the Soviet Union in Africa and

Anwar el-Sadat of Egypt, Jimmy Carter of the United States, and Menachem Begin of Israel worked together on a peace treaty.

elsewhere began to increase. Communist Cuba also sent troops to Africa. President Ronald Reagan took office in 1981. He began to stress the danger of Communist actions. Like President Carter, Reagan condemned the sending of Soviet troops into Afghanistan. Reagan also criticized the Soviet Union and other Communist nations for sending arms to rebels in El Salvador.

REVIEW

CHECK YOUR FACTS

1. Which side did the American government support in the Vietnam War?

2. Which President sent many American troops to fight in Vietnam?

3. The Vietnam War spread to two neighboring nations. What were these nations?

4. Which American President helped bring about a peace treaty between Egypt and Israel?

THINK ABOUT IT

What was the reaction of the American people to World War II? How did the reaction to the Vietnam War differ?

Lesson 8: New Americans

FIND THE WORDS

quota   national-origins system
refugee   sponsor

In 1921, the United States Congress passed an immigration law. This law limited the number of people who could come to the United States to live. It was the first time such a limit had been set.

In 1924, Congress passed another immigration law. This set up a system of immigration that was to last until the 1960s. Starting in 1929, only 150,000 immigrants could enter the country each year. The law also said how many people could come from each foreign nation. Each nation had a different quota. **A quota** is a certain share of the whole amount. Each nation's quota was based on its share of the United States population in 1920. This was known as the **national-origins system** of immigration.

Over the years, many immigrants had come to the United States from Europe. Particularly in the earlier years, most had come from Northern and Western Europe. So the proportion of the United States population from those areas was high. Thus, the nations of Northern and Western Europe had high quotas. In more recent years, more immigrants had started to come from Southern and Eastern Europe. However, the proportion of the total United States population from those areas was still fairly low. Thus, the nations of Southern and Eastern Europe had lower quotas. Asians and Africans were not allowed to immigrate at all.

The national-origins system affected the sources of immigration and helped reduce it overall. Immigration was also discouraged by the Great Depression of the 1930s. During that time, there were few jobs to be had in the United States. So not many immigrants wanted to come. Then World War II was fought. The war made it difficult for people to move about freely. After the war, new immigration laws were passed. Some American soldiers serving overseas had married foreigners. In 1946, they were allowed to bring their families to the United States.

In 1948, 1950, and 1953, Congress passed more special immigration laws. These laws helped refugees (REF yoo JEEZ) come to the United States. **Refugees** are people who leave their country to escape danger or death. Most of

More than 300,000 people fled from Vietnam in boats. These boat people waited at sea to be rescued.

In 1980, a boatlift brought thousands of Cubans to Florida.

the refugees were from Germany, Hungary, the Soviet Union, Poland, and Yugoslavia. Many of them were Jews. They wanted to live in freedom and to worship as they pleased. A 1952 law set up quotas for nations in Asia and other areas.

New Immigration Laws

In 1965, Congress changed the basic immigration law. A new system of quotas was set up. Each year, 170,000 immigrants could come from the Eastern Hemisphere. Each year, 120,000 could come from the Western Hemisphere. Thanks to this law, many Asians could come to the United States again. Many Asians came from India, Korea, and the Philippines. Later, many came from Vietnam.

In 1978, Congress changed the immigration laws once more. The separate quotas for the two hemispheres were dropped. There was still a limit of 290,000 immigrants a year. But now people could come from any part of the world.

Cuban and Vietnamese Refugees

Several times, Congress has let large numbers of refugees enter the United States. In 1959, a Communist government took over in Cuba. Thousands of Cubans left their country. Many came to the United States as refugees. In 1980, the Cuban government said that others who wanted to leave could do so. Hundreds of boats left Florida to pick up refugees from Cuba. This "boatlift" brought more than

100,000 Cubans to the United States.

In 1973, the United States withdrew its troops from Vietnam. Soon, a Communist government gained power there. Then, thousands of Vietnamese left their homeland. Many feared for their lives because they had helped the Americans.

There were also many Chinese people living in Vietnam. Later, the Vietnamese government forced many of them to leave. More than 300,000 people fled from Vietnam on boats. Many times, these "boat people," as they were called, had nowhere to go. They often suffered great hardships. Between 1975 and 1979, the United States took in over 200,000 refugees from Vietnam. In recent years, refugees have also fled from wars in Cambodia and Laos.

A New Start

Almost all immigrants have problems when they come to a new land. Many must learn a new language. All have to find new jobs and homes. Immigrants also have to find new friends. They have to learn new ways of doing things.

In recent years, many Americans have tried to help the refugees. Thanks to their help, many of the immigrants' problems have been eased. The United States government helps refugees learn English. It also helps find sponsors for them. A **sponsor** is someone who agrees to be responsible for one or more refugees. Sponsors help refugees find homes and jobs. They help them make a new start. Thanks to American sponsors, many refugees are making new lives.

REVIEW

WATCH YOUR WORDS

1. Under the national-origins system, each nation had a ___.
   refugee   sponsor   quota

2. ___ are people who leave their countries to escape danger or death.
   Refugees   Sponsors   Quotas

CHECK YOUR FACTS

3. When was the national-origins law passed?

4. What events limited immigration in the 1930s and 1940s?

5. From what nations have many refugees come to the United States in recent years? Name two.

THINK ABOUT IT

Are there any recent immigrants in your community? From what nations did they come?

Lesson 9: The Space Age

"That's one small step for a man, one giant leap for mankind." With these words, American astronaut Neil Armstrong became the first person to walk on the moon. Neil Armstrong and Edwin Aldrin reached the moon on July 20, 1969, on the *Apollo 11* mission. This exciting moon landing was the high point of America's space program.

The space age began on October 4, 1957. On that day, the Soviet Union put the first satellite, *Sputnik I*, into orbit around the Earth. Other Soviet successes in space followed. The Soviets put the first satellite into orbit around the moon in 1959. In 1961, they sent the first person into space. He was Yuri Gagarin. In 1963, they sent the first woman into space. She was Valentina Tereshkova.

The Soviet space program was a challenge to the United States. The first American satellite was *Explorer I*. It went into orbit on January 31, 1958. In May 1961, President John F. Kennedy said that the United States would put a person on the moon "before this decade is out." During that same month, Alan Shepard became the first American to travel in space. In 1962, John Glenn became the

American astronaut Neil Armstrong was the first person to walk on the moon.

first American to orbit the Earth. From 1961 to 1966, the United States prepared for the trip to the moon with the Mercury and Gemini programs.

The Apollo moon program sent astronauts into Earth orbit in 1968. Several practice missions around the moon or the Earth followed. After *Apollo 11* in 1969, five more landings were made on the moon. The last was in 1972. The United States then sent astronauts on long trips in Earth orbit aboard Skylab, a space station. The space shuttle, a combined spacecraft and airplane, will be

In April 1981, the space shuttle *Columbia* blasted off on its first round-trip flight. The shuttle is the first reusable spaceship.

the main American space effort of the 1980s. In April 1981, the first successful flight of the space shuttle *Columbia* took place.

Meanwhile, the Soviets continued their space program. The Soviets stressed long flights in orbit. They did not send people to the moon. In 1975, an American Apollo spacecraft docked with a Soviet Soyuz craft. This joint mission showed that the two nations could work together in space.

The space age has included much more than the exciting trips people have made into space. American and Soviet spacecraft have studied the moon, the planets, and the sun. The Soviet Union concentrated on the planet Venus. The United States sent many Mariner spacecraft to Mars. The American Viking spacecraft landed on Mars in July 1976. The American Pioneer and Voyager spacecraft sent back beautiful pictures of Jupiter and Saturn.

Some of the most important spacecraft have stayed close to the Earth. Every day we see pictures of the Earth sent back by weather satellites. These have been of great help in predicting the weather. Telephone calls and live television pictures come from overseas through communications satellites. Scientific satellites study the Earth and the skies. Military satellites spy on other nations.

Some people have questioned the huge amounts of money spent on space. They suggest that we should pay attention to problems here on Earth, instead. Yet the space program has brought many new inventions. They have made our lives better. Besides this, space is the last frontier. It is a challenge to people everywhere. President Kennedy said it very well in 1962:

"We choose to go to the moon in this decade and do the other things, not because they are easy, but because they are hard; because that goal will serve to organize and measure the best of our energies and skills. . . . Many years ago the great British explorer George Mallory, who was to die on Mount Everest, was asked why did he want to climb it, and he said, 'Because it is there.' Well, space is there, and . . . the moon and the planets are there, and new hopes for knowledge and peace are there."

FUN FACTS

What is a lunatic? *Luna* is a Latin word meaning moon. So a lunatic is a person who is "moonstruck." For many centuries some people believed that sleeping in moonlight could make a person crazy. Even today, people believe that a full moon makes people nervous and excited.

Astronauts found the moon to be a dead world without air or water. But for thousands of years, people believed that some form of life existed on the moon. There was the "man in the moon," who was put there for stealing. Other people told of insects, demons, and even a lunar city.

REVIEW

CHECK YOUR FACTS

1. In what year did people first land on the moon? Who were they?

2. What nation put the first satellite into orbit around the Earth?

3. Which American President set the goal of reaching the moon?

4. What is the main American space effort of the 1980s?

5. Name two kinds of satellites that affect our lives every day.

THINK ABOUT IT

List some arguments for and against space travel.

Lesson 10: Into the Future

FIND THE WORDS

bicentennial   Watergate Scandal
energy   environment   scarcity
black lung   pollution   inflation
productivity   investment
savings   efficient

On July 4, 1976, the United States celebrated its 200th birthday. This birthday was called the **bicentennial** (BY sen TEN ee ul). This was a day of many celebrations. It was also a time when many American citizens looked at the problems facing the nation.

Honesty in Government

Honesty in government is one concern of Americans. The muckrakers in the early 1900s made the nation aware of politicians who were not acting properly. In the 1970s, some politicians were still behaving dishonestly. Some people who worked for President Richard Nixon broke into an office in the Watergate building in Washington, DC. They were probably trying to spy on the candidate running against President Nixon in 1972. Newspaper reporters found out more about the spying and who

The United States celebrated its 200th birthday on July 4, 1976. Here, fireworks light up the night sky around the Statue of Liberty.

was involved. This caused many people to become suspicious of the President and of other people in the government.

President Nixon tried to help his friends. He wanted the people to believe his friends had done nothing wrong. But this made many people even more suspicious. Many felt that perhaps he, too, had done something illegal. Most people did not feel that a President of the United States should break the law. Congress thought about removing Nixon from the office of President. Before they could do that, he chose to resign. The events leading to his resignation became known as the **Watergate Scandal.** After this, laws were passed to help increase honesty in government.

Violence in America

On March 30, 1981, Americans were shocked to hear that President Ronald Reagan had been shot. As he left a hotel in Washington, DC, a gunman fired six shots at him. One bullet struck the President in the chest. Three other bullets wounded men near him. Fortunately, the President recovered from his wound. He was back at the White House in about 2 weeks.

But many Americans asked themselves: "What is happening to us? How can we protect our leaders?" People remembered their shock on November 22, 1963. Then, President John Kennedy was shot and killed in Dallas, Texas. The nation and the world mourned for days. The leaders of nations from all over the world flew to Washington. They wanted to show their feelings for the dead President and for the American people.

But there were many shocks awaiting the American people during the 1960s. Dr. Martin Luther King, Jr., the leader of the civil rights movement, was shot and killed on April 4, 1968. This happened in Memphis, Tennessee. Two months later, Robert Kennedy was shot and killed in Los Angeles, California. Robert Kennedy was the brother of President John Kennedy. He was running for President, himself, when he died.

Americans were reminded again and again about violence in the United States. But people did not seem to know what to do about it. Some said that all guns should be banned. Others said that taking guns away from people would mean that only criminals would have guns. But most people felt that something had to be done to stop violent crime.

Problems of Energy

A nation with as much industry and transportation as the United

The United States needs to find ways to provide its people with energy. Some people think that atomic reactors are the answer.

States faces an important challenge. It needs energy to keep everything running. **Energy** means power. Electricity is a form of energy. It makes light bulbs, refrigerators, record players, televisions, and air conditioners work. Gasoline is another form of energy. It powers our cars, trucks, and airplanes. Coal is another form of energy. It is used to heat many homes and factories and to make electricity.

The United States is a land rich in natural resources. Water, petroleum, and coal are resources. They have been used to produce the energy the nation has needed. But as the population of the United States grows larger, the nation needs more and more energy. The petroleum in the United States cannot provide as much energy as the nation needs.

The United States has begun to buy more than half the petroleum it uses from other nations. These nations demand very high prices for their petroleum. Many people in the United States cannot afford to pay these prices. Ways must be found to provide the American people with the energy they need at a price they can afford.

Resources and the Environment

The natural resources of the United States give its people more than just energy. People breathe the air. They drink the water and use it in many other ways. They grow food in the soil. They cut wood and hunt animals in the forests. Americans do not just use the waters and the land in practical ways. They also enjoy the rivers, lakes, and oceans of their nation. They love its forests, mountains, and valleys. All these things—the air, the water, the land, and the plants and animals—are natural

The United States has been called "America the Beautiful." Some people fear that too much development can destroy much natural beauty.

resources. Together, all these natural surroundings make up the **environment.**

In the past, Americans have acted as though there were no end to the forests and other resources. Generations of settlers burned or cut down the forests to make room for farms. There always seemed to be plenty of forests left. But by 1900, this was no longer true. Americans now know that if they use up too many resources, soon there will not be any left. There will be a **scarcity** of resources. That means that there will not be enough resources to meet people's needs.

Americans have also learned that some activities can destroy the environment and the people

living in it. For example, coal mining is dangerous work. Coal miners often suffer from an illness called **black lung** disease. Many have died from it. Very often, too, the ways that coal is taken from the Earth destroy the land.

There are other dangers to the environment. An important problem is **pollution,** the putting of wastes into the air and water. When automobiles and factories burn gasoline and coal, certain waste products get into the air. These wastes can harm living things. When people breathe polluted air, they can get sick and even die.

Some factories throw their waste products into nearby bodies of water. These wastes often pollute the water. They harm and sometimes kill fish and plants. Birds and other animals feed and drink in these polluted waters. They often get sick or die. Sometimes, water pollution threatens to wipe out whole groups of living things. People who drink such water or eat things taken from it can also be affected. Protecting our natural environment is an important challenge for the future.

Economic Problems

In recent years, the United States and other nations have suffered from inflation. **Inflation** is a drop in the value of money. It means that the same goods cost more. You have learned that the United States buys much of its petroleum from other nations. In part, inflation has been caused by large increases in the price of this petroleum.

Inflation has also been created by a decline in productivity in the United States. **Productivity** refers to how many goods a worker can make. In large part, this depends on how good factories and machines are. In recent years, workers' wages have been going up. But workers have not been producing any more goods. Thus, to pay the higher wages, companies have increased the prices of their goods. This causes inflation.

One of the main reasons that productivity has not been increasing has been a lack of investment. **Investment** takes place when companies build factories and buy new machines. The money for investment comes from **savings.** These are funds that people set aside for use in the future. Recently, companies have not been building many factories or buying many new machines. Workers have had to make goods in old factories with old machines. These old factories and machines are less **efficient.** That means that they produce fewer goods or cost more to run. Workers who use them have lower productivity. There has

also been less investment because Americans have been saving less. There has been less money available for companies to borrow and use for investment.

Productivity, investment, and savings have fallen in the United States. But they have risen in other countries. Japan is using new factories and machines to produce goods very efficiently. American companies have lost sales to the Japanese around the world and even in the United States. To remain strong, the American economy must meet this challenge from other nations.

President Ronald Reagan took

Water pollution is a danger to the environment. People who swim in polluted water can get sick.

President Ronald Reagan took office in 1981. He promised to help the economy by cutting taxes and government spending.

office in 1981. He promised to do something about the problems of the American economy. To cure inflation, he proposed cutting government spending. To increase savings, investment, and productivity, he suggested cutting taxes. That way, money that would have gone to the government could be used to rebuild industry. However, the President also planned to increase spending on national defense. This could add to inflation. You can see that the problems of the American economy are all connected to one another. You can also see that solving these problems will be a difficult challenge.

REVIEW

WATCH YOUR WORDS

1. ____ is a decrease in the value of money.
   Investment   Scarcity   Inflation

2. ____ refers to how many goods a worker can make.
   Investment   Productivity   Energy

3. ____ means power.
   Inflation   Productivity   Energy

CHECK YOUR FACTS

4. Give three examples of violence against American leaders.

5. The United States (does/does not) produce all the petroleum it needs.

6. What will happen if the United States keeps on using too many of its resources?

7. Name two places in the environment where there is pollution.

CHAPTER REVIEW

WATCH YOUR WORDS

1. ____ is telling people about products or services.
   Productivity Advertising
   Discriminating

2. A(n) ____ is a community near a city where some city workers live.
   suburb relocation camp
   environment

3. The ____ was invented by American scientists during World War II.
   concentration camp cold war
   atomic bomb

4. ____ is the kind of economy the United States has.
   Socialism Capitalism Investment

5. ____ are people who leave their country to escape danger or death.
   Refugees Nisei Muckrakers

6. To ____ is to increase greatly.
   concentrate escalate embargo

7. A(n) ____ is a halt in the sale of a product to a nation.
   scarcity scandal embargo

8. ____ are funds put aside for future use.
   Stocks Savings Inflation

9. ____ takes place when companies build factories or buy new machines.
   Investment Escalation Inflation

10. Old machines tend to be less ____ than new ones.
    atomic efficient capitalist

11. The ____ was the 200th birthday of the United States.
    bicentennial inflation
    celebration

12. Coal miners get a disease called ____.
    pollution inflation black lung

CHECK YOUR FACTS

13. List three important things that happened in the 1920s.

14. What President was responsible for the New Deal?

15. What were the two groups of nations that fought World War II called?

16. What two nations "fought" the cold war after World War II?

17. Name two wars in which the United States fought after World War II.

18. How do new factories and machines help improve productivity?

THINK ABOUT IT

19. List three good things and three bad things about the 1920s.

20. The Social Security system started under the New Deal. What is Social Security? Why is it important?

21. How were relocation camps like concentration camps? How were the two different?

22. What is the difference between a "hot" war and a "cold" war? Give an example of both kinds of war.

23. Many Americans believe we should continue to explore outer space. Others feel we should spend the money to solve problems at home. What do you think? Why?

24. The United States has many problems to solve. What do you think is the most important problem? What would you do to solve it?

25. The United States also has many opportunities. What are some good things that you think may happen in the future?

UNIT REVIEW

WATCH YOUR WORDS

advertising	atomic bomb	Great Depression	Prohibition
alliances	Axis	isolationism	reformers
Allied Powers	Central Powers	migration	stocks
Allies	congestion	muckrakers	subways
armistice	drought	neutral	suffrage
assassinated	erosion	Progressives	U-boat

In 1900, cities were growing in part because of ___ from the farms. The crowds of people and vehicles caused ___ . Some cities built ___ to help people get around. The ___ tried to change things for the better. The ___ wrote about the problems created by big business. The ___ founded a political movement to do something about the problems.

World War I began when an Austro-Hungarian leader was ___ . The European nations were divided into two ___ . Germany, Austria-Hungary, and the Ottoman Empire were the ___ . Their opponents were called the ___ . At first, the United States was ___ . However, a submarine, the ___ , helped bring the Americans into the war. Finally, in 1918, a(n) ___ was signed. It ended World War I. Partly as a result of the war, women's ___ was approved in the United States.

During the 1920s, ___ told people about the many new products. ___ helped gangsters to get rich. The ___ followed the good times. It brought hard times in the 1930s. The prices of ___ fell. There was ___ on the Great Plains and much soil ___ in farming areas.

In spite of the policy of ___ , the United States entered World War II. It fought with the ___ against the ___ . A new weapon, the ___ helped end the war.

CHECK YOUR FACTS

1. What were two important things that President Theodore Roosevelt did?
2. What kind of fighting took place in Western Europe during World War I?
3. In what year did World War I begin? When did it end?
4. Did the United States sign the Treaty of Versailles? Why, or why not?
5. What work did many women do during both world wars?
6. What are two names that have been used for the 1920s?
7. What President had the Bonus Army driven out of Washington?
8. What was President Franklin Roosevelt's program called?
9. When did the U.S. economy fully recover from the Great Depression?
10. What dictators came to power in Germany and Italy in the 1930s? What party did each lead?
11. Why was Germany so successful at the beginning of World War II?
12. What people were put into concentration camps in World War II?

13. What caused the United States to enter World War II?

14. Against what nation were atomic bombs used in World War II?

15. During World War II, what did Americans have to use along with money to buy many goods?

16. During World War II, the armed forces were (integrated/segregated).

17. What are two names for the kind of economy the United States has?

18. Name three areas in which women have made gains in recent years.

19. What nation seized a group of Americans as hostages in 1979?

20. In what year was the first satellite put into orbit around the Earth? In what year was the first moon landing made?

KNOW YOUR PEOPLE

21. Neil Armstrong
22. Amelia Earhart
23. Yuri Gagarin
24. Charles A. Lindbergh
25. Alan Shepard
26. Valentina Tereshkova

A. first person to fly alone from Honolulu to California

B. first person to fly alone across the Atlantic

C. first person to walk on the moon

D. first person to travel in space

E. first woman to travel in space

F. first American to travel in space

THINK ABOUT IT

27. How did life change in the United States between 1900 and 1929? List as many changes as you can.

28. Was World War I called by that name when it was being fought?

29. What caused World War II? List as many causes as you can.

30. Why have many refugees come to the United States in recent years? What problems do they face?

31. Suppose you were writing a history of the 20th century. What do you think were the five most important things that happened between 1900 and 1982? Tell why.

TRY SOMETHING NEW

32. Pretend that it is March 1917. German U-boats are attacking ships. Germany is trying to get Mexico to take sides against the United States. Make a poster. Show why the United States should enter the war in Europe.

33. Pretend that it is 1918. Draw a poster in support of women's suffrage.

PUT IT ALL TOGETHER

34. Make two charts labeled "World War I" and "World War II." On the first, make two columns headed "Allied Powers" and "Central Powers." On the second, put columns for "Allies" and "Axis." List each nation under the correct column: Austria-Hungary, Serbia, Russia, Germany, France, Great Britain, Ottoman Empire, Bulgaria, United States, Italy, Japan, Soviet Union. Put a star by the nations that fought in both wars.

1 THE UNITED STATES AND ITS NEIGHBORS

Lesson 1: The United States and the American People

FIND THE WORD

communication

The people of the United States live in a large nation. Their country covers 9,363,353 square kilometers (3,615,191 square miles). There are more than 226 million people in the United States. Only three nations have more people.

These three nations are China, India, and the Union of Soviet Socialist Republics.

The United States is also a powerful and rich nation. It has a large army, navy, and air force. It has more factories and businesses than any other nation.

The system of transportation in the United States reaches even the smallest town in the nation. It is

344

In different parts of the United States, large roads have different names. In Los Angeles, this road is called a freeway.

HARRISVILLE PUBLIC LIBRARY

LIBRARY HOURS

MON.	6:00-8:00
WED.	3:00-5:00
FRI.	4:00-6:00

People in the United States share an interest in learning. The nation has many libraries.

fairly easy for people to move from place to place. There are waterways, highways, railroads, and airlines connecting all parts of the nation.

The United States also has a very good system of communications. **Communication** includes all the ways people send or get messages. Telephones, radios, televisions, newspapers, and magazines are all part of this system. They help people find out what is going on in the rest of the world. They help people keep in touch with one another.

People in the United States are like one another in many ways. They share many beliefs. You will read about some of these beliefs later. Most share a common language, English. Americans also share a common government. They are expected to follow the same laws.

Americans can use many of the same objects. They drive the same kinds of cars. They use the same brands of goods. You could travel all around the nation and still find most of the same things you see every day.

But the people of the United States are also different in many ways. They are different in the amount and kinds of things they have. The poor, the wealthy, and those in between do not live in the same way. The people have many different interests and abilities.

Americans have come from different parts of the world. Some are still arriving. They have brought different ways of living, talking, and thinking with them. They have settled in different parts of the country. *Where* they live sometimes makes the *way* they live different. Often, jobs are different in different parts of the nation. The ways people have fun and the kinds of music they enjoy often differ.

Some people say that these differences are among the things that make the United States great.

FUN FACTS

Today it is easy to communicate with people far away. We can either telephone or write a letter and take it to the post office. But 5000 years ago, there weren't any post offices. Ancient rulers employed runners who memorized a message. They went on foot from one place to another and repeated the message aloud. There wasn't any need for a more developed system. Few people in those days could read or write.

The earliest "letter" was carved on clay or bronze. Later, letters were carved on bone or wood and protected by a wax coating. Still later, letters were written on the skins of animals and on paper called parchment.

The first American postal system appeared in 1639. Richard Fairbanks received permission from the Massachusetts Colony to dispatch ship mail from his home in Boston. He was paid one cent for every letter he handled.

REVIEW

CHECK YOUR FACTS

1. How does the United States rank in population among the world's nations?

2. In what ways is the United States rich?

3. What is the difference between transportation and communication?

4. List some ways in which the people of the United States are alike.

5. List some ways in which the American people are different.

THINK ABOUT IT

People have come to the United States from all over the world. How has this made the United States a more interesting, exciting nation?

Lesson 2: Where Americans Live

FIND THE WORDS

county   urban area   rural area
population-density map   census

On page 348 is a political map of the United States. This map shows the 50 states. The names of the states are abbreviated, or shortened. These are the short forms that the post office uses. Find DC on the map. DC stands for the District of Columbia. We call this district Washington, DC.

Washington, DC, is the capital of the United States. The national government is located there. Each state has a capital where the state government meets. You can find state capitals on the map on pages 8 and 9. Each state is also divided into counties. A **county** is a unit of local government.

Today, 75 of every 100 people in the United States live in urban areas. **Urban areas** are towns and cities with more than 2500 people in them. **Rural areas** are farms or

POPULATION OF THE UNITED STATES

ALASKA

Kilometers 0 — 1000
SCALE
Miles 0 — 1000

HAWAII

Kilometers 0 — 200
SCALE
Miles 0 — 200

San Francisco
Las Angeles
San Diego
Dallas
Houston
Detroit
Chicago
New York
Philadelphia
Washington, DC
1850 1800
1950
1980 1900

Kilometers 0 — 500
SCALE
Miles 0. — 500

PEOPLE	
Per Square Kilometer	Per Square Mile
under 10	under 25
10 to 50	25 to 125
50 to 100	125 to 250
over 100	over 250

KEY	
—— National Borders	● Centers of Population
---- State Borders	● Cities

UNITED STATES

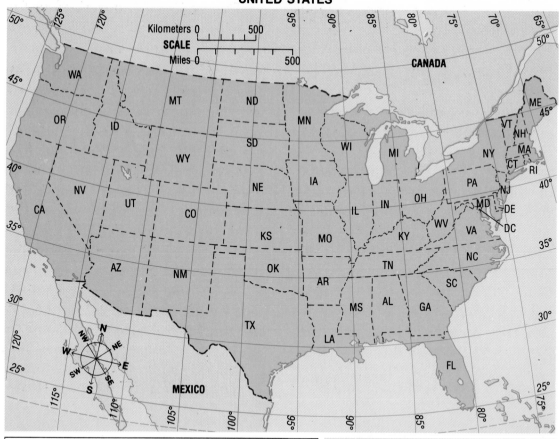

SCALE
Kilometers 0 — 500
Miles 0 — 500

CANADA

MEXICO

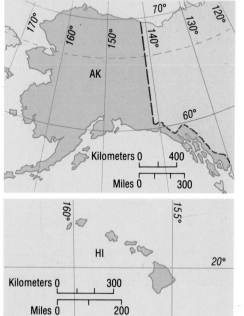

KEY

States:

AL Alabama	KY Kentucky	ND North Dakota
AK Alaska	LA Louisiana	OH Ohio
AZ Arizona	ME Maine	OK Oklahoma
AR Arkansas	MD Maryland	OR Oregon
CA California	MA Massachusetts	PA Pennsylvania
CO Colorado	MI Michigan	RI Rhode Island
CT Connecticut	MN Minnesota	SC South Carolina
DC District of Columbia	MS Mississippi	SD South Dakota
DE Delaware	MO Missouri	TN Tennessee
FL Florida	MT Montana	TX Texas
GA Georgia	NE Nebraska	UT Utah
HI Hawaii	NV Nevada	VT Vermont
ID Idaho	NH New Hampshire	VA Virginia
IL Illinois	NJ New Jersey	WA Washington
IN Indiana	NM New Mexico	WV West Virginia
IA Iowa	NY New York	WI Wisconsin
KS Kansas	NC North Carolina	WY Wyoming

AK

Kilometers 0 — 400
Miles 0 — 300

HI

Kilometers 0 — 300
Miles 0 — 200

are country towns and villages with fewer than 2500 people. About 20 of every 100 Americans live in country towns or villages. About 5 out of 100 live on farms.

Look at the **population-density map** of the United States on page 347. This is a kind of distribution map. It shows where people lived at the time of the last census. Every 10 years, the government takes a **census,** or count, of the population. Examine the map. Study the map key. The color red stands for the most crowded areas. Notice that the Northeast is one of the most heavily populated regions. Few people live in the areas colored light green. Much of this land is in the western United States.

The center of population for the United States is marked with a circle on your map. A north-south line and an east-west line cross on that spot. As many people live north of that place as live south of it. As many people live east of that place as live west of it. The center of population moves from year to year, as people move from place to place. Since the early days of the United States, the center of population has been moving west.

The center of population shown on the map is only for the 48 states between Canada and Mexico. It does not include the states of Alaska and Hawaii. It does not include the island of Puerto Rico.

REVIEW

WATCH YOUR WORDS

1. A___is a division of a state.
   county   government   census
2. In the ___ , the government counts the population.
   county   census   distribution

CHECK YOUR FACTS

Look at the Maps

3. What states border on Texas? What nation borders on Texas?

4. What do IA and ID stand for?
5. The Atlantic Coast from Massachusetts down to Virginia is heavily populated. Find two other areas with large populations.

THINK ABOUT IT

Many people live in the eastern half of the United States and on the West Coast. Fewer people live in between. What reasons can you think of for this?

Lesson 3: Canada and the Canadian People

FIND THE WORDS

Parliament   prime minister   province

The nation of Canada shares the North American continent with the United States. Canada is a little larger than the United States. It has 9,976,128 square kilometers (3,851,787 square miles). About 226 million people live in the United States. How many do you think live in Canada?

If you said about 200 million for Canada, you guessed wrong. Canada has only about 23 million people. This is a small population for such a large nation. Most Canadians live in the south near the border with the United States. Few people live in northern Canada. The climate there is very cold.

As in the United States, there are many differences within Canada. The Rocky Mountains are in the west. The Great Plains are in the center. The Canadian Shield, or Laurentian Plateau, is in the east. In the far north is an area called the Arctic. Ways of living are different in Canada's regions.

The Innuit sometimes build snow houses, called igloos, to protect themselves from the cold.

WHERE WE ARE IN TIME AND PLACE

THE GROWTH OF CANADA

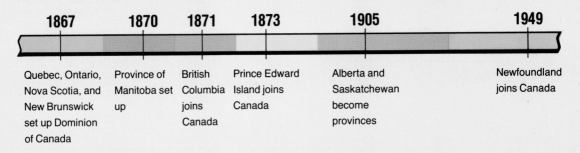

1867	1870	1871	1873	1905	1949
Quebec, Ontario, Nova Scotia, and New Brunswick set up Dominion of Canada	Province of Manitoba set up	British Columbia joins Canada	Prince Edward Island joins Canada	Alberta and Saskatchewan become provinces	Newfoundland joins Canada

POLITICAL MAP OF CANADA

ARCTIC OCEAN

160° 120° 110° 100° 90° 80° 70° 60° 50°

GREENLAND (DENMARK)

Baffin Bay

30°

Yukon

ALASKA (U.S.)

150°

70°

YUKON TERRITORY

Great Bear Lake

ARCTIC CIRCLE

NORTHWEST TERRITORIES

Whitehorse ★

Mackenzie River

ROCKY COAST MTS. MOUNTAINS

Yellowknife ★

60°

ATLANTIC OCEAN

40°

Great Slave Lake

140°

BRITISH COLUMBIA

Peace River

LABRADOR

NEWFOUNDLAND

50°

ALBERTA

SASKAT-CHEWAN

Nelson River

Hudson Bay

PACIFIC OCEAN

Fraser River

MANITOBA

Lake Winnipeg

QUEBEC

St. John's ★

Laurentian Highlands

PRINCE EDWARD ISLAND

Edmonton ●

Saskatoon ●

Vancouver ●

Calgary ●

Winnipeg ★

St. Lawrence River

Charlottetown ★

NOVA SCOTIA

130°

Victoria ●

Regina ★

ONTARIO

Quebec ★

Halifax ★

NEW BRUNSWICK

Montreal ●

40°

Lake Huron

✪ Ottawa

Fredericton ★

KEY

- - - - National Borders
- - - - Provincial Borders

✪ National Capital
★ Provincial Capitals
● Cities

GREAT LAKES

Lake Superior

Lake Michigan (U.S.)

UNITED STATES

Lake Ontario

Toronto ★

Niagara Falls

Lake Erie

Miles 0   500

SCALE

Kilometers 0   500

351

Most people in the province of Quebec speak French. That is why signs are in French.

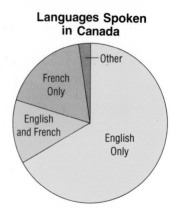

Languages Spoken in Canada

Other
French Only
English and French
English Only

The Eskimos of North America are properly called the Innuit (IN yoo it). *Innuit* is their word for "people." Canada has 15,000 Innuit. Many of them live in the Arctic. The Arctic is one of the coldest parts of North America. In the winter months, it can get as cold as −40°C (−40°F).

There are more than 300,000 American Indians in Canada. Many of them live on reservations. Some live and work in Canada's cities.

Most Canadians, like most Americans, have European backgrounds. About half have English ancestors. About one-third have French ancestors. English and French are the two official languages of Canada. All documents published by the national government are written in both languages. In some parts of Canada, there are separate French schools and English schools. In other places, there are schools where classes are taught in both languages.

The national government of Canada meets in Ottawa (OT uh wuh), the capital city. Laws are made for the nation by the members of the **Parliament.** The Canadian Parliament is like the United States Congress. A **prime minister** is the head of the Canadian government. The Canadian prime minister is like the American President. As in the United States, the leaders of the Canadian government are elected by the people.

Canada is divided into 10 provinces and 2 territories. A **province** is similar to an American state. Each province has its own government. The Canadian territories are like the territories that used to exist in the United States. Many states of the United States were once territories. The Canadian territories have their own governments. However, they are less independent of the national government than provinces are. Few people live in the territories because it is so cold there.

Canada has many natural resources. It has fertile land for crops. It has great forests that supply timber. It also has valuable minerals, such as petroleum and natural gas.

Americans own about half of all Canadian factories. Money from the United States has helped to build many businesses in Canada. Many Canadians are not so

Timber is an important resource in Canada.

sure this is a good thing. Canada is a separate nation. Canadians want to have greater control over all the resources of their nation.

Canada and the United States are friendly neighbors. The International Peace Garden is one of the monuments built in honor of this friendship. The people of Manitoba and North Dakota gave the land for the garden.

REVIEW

WATCH YOUR WORDS

1. In Canada, the ___ makes the laws for the nation.
   prime minister   province
   Parliament

2. A Canadian ___ is like an American state.
   territory   province   Parliament

CHECK YOUR FACTS
Look at the Map
3. What city is the capital of Canada?

4. Name the two Canadian territories.

5. Name the capital of Saskatchewan. Of British Columbia.

6. What oceans border on Canada?

THINK ABOUT IT

Canada is a little larger than the United States. However, it has only about one-tenth as many people. What reasons can you think of for this?

Lesson 4: Mexico and the Mexican People

FIND THE WORDS

federal district

The third large nation on the continent of North America is Mexico. Mexico covers 1,972,544 square kilometers (761,600 square miles). About 74 million people live in Mexico. Mexico has much less land than Canada. But it has many more people.

Of every 100 Mexicans, about 25 are American Indians. Their ancestors lived in Mexico thousands of years ago. About another 8 of every 100 have Spanish or other European backgrounds.

Their ancestors came to Mexico during and after the 1500s. The remaining 67 out of 100 are mestizos. Mestizos have both Spanish and American Indian ancestors. Most people in Mexico speak Spanish.

About 67 out of every 100 Mexicans live in urban areas. Most of them live on a plateau in central Mexico. One of the reasons is the

This picture shows a modern shopping center in Mexico.

354

climate. Look at the map on page 56. What is the climate like in the middle of Mexico?

Mexico is divided into 31 states and 1 federal district. The Mexican states are like the American states. The **federal district** is the area around the capital, Mexico City. It is like the District of Columbia in the United States. Mexico is like the United States in other ways, too. A president heads the national government of Mexico. The members of a congress make the laws for Mexico as a whole. These leaders of Mexico's

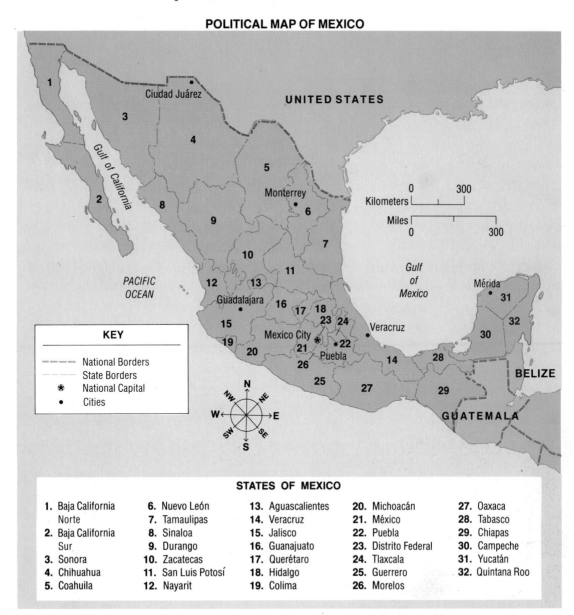

POLITICAL MAP OF MEXICO

KEY
- --- National Borders
- ···· State Borders
- ✳ National Capital
- • Cities

STATES OF MEXICO

1. Baja California Norte	6. Nuevo León	13. Aguascalientes	20. Michoacán	27. Oaxaca
2. Baja California Sur	7. Tamaulipas	14. Veracruz	21. México	28. Tabasco
3. Sonora	8. Sinaloa	15. Jalisco	22. Puebla	29. Chiapas
4. Chihuahua	9. Durango	16. Guanajuato	23. Distrito Federal	30. Campeche
5. Coahuila	10. Zacatecas	17. Querétaro	24. Tlaxcala	31. Yucatán
	11. San Luis Potosí	18. Hidalgo	25. Guerrero	32. Quintana Roo
	12. Nayarit	19. Colima	26. Morelos	

Old and new meet and mix in Mexico. Above, on the right, is a beautiful old Spanish building. The other picture shows modern Mexico.

government are elected by the Mexican people.

Mexico and the United States have not always been friends. Much of the southwestern part of the United States once belonged to Mexico. You have read about the war between Mexico and the United States in the 1840s.

Today, Mexico and the United States are good neighbors again. Many Mexicans have relatives in the United States. The two nations now help each other.

REVIEW

CHECK YOUR FACTS

1. Which nation has more land, Canada or Mexico? Which has more people?

2. What language do most Mexicans speak?

3. Do most Mexican people live in rural areas or urban areas?

4. What area of Mexico is like the District of Columbia?

5. List four ways in which Mexico and the United States are alike.

THINK ABOUT IT

Do you live in a part of the United States that once belonged to Mexico? Do you live in an area that once belonged to France or Spain?

Lesson 5: Sharing North America

FIND THE WORD

reservoir

It is important to know about our neighbors. What happens in Canada and Mexico affects the United States in many ways. Neighboring nations also have many things in common.

Canada, the United States, and Mexico share many physical features. For example, all three nations have long coastlines. Look at the map of North America on page 44. Notice that mountains run all the way down the west side of the continent. All three nations have mountains in the east and west and flat land in the middle. Canada and the United States share the Rocky Mountains, the Great Plains, and the Great Lakes. The United States and Mexico share the Rio Grande and the Colorado River. Sharing physical features means that the nations are alike in other ways. For example, nations with coastlines usually have ports. Canada, Mexico, and the

The United States and Canada built the St. Lawrence Seaway.

The United States buys cattle from Mexico.

United States all have port cities. They can send ships loaded with goods to each other.

Neighboring nations can work together to make things better for their peoples. Canada and the United States built the St. Lawrence Seaway together. This seaway opened up the St. Lawrence River to oceangoing ships. Now ships can sail through the seaway. They can carry goods from the Atlantic Ocean to any city on the Great Lakes. They can go to Toronto, Detroit, or Chicago. The two nations also built dams on the Columbia River. These dams produce electric power for both Canada and the United States.

Canada and the United States trade with one another. Canada has resources the United States needs. Some of these resources are petroleum and timber. The United States manufactures many products Canada needs. Of the goods Canada buys from other nations, 71 percent come from the United States. Among these goods are cars, appliances, and other machines. Of the goods Canada sells to other nations, the United States buys about 67 percent.

Neighbors share problems, too. Pollution is one problem Canada and the United States share. Both nations suffer from the pollution of the Great Lakes. Big factories

In Laredo, Texas, people often walk across the border to shop in Mexico.

along the shores dump waste water into the lakes. Lake Erie is so dirty that swimmers cannot go into the water in many places. The Chicago River is badly clogged with wastes. A few years ago, this river actually caught fire!

In 1909, Canada and the United States started the International Joint Commission. It is the commission's job to clean up the lakes. Today, American and Canadian scientists are working on the problem of pollution together.

The southwestern part of the United States is next to the northern part of Mexico. Both of these areas are dry and need water. The Rio Grande flows along the border between them. Together, the United States and Mexico have built dams on the Rio Grande. The dams keep the river from flooding when there are heavy rains. These dams also hold back water in lakes called **reservoirs**

359

(REHZ ur VWAHRZ). This water is used to irrigate farmlands. It is piped into cities and towns as well. Mexico and the United States finished one of these dams in 1969. The reservoir behind this dam stores water for the use of both nations. They named the dam Amistad Dam. *Amistad* means "friendship" in Spanish.

American and Mexican scientists have worked together to save groups of animals that are in danger of being wiped out. They helped save the birds on Raza Island in Baja (BAH hah) California, a part of Mexico. In 1964, Raza Island was set aside for wild animals. Elephant seals, Guadalupe fur seals, and gray whales are also protected by both nations.

Another way Mexico and the United States help one another is in industry. American businesses want workers. Mexicans need jobs. So "twin factories" have been set up in cities along the border between the two nations. Mexicans do the work in their factory. The products are then taken to the American twin factory. There they are packaged and sent away to be sold.

The two nations also trade with one another. The United States buys cattle and other farm products from Mexico. It also buys minerals, such as natural gas and petroleum. Mexico buys machinery from the United States. Mexico also has visitors from the United States. These tourists are important to the Mexican economy.

Canada, Mexico, and the United States work together to protect wild animals. Together they try to solve water problems. They help each other by cleaning polluted air and water. They trade with one another. These are ways in which nations that share a continent can help one another.

REVIEW

CHECK YOUR FACTS

1. Name two land features shared by the United States and Canada.
2. How can ships sail from the Atlantic Ocean to the Great Lakes?
3. What nation is Canada's most important trading partner?
4. What major problem do Canada and the United States share?
5. What important problem do northern Mexico and the southwestern United States share?

THINK ABOUT IT

Do you live closer to Canada or to Mexico? Have you ever visited those nations? Have you met any Canadians or any Mexicans?

WATCH YOUR WORDS

1. ____ includes the ways people send or get messages.
   Transportation   Communication
   Government

2. A Canadian ____ is like an American state.
   province   prime minister   territory

3. Mexico City is located in the ____ .
   congress   state   federal district

4. A lake for holding back water is a ____ .
   dam   reservoir   seaway

5. In Canada, national laws are made by the ____ .
   province   prime minister
   Parliament

CHECK YOUR FACTS

6. Rank the three large nations of North America according to size.

7. Rank the three large nations of North America according to population.

8. How does the United States rank in population among the nations of the world?

9. Name the capitals of the United States, Canada, and Mexico.

10. How does the United States government know how many Americans there are?

11. What are the two main languages of Canada?

12. What group lives in the Arctic region of Canada?

13. Who is the leader of the government of Canada?

14. What are the three main groups of people who live in Mexico?

15. What language do most people in Mexico speak?

USE YOUR MAPS

16. Look at the population-density map of the United States on page 347. What parts of the United States are heavily populated? What parts have few people?

17. Look at the political map of the United States on page 348. Name the states that border Canada.

18. Look at the political map of the United States again. Name the states that border Mexico.

19. Look at the political map of Canada on page 351. What is the smallest Canadian province? What province separates two parts of the United States?

20. Look at the political map of Mexico on page 355. What area of Mexico has many small states.?

THINK ABOUT IT

21. Why are good systems of transportation and communication important in a large nation?

22. What reasons can you think of for taking a census?

23. What problems can arise when two languages are spoken in the same nation?

24. Most Mexicans speak Spanish. What other kinds of languages do you think might be spoken in Mexico?

25. *International* means "between or among nations." Why is pollution of the air and water an international problem?

CHAPTER 2

THE PEOPLE OF THE UNITED STATES

Lesson 1: The United States and Its Culture Groups

> **FIND THE WORDS**
>
> culture   culture group   society
> dominant culture   subculture

People have come to the United States from all parts of the world. They have arrived at different times in our history. Some groups have kept closer to their original ways than other groups have.

Some people in the United States may be different from you in certain ways. They may wear clothing or eat food that differs from yours. They may not speak the same language that you do. They may not believe in some of the things you believe in.

We usually like people who are like us. We understand them. We feel comfortable with them. It is sometimes hard for us to understand people who are different from us. Sometimes, we dislike them because they are different.

The Amish are one of many culture groups in the United States. These Amish children are outside their one-room schoolhouse.

An American Indian mother watches as her daughter learns to weave.

But learning about people who are not like you is important. It is useful to learn about different ways of doing things. You can compare other people's ways with your own ways. When you do that, you learn more about yourself. You also understand other people better. Comparing is an important way of learning.

One way to learn about different groups of people is to study their way of living. A group's way of living is its **culture.** Culture includes the behavior, beliefs, and language that are shared by the members of a group.

People who share the same culture form a **culture group.** There are many culture groups in the United States. These groups live in one nation. They have to follow the same laws. Thus, together they form a larger **society.** In a society, one culture group may be larger or more powerful than the others. The culture of such a group is then the **dominant culture** of the society. The major culture group in the United States is British-American. So the British-American culture is the dominant culture. The minor culture groups in a society are called **subcultures.** The

Many Americans came to the United States on immigrant ships like this one.

United States has many subcultures. There are Italian-American, Afro-American, Mexican-American, and Chinese-American subcultures. Can you name more?

In this book, you have learned about several culture groups in the United States. You have also learned a great deal about yourself and your own culture.

REVIEW

WATCH YOUR WORDS

1. British-American is the ____ culture in the United States.
   dominant   minority   sub

2. Minor culture groups are called ____.
   societies   subcultures   dominants

3. A group's way of living is its ____.
   society   culture   dominance

CHECK YOUR FACTS

4. What does a group's culture include? Name three things.

5. List five culture groups of the United States.

THINK ABOUT IT

6. To what culture group does your family belong?

7. Why is it important to learn about culture groups different from your own? Give two reasons.

Lesson 2: Behavior, Language, and Beliefs in a Culture

FIND THE WORDS

behavior   language   belief
norm   value

People in culture groups do things in ways that are alike, or similar. They fix food in ways that are alike. They furnish homes in similar ways. They raise their children in similar ways. They dress very much alike. They make decisions in ways that are alike. These are all kinds of behavior. **Behavior** is how people act or what they do.

Many United States families still celebrate special occasions from their original countries. Pictured here are a Ukrainian folk dance, a Norwegian parade, and a Chinese New Year celebration.

You share many kinds of behavior with others in your culture group. Suppose you were talking to someone you did not know very well. How close would you stand to that person? You would probably choose a distance that is comfortable for you. Did you know that this distance is influenced by your culture?

In some cultures, people stand very close to persons they do not know very well. Sometimes, they almost touch each other. In other cultures, strangers stand far apart. Each culture shares a different kind of behavior. Now suppose a member of a "closer" culture tried to talk to a member of a "farther" culture. What would happen? Probably, each would feel that the other person had bad manners.

Usually, we do not think about our own ways of doing things. We only notice them when we see someone who behaves in a different way. Suppose you were given a prize in front of your class. What would your classmates do? If they clapped their hands, would you clap your hands with them? Probably, you would not. But in some cultures, it is the right thing to do. Clapping along with your audience shows that you appreciate them, too.

Sharing behavior does not mean that everyone in a group

Members of a culture group share behavior. Each person's skills and circumstances differ. But a disability need not keep a person from taking part.

In some neighborhoods, signs are in English and a second language.

does exactly the same things all the time. Each person does many things in her or his special way.

People in the same culture group also share a language. A **language** includes words and the ways they are used. The language you learn as a child lets you communicate with other members of your group. But language does more than that. It also shows what is important in a culture. It shows how the people of a culture think. One culture, for example, does not know about war. The people do not understand this idea. Their language has no words for *war* or *weapon*.

People in culture groups share many beliefs. A **belief** is something that people think is right or wrong, good or bad, true or false.

People in the same culture group usually agree on what behavior is right or wrong. Such an agreement about behavior is called a norm. A **norm** is a shared belief about how the members of a group should behave.

Most norms are not written down. But everyone in the group knows what the norms are. For example, people believe that telling lies is wrong behavior. Do you know how children learn not to lie to other people? They learn from their parents and teachers. Parents and teachers tell children that lying is wrong. Children also learn by watching what others do. By being around honest and truthful people, children learn to be honest and truthful, too.

People in a culture group often share beliefs about what is important or not important. Beliefs about what is important are called **values.** Suppose you believe that a thing, a person, or an idea is important. That means you value that thing, person, or idea. The choices you make are based on your values.

People use words like *good* and *bad* when they talk about their values. They choose the things they think are good or best. For example, suppose someone finds a wallet full of money. The finder believes being honest is important. She has an idea of herself as being an honest person. She values her honesty more than the money in the wallet. Keeping the wallet would be bad. It would hurt the person who lost it. Returning it would be good. So the finder chooses what she values more—her honesty. She gives up what she values less—the money. She returns the wallet.

Different cultures sometimes have different values. Some groups value people who spend large amounts of money. Other groups value people who save money or do not waste anything. Some groups value winning and trying to be best. Other groups value working together and sharing.

FUN FACTS

Salt is a common sight on many dinner tables. You probably put salt on a lot of the foods you eat. But have you ever spilled salt at the table?

Long ago, many people in different cultures believed that spilling salt would bring them bad luck. To avoid bad luck, a person would throw a few grains of salt over the left shoulder. People who did this believed that evil spirits, with lots of nasty little plans, stood behind their left shoulder. They believed that good spirits stood behind their right shoulder. They thought that throwing salt in the evil spirits' eyes would distract the spirits. Then the evil plan might be forgotten.

The next time you spill salt at the table and decide to avoid some bad luck, however, be careful where you throw those grains. They may not land in your evil spirits' eyes at all, but on one of your friends. If that happens, you will have sprinkled your friend with some grains of bad luck. Or so many people believed.

Freedom of religion is an important value in the United States.
At left, a family celebrates the Jewish harvest festival of
Sukkoth. At right, Episcopalian monks worship together.

REVIEW

WATCH YOUR WORDS

1. Beliefs about what is important are
   ___ .
   behaviors   cultures   values
2. A ___ is something people think is
   right or wrong.
   belief   language   culture
3. A ___ is a shared belief about how
   people should behave.
   good   norm   behavior

CHECK YOUR FACTS

4. Define *behavior*.

5. What are some kinds of behavior
   that people in a culture share?

THINK ABOUT IT

6. Think of some things that people in
   different cultures do differently.
   List as many examples as you can.
7. How could learning another language help you understand another
   culture better?
8. List some words you use to show
   respect for other people.

Lesson 3: How People Are Alike and Different in the United States

FIND THE WORDS

cultural pluralism   democracy
majority rule   election   voting
minority

When a country has many different culture groups, we say that it has **cultural pluralism.** This means that different kinds of behavior, different languages, and different beliefs are found within the same country.

The United States has many different culture groups. But the people of the United States are alike in many ways, too. Some important beliefs are shared by most Americans.

Among the most important beliefs that most Americans share are certain ideas about government. Most Americans believe in democracy. **Democracy** is government by the people. In practice, there is **majority rule.** This means

People in the United States share a national government. It is symbolized here by the White House, the President's home.

British-Americans, Chinese-Americans, and Mexican-Americans share many beliefs about what is important.

that the majority—the largest group—decides who will run the government. The majority also decides which laws will be approved. The majority expresses its will through elections. In an **election,** the people choose between candidates who want to be government leaders. Sometimes, the people also approve or reject laws. Choosing leaders and approving or rejecting laws is called **voting.**

Most Americans believe in rule by the majority. But they do not believe that the majority should have complete power. They believe that all citizens have rights. Rights are privileges and protections that people have just because they are citizens. Rights

371

Americans value the right of each person to get a good education. The women at the left have learned to communicate in sign language.

protect the people from the power of the government. They protect **minorities,** the smaller groups, from the power of the majority.

Along with rights, Americans have responsibilities. They have the responsibility to protect and defend their rights and freedoms. They have the duty to be good citizens of the United States.

REVIEW

WATCH YOUR WORDS

1. Smaller groups are called ___.
   majorities   minorities   cultures

2. ___ means that the people should run the government.
   Democracy   Voting   Free speech

3. Under ___ , the largest group makes the decisions.
   elections   majority rule
   cultural pluralism

4. Citizens choose leaders in ___ .
   elections   majority rule
   free speech

5. What citizens do in elections is called ___ .
   cultural pluralism   rights   voting

CHECK YOUR FACTS

6. What does *cultural pluralism* mean?

7. Under majority rule, who chooses the leaders who will run the government?

8. What happens when an election is held?

9. What are rights? Why are they so important?

THINK ABOUT IT

10. Many people who have the right to vote do not vote. Do they share in majority rule?

11. What are some beliefs that most Americans share? List as many as you can.

CHAPTER REVIEW

WATCH YOUR WORDS

1. People who share the same culture form a ___ .
   language   norm   culture group

2. The culture groups within one nation form a ___ .
   subculture   society   government

3. ___ is how people act or what they do.
   Behavior   Society   Culture

4. ___ includes words and how they are used.
   Society   Language   Culture

5. A nation that has many different culture groups has ___ .
   elections   cultural pluralism
   society

6. The behavior, beliefs, and language of a group make up its ___ .
   society   values   culture

7. The largest culture group in a society is the ___ culture.
   dominant   sub   minority

8. A society in which the people govern themselves has ___ .
   pluralism   democracy   minorities

9. In ___ rule, the largest group decides who will run the government.
   minority   cultural   majority

10. The people choose leaders and sometimes approve laws in ___ .
    society   communication   elections

CHECK YOUR FACTS

11. What do people in a culture share?

12. What is the dominant culture in the United States?

13. What are the smaller culture groups in a society called?

14. What is a norm? Are norms usually written down?

15. In what two important ways do children learn norms?

16. What are values?

17. When there is cultural pluralism in a nation, what kinds of things differ?

18. Do different culture groups ever share some of the same beliefs?

19. What do people do when they vote?

20. What protects minorities from the power of the majority?

THINK ABOUT IT

21. Why does the United States have different culture groups?

22. How can language show what is important in a culture? Give two examples of your own.

23. Suppose you wanted to teach a norm to a younger brother or sister. What would you do?

24. Suppose a salesclerk gave a customer too much change. What should the customer do? How does this show the customer's values?

25. Do the majority of voters always express the will of the majority of Americans? Why, or why not?

TRY SOMETHING NEW

26. Make a chart labeled "United States Citizenship." At the top, make two columns headed "Rights" and "Responsibilities." Then list your rights and duties as an American citizen.

WATCH YOUR WORDS

Use the words below to fill in the blanks. Use each term only once.

behavior	democracy	Parliament
beliefs	dominant culture	prime minister
census	elections	provinces
communication	federal district	reservoirs
counties	language	rural areas
cultural pluralism	majority rule	society
culture	minorities	urban areas
culture groups	norms	values

The United States is a large nation. It has a good system of ____ that helps people keep in touch. The United States is divided into 50 states. The states are divided into ____. Most Americans live in the cities or suburbs in ____. Only about one-fourth live in the towns, villages, and farms in ____. Every 10 years, the government takes a ____ of the people.

Canada is divided into 10 ____ and 2 territories. In Canada, laws are made for the nation by the ____. The ____ is the leader of the government. Mexico has a ____, which is like the District of Columbia. Together, Mexico and the United States have built dams to hold back scarce water in ____.

A group's way of living is its ____. It includes the group's behavior, beliefs, and language. In the United States, there are many ____ with different ways of living. Together, these groups form a larger ____. The ____ in the United States is British-American.

Members of culture groups share many kinds of ____, or ways of acting. They speak the same ____. They have the same ____ about what is right or wrong. They agree on ____, which are unwritten rules about how people should behave. They share the same ____, or beliefs about what is important.

Having many culture groups, the United States has ____. Yet most Americans share a belief in ____ as the best form of government. In practice, there is ____ in the government of the United States. The people express their will by voting in ____. Nonetheless, the rights of ____ are protected from the majority in the United States.

CHECK YOUR FACTS

1. What three nations have more people than the United States?

2. The center of population in the United States has been moving (east/west).

3. Which nation has more land, the United States or Canada?

4. Why do few people live in northern Canada?

5. Most Mexicans are (Spanish/mestizos).

6. What mountains, plains, and lakes do the United States and Canada share?

7. What two rivers do the United States and Mexico share?

8. What waterway did the United States and Canada build to improve shipping?

9. What have the United States and Mexico built to help save water to be used for irrigation?

10. What does the United States buy from Canada? From Mexico?

USE YOUR MAPS AND GRAPH

For questions 11 through 22, use the map of the United States on page 348. Match the postal abbreviations with the states that the abbreviations stand for.

11. CA	**A.** Nebraska
12. IA	**B.** Minnesota
13. MS	**C.** Mississippi
14. AK	**D.** Iowa
15. MI	**E.** California
16. CO	**F.** Alaska
17. MN	**G.** Colorado
18. MA	**H.** Idaho
19. AL	**I.** Michigan
20. NE	**J.** Alabama
21. NV	**K.** Massachusetts
22. ID	**L.** Nevada

23. Look at the political map of Canada on page 351. What is the capital of Canada? What are the capitals of Ontario and Manitoba?

24. Look at the pie graph on page 352. What language do the greatest number of Canadians speak?

25. Look at the political map of Mexico on page 355. What nation borders southeastern Mexico?

26. Look at the population-density map of the United States on page 347. Find New York City, Chicago, Los Angeles, and Philadelphia. They are the nation's largest cities. Are these cities surrounded by areas of high population density?

27. Find three other areas of high population density in the United States. Name the city that is the center of each of these areas.

THINK ABOUT IT

28. The center of population for the United States has been moving westward since 1790. What do you think are the reasons for this?

PUT IT ALL TOGETHER

29. Draw or trace an outline map of North America. Put these places on the map and label them. Include a map key.

   a. The United States, Canada, and Mexico
   b. The Great Lakes and the Rio Grande
   c. Your state, with its name and borders
   d. The capital of your state
   e. The states that border your state
   f. Washington, DC, Ottawa, and Mexico City

GLOSSARY

abolitionist (AB uh LISH un ist) a person who wanted to end slavery (205)

alien (AY lee un) a foreigner (260)

alliance (uh LY uns) an agreement between nations to work together and support each other (295)

Allied Powers in World War I, Russia, France, Britain, Italy, Japan, and the United States (295)

Allies (AL EYEZ) in World War II, the United States, Britain, France, and the Soviet Union (311)

amendment a change in the Constitution (163)

arid dry: said of land or climate (53)

armistice (AHR muh stis) an agreement to end a war (296)

Articles of Confederation (kun FED uh RAY shun) the 1781 agreement that set up the first government of the United States (154)

assembly (uh SEM blee) **1** a meeting **2** a group of representatives who meet to make laws (116)

assembly line a line of workers and machines in a factory, each doing a different thing to the product (230)

Axis (AK sis) in World War II, Germany, Italy, and Japan (310)

bicentennial (BY sen TEN ee ul) the 200th birthday of the United States (333)

bill a written plan for a new law (160)

Bill of Rights the first 10 amendments to the U.S. Constitution (163)

blockade keeping a port or city blocked so supplies cannot get in or out (216)

border a line that divides two nations or parts of nations (37)

boycott to stop buying or using certain goods or services, as a form of protest (134)

burgess (BUR jis) an elected representative in the colony of Virginia (97)

Cabinet the group of advisers who head departments and help the President make decisions (166)

capital a city where the government of a state or nation meets (45)

capitalism (KAP uh tuh LIZ um) an economy in which private individuals own property and run businesses (319)

cardinal directions north, south, east, and west (34)

cartographer (kahr TOG ruh fer) a mapmaker (32)

cash crop a crop grown to be sold (99)

census a count of the population (349)

Central Powers in World War I, Germany, Austria-Hungary, the Ottoman Empire, and Bulgaria (295)

charter a government paper that grants a person or group special rights (105)

climate the average weather a place has over a long period of time (23)

coal a black, rocklike mineral found in the ground, used as a fuel (49)

cold war a tense condition in which nations are enemies but are not actually at war (317)

colony **1** an area of land ruled by a foreign or "parent" country **2** a group of people who settle in such a place (88)

communication (kuh MYOO nuh KAY shun) all the ways people send or get messages (345)

communism (KOM yuh NIZ um) an economy in which the government owns and runs all businesses and there is no private property (195)

compass a map drawing of arrows that point north, south, east, and west (34)

compromise (KOM pruh MYZ) an agreement in which each side gives something up (157)

confederacy (kun FED ur uh see) a group of states or tribes that join together (77)

Confederacy the Southern states that fought against the Union in the Civil War (213)

Congress the legislative branch of government in the United States (160)

Constitution the written plan of government and basic law of the United States (157)

continent one of the seven large masses of land on Earth (43)

culture a group's way of living, including behavior, beliefs, and language (363)

currency the money issued by a government (167)

declaration (DEK luh RAY shun) a formal statement or announcement (138)

delta an area of rich soil dropped by a river before it flows into the ocean (22)

democracy (di MOK ruh see) government by the people (370)

dictator (DIK TAY tur) a ruler who has complete power over a government (310)

discrimination (dis KRIM uh NAY shun) treatment that is unequal or unfair (260)

distribution (DIS truh BYOO shun) the way things are spread or scattered over an area (39)

division of labor the dividing up of work so that different workers do different jobs (228)

draft a law that requires people to join the armed forces (217)

drainage basin the land area drained by a group of rivers (59)

economy (i KON uh mee) the way in which people produce and distribute goods and services (317)

elevation the height of land above sea level (33)

embargo a ban on foreign trade in a particular product, such as oil (325)

enterprise new ideas and extra effort used to reach a goal (251)

entrepreneur (AHN truh pruh NUR) someone who sees an opportunity and sets up a new business (236)

equal-area projection a map that keeps land areas the right size (29)

equator (i KWAY tur) an imaginery line around the middle of Earth (26)

executive (eg ZEK yuh tiv) **branch** the branch of government that carries out the laws (160)

export v. (ek SPORT) to sell (a product) to another country n. (EKS port) a product sold by one country to another (119)

federal of a nation made up of states (157)

federal district a special area where the capital of a nation is located (355)

forty-niner someone who came to California in 1849 to look for gold (190)

free enterprise an economy run by private individuals and businesses (319)

frontier (frun TIR) an unsettled area just beyond a settled region (173)

geographer (jee OG ruh fur) an expert who studies physical facts about places on Earth (17)

globe a round model of Earth (26)

grid system a pattern of squares on a map (26)

hemisphere (HEM uh SFIR) one of the four half circles that Earth can be divided into: the Northern, Southern, Eastern, or Western Hemisphere (26)

historian (hi STOR ee un) a person who writes or studies records of the past (16)

House of Representatives one of two parts of Congress (160)

immigrant (IM i grunt) a person who comes to settle in a new country (241)

import v. (im PORT) to buy (a product) from another country n. (IM port) a product bought by one country from another (120)

indentured (in DEN chured) **servant** a person whose way was paid to the colonies in return for work without pay for a set period (92)

industry (IN duh stree) **1** the manufacturing and sale of goods and services **2** all the businesses that supply a certain product or service **3** steady effort to get work done (234)

inflation a rise in the cost of goods and services, making money worth less (336)

intermediate directions northeast, northwest, southeast, and southwest (34)

interrupted projection a map with gaps in the ocean areas (31)

irrigation supplying land with water that comes from somewhere else (54)

isolationism (EYE suh LAY shuh NIZ um) a national policy of not getting involved with other nations (311)

judicial (joo DISH ul) **branch** the branch of government that decides whether laws have been obeyed or broken (160)

key a list explaining the symbols and colors used on a map (32)

landforms the shapes of land on Earth. Mountains, hills, plains, and plateaus are landforms. (18)

legislative (LEJ is LAY tiv) **branch** the branch of government that makes the laws (160)

lines of latitude (LAT uh TOOD) the lines on a map or globe that run east and west. They measure distance north and south of the equator. (26)

lines of longitude (LON juh TOOD) the lines on a map or globe that run north and south. They measure distance east and west of the prime meridian. (26)

majority rule decision-making by the largest group of voters (370)

map a flat drawing of Earth or a part of Earth (29)

mass production making a great many goods by using machines (228)

melting pot a place where peoples from many different cultures come together to live (262)

Mercator (mur KAY tur) **projection** a map on which the lines of latitude and longitude are both parallel. This makes land areas distorted near the poles. (29)

merchant a person who buys goods in order to sell them for a profit (113)

meridian (muh RID ee un) a line of longitude (26)

mesa (MAY suh) a hill with steep sides and a flat top (20)

migration (my GRAY shun) movement from one place to another (288)

minority (my NOR uh tee) a group making up less than half of the whole (372)

mouth the place where a river flows into the ocean (22)

neutrality (noo TRAL uh tee) not taking sides or taking part in a war (168)

ocean one of the four very large bodies of salt water on Earth (21)

parallel (PAR uh LEL) a line of latitude (26)

Parliament (PAHR luh munt) the lawmaking group, or legislature, in some nations, such as Great Britain and Canada (129, 352)

peninsula (puh NIN suh luh) a piece of land almost surrounded by water (21)

petroleum (puh TROH lee um) a thick, dark liquid found in the ground, used as a fuel; oil (50)

Pilgrims a group of English Protestants who believed that religious worship should be plain, simple, and strict (104)

pioneer (PY uh NIR) one of the first to explore or settle in a new area (176)

plantation (plan TAY shun) a large farm where crops are raised (100)

planter a person who owns a farm on which cash crops are raised (100)

plateau (pla TOH) an area of high, flat land (20)

political map a map that shows the borders of cities, states, or nations (33)

political party a group of people with similar ideas about how to run a government (169)

population-density map a map that shows how many people live in different parts of a country or continent (349)

port a town on the water where ships can load and unload people and goods (115)

prairie a large area of flat or rolling grassland with few trees (50)

precipitation (pri SIP uh TAY shun) the amount of water that falls from the air as rain, mist, snow, sleet, or hail (57)

President the leader of the United States (160)

prime meridian (muh RID ee un) the imaginary line at which longitude starts. It passes through Greenwich, England. (36)

prime minister the head of the government in many nations (352)

productivity (PROH duk TIV uh tee) the number of goods or services a worker can produce (337)

projection (pruh JEK shun) the way sizes and shapes of places on Earth are changed on a map (29)

province a part of Canada that is like a state in the United States (352)

Puritans (PYOOR uh tunz) a religious group that wanted to make the Church of England plain and simple (92)

Quakers the Society of Friends, a group of Protestants who live simply and believe that war is wrong (117)

ration (RASH un) to limit the amount of (goods) a person is allowed to buy (315)

reaper a machine that cuts down a crop and drops it in piles (227)

refugees (REF yoo JEEZ) people who leave their country to escape danger or death (327)

region (REE jun) a large area with the same kind of landforms or climate (43)

representative (REP ri ZEN tuh tiv) **1** a person chosen to speak or act for a group **2** a member of the House of Representatives (97)

reservation (REZ ur VAY shun) an area of land set aside for a group of American Indians (276)

revolution (REV uh LOO shun) **1** a war which the people of a country fight to change the government (129) **2** any great change in the way people think, work, or live (226)

rural area a country town, village, or farming region with fewer than 2500 people (347)

scale a diagram that shows what a map distance equals in real distance (32)

sea level the surface of the ocean (33)

secession (si SESH un) the withdrawing of the Southern states from the Union before the Civil War (213)

secretary the head of any of the departments in the President's Cabinet (166)

Senate one of two parts of Congress (160)

session a meeting or series of meetings of a legislature, such as Congress (308)

socialism an economy in which the government owns and runs the businesses but people keep some private property (317)

source the place where a river starts (22)

stereotype (STEH ree oh TYP) the false idea that everyone in a group is much the same (255)

stock shares owned in a company (306)

suffrage the right to vote (299)

suffragist (SUF ruh jist) someone who fights for the right to vote (299)

Supreme Court the most powerful court in the United States (161)

tariff (TAIR if) a tax on imports (209)

taxes money that people pay to support their government (129)

temperature the amount of heat that is in the air (57)

territory an area with less power and independence than a state (176)

thresher a machine that separates the grains of wheat from the rest of the plant (227)

time line a chart that shows the dates of important events in order (67)

trade **1** a way of making a living by doing skilled work with the hands **2** the business of buying and selling goods (113)

transportation the movement of people or goods (50)

treaty an agreement between nations (143)

unconstitutional (UN kon stuh TOO shun ul) not agreeing with the United States Constitution (162)

Union the Northern states that fought against the Confederacy in the Civil War (215)

urban area a town or city with more than 2500 people (347)

veto (VEE toh) to stop (a bill) from becoming law: said of the President or a governor (161)

volunteer (VOL un TIR) **1** someone who offers to work without pay (122) **2** someone who freely chooses to join the armed forces (217)

weather the condition of the air (23)

INDEX

King, Dr. Martin Luther, Jr.,
    322, 334
Kiowas, 268
Korean War, 320
Kosciusko, Thaddeus, 150

Laos, 324, 325
latitude, 26
laws, 161, 162
Lazarus, Emma, 249
League of Nations, 297
Lee, General Robert E., 217,
    218, 219
legislative branch of
    government, 160, 161
Lewis and Clark, 180
Lewis, Meriwether, 180
Lincoln, President Abraham,
    213–214, 216–219, 221
Lindbergh, Charles A., 305
longitude, 26
"Lost Colony," 89, 91
Louisiana Purchase, 180
Loyalists, 149
Luey Gim Gong, 254
Lusitania, 296

Madison, President James,
    157, 170
Magellan, Ferdinand, 83
majority rule, 370–371
manufacture, 130, 234, 236
Mao Tse-tung, 317
maps, 32–34
  list of, 4
Marshall, James, 189–191
Maya, 70–72
Mayflower, 104
McClellan, George, 216
McCormick, Cyrus, 227
Meade, General, 218
Meat Inspection Act, 292
melting pot, 262
mercator projection, 29, 30
merchants, 113–114
mesa, 20
mestizos, 192, 354
Mexican-Americans, 192–193
Mexico, 354–360
  government of, 355–356
  map of, 355
  people of, 354
  and United States, 356,
    357–360
  war with, 187–188
Middle East conflict, 325–326
migration, 288
minorities, 372
Mississippi River, 58, 59

Missouri River, 58, 59
Mitchell, Maria, 299
Monroe, President James, 170
Montezuma II, 84–85
Morgan, J.P., 237
Morse, Samuel, 231
Mott, Lucretia, 299
muckrakers, 290–291
Mussolini, Benito, 310

Napoleon, 180
Natchez culture, 76–77
national-origins system, 327
natural resources, 335–336
Nazi Party, 310
New Amsterdam, 115
New Deal, 307–308
New Netherland, 115–116
Nez Percé, 274
Nisei, 316
Nixon, President Richard M.,
    324–325, 333–334
North America, maps of
  climate, 25, 56
  physical, 44
  resources, 47–48
  settlements in 1630, 89
nuclear weapons
  atomic bomb, 312–313, 316,
    317
  banning of, 320, 325

Oregon, 185, 186
Otis, Elisha G., 238
Paine, Thomas, 145–146, 151
Parks, Rosa, 321
Paul, Alice, 301
Pawnee, 268
Pearl Harbor, 311
Penn, William, 116–118
petroleum, 236, 335, 358
Philadelphia, 119–122
Philippine Islands, 258, 261,
    262
physical maps, 10–11, 44
Pilgrims, 104–105
plantations, 101, 102–103
Plymouth, 104
Pocahontas, 96, 97
political maps, 8–9, 12–13, 33,
    294, 309, 318, 348, 351,
    355
political parties, 169–170
Polk, President James K., 188
Poor, Salem, 137
population of United States,
    344
  map of 347
Postmaster General 166, 167

Powhatan, 96
President, 160, 165–166, 188
printing press, 232
Progressives, 292–293
Prohibition, 304
pueblos, 75
Puerto-Rican Americans, 194
Pure Food and Drug Act, 292
Puritans, 92, 105–106, 111–112

Quakers, 117–118
Quetzalcoatl, 84

railroads, 230, 231, 236, 240,
    253–254
Raleigh, Sir Walter, 89, 91,
    241
Reagan, President Ronald,
    326, 334, 337–338
Reconstruction, of the South,
    221–224
reformers, 289, 290–293
refugees, 327–329
relocation camps, 316
Republican Party, 170
resources, 335–336
  maps, 40, 47–48, 102
Revere, Paul, 134
rights, 159, 321–323, 371–372
Rillieux, Norbert, 206
rivers, 22, 58, 59–60
Roaring Twenties, 304
Rockefeller, John D., 236–237,
    290
Rolfe, John, 97
Roosevelt, President Franklin
    D., 307–308, 313
Roosevelt, President
    Theodore, 259, 292
rural areas, 347, 349
Russia, 294–296; see also
    Soviet Union
Ruth, Babe, 305

Sacajawea, 180
Samoset, 105
Sampson, Deborah, 137
scalawags, 222
segregation, 222, 224, 315,
    321–322
Senate, 160
separatists, 104
Shays, Daniel, 156
Shepard, Alan, 330
Shoong, Joe, 257
Shoshone, 180
Sioux, 268, 272
slavery, 100–103, 202–214,
    217–218

CREDITS

Maps by Continental Cartography (except 33, 35, 37, 40, 68, 81, 85, 89, 140, 175, 211, 278, 355). 24, 67, 84, 98, 101, 129, 175, 180, 195, 213, 241, 247, 318, 351: Charts and Time Lines by Function Thru Form Inc. **14:** NYPL Picture Collection. **15:** (BL) Hugh Rogers/Monkmeyer; (BR) L. L. T. Rhodes/Taurus. **16:** Mel Horst. **18:** Russ Kinne/Photo Researchers. **20:** Sylvia Johnson/Woodfin Camp. **21:** Manuel Rodriguez. **26:** Michal Heron/Monkmeyer. **32:** Elihu Blotnik/Woodfin Camp. **42:** Dan Budnik/Woodfin Camp. **43:** George Hall/Woodfin Camp. **46:** Erich Hartmann/Magnum. **49:** Ken Foster/Photo Researchers. **50:** Information Canada Phototeque. **52:** John Running/Stock, Boston. **53:** (L) Van Bucher/Photo Researchers; (R) Georg Gerster/Photo Researchers. **54:** Craig Aurness/Woodfin Camp. **55:** Al Satterwhite/Image Bank. **58:** Georg Gerster/Photo Researchers. **60:** Robert Philips/Image Bank. **64–65:** Hope of Jamestown, John Gadsby Chapman, Collection of Mr. and Mrs. P. Mellon. **66:** NYPL Picture Collection. **69:** L. L. T. Rhodes/Taurus. **70:** Dick Hufnagle/Monkmeyer. **71:** Monkmeyer Press Photo. **72:** American Museum of Natural History. **73:** NYPL Picture Collection. **74:** NYPL Picture Collection. **76:** Martin J. Dain/Magnum. **77:** American Museum of Natural History. **78:** Library of Congress. **79:** Library of Congress. **80:** Courtesy, The Mariner's Museum, Newport News, Va. **82:** Library of Congress. **86:** Culver Pictures. **87:** NYPL Picture Collection. **90:** La Salle's Expedition, George Catlin, National Gallery of Art. **91:** NYPL Picture Collection. **94:** NYPL Picture Collection. **95:** A. H. Robbins Co. **96:** Courtesy of American Heritage.

100: *The Plantation*, Metropolitan Museum of Art, Garbisch Collection. **101:** Bettmann Archive. **105:** Bettmann Archive. **106:** New York Historical Society. **108:** NYPL Picture Collection. **109:** Pilgrim Society. **110:** NYPL Picture Collection. **112:** (T) Bettmann Archive; (B) Boston Society. **113:** Bettmann Archive. **116:** Museum of the City of New York, Davies Collection **117:** The Historical Society of Pennsylvania, Abby A. Rockefeller Collection. **119:** Historical Society of Pennsylvania. **120:** Bettmann Archive. **121:** Bettmann Archive. **126–127:** NYPL Picture Collection. **128:** NYPL Picture Collection. **130:** (L) Massachusetts Historical Society; (R) The John Carter Brown Library, Brown University. **131:** Metropolitan Museum of Art. **132:** Shelburne Museum. **133:** NYPL Picture Collection. **134:** Connecticut Historical Society. **135:** Delaware Art Museum. **136:** Delaware Art Museum. **137:** Bettmann Archive. **139:** U.S. Naval Academy Museum. **141:** Valley Forge Historical Society. **142:** Indiana Historical Bureau. **143:** Bettmann Archive. **144:** NYPL Picture Collection. **145:** (T) Kennedy Galleries; (BL) NYPL Picture Collection; (BR) NYPL Picture Collection. **146:** (T) NYPL Picture Collection; (B) Culver Pictures. **147:** NYPL Picture Collection. **148:** Metropolitan Museum of Art. **150:** *George Washington, Lafayette and Tench Tilghman at Yorktown*, Charles Willson Peale, Maryland Commission of Artistic Property. **151:** Bettmann Archive. **153:** NYPL Picture Collection. **154:** Bettmann Archive. **155:** Bettmann Archive. **158:** Virginia Museum, Garbisch Collection. **159:** NYPL Picture Collection. **162:** William S. Weems/Woodfin Camp. **164:** Bettmann Archive. **165:** Library of Congress. **168:** (L) NYPL Picture Collection; (R) Yale Art Gallery. **169:** Archive of Bay Village/Smithsonian Institute. **171:** Scala/EPA, Inc. **173:** NYPL Picture Collection. **174:** NYPL Picture Collection. **177:** State Historical Society of Missouri. **178:** Bettmann Archive. **179:** Bettmann Archive. **181:** (T) Montana Historical Society; (B) Museum of the American Indian. **182:** Museum of the American Indian. **183:** Woolaroc Museum, Oklahoma. **184:** NYPL Picture Collection. **185:** Bettmann Archive. **186:** The Butler Institute, Cincinnati. **187:** Bettmann Archive. **189:** Southwest Museum, Los Angeles. **190:** Bettmann Archive. **192:** Witte Museum. **196:** Michal Heron/McGraw-Hill. **200–201:** Metropolitan Museum of Art. **203:** (T) Culver Pictures; (B) Bettmann Archive. **204:** Granger Collection. **207:** (TL) Bettmann Archive; (TR) Library of Congress; (B) Bettmann Archive. **208:** Granger Collection. **212:** (T) Bettmann Archive; (B) Culver Pictures. **213:** Library of Congress. **214:** (L) Bettmann Archive; (R) Museum of the Confederacy. **215:** Henry Steele Commager, Houghton Mifflin, 1951. **216:** Library of Congress. **217:** Library of Congress. **218:** Seventh Regiment, N.Y. **219:** Culver Pictures. **220:** Library of Congress. **221:** Bettmann Archive. **223:** (T) Library of Congress; (B) Culver Pictures. **224:** Bettmann Archive. **226:** NYPL Picture Collection. **227:** National Canning Association. **228:** Yale University Art Gallery, Garvan Collection. **229:** (T) Culver Pictures; (B) NYPL Picture Collection. **231:** (T) NYPL Picture Collection; (B) Culver Pictures. **232:** Culver Pictures. **234:** Culver Pictures. **235:** Culver Pictures. **237:** Culver Pictures. **238:** Library of Congress. **239:** AT&T. **242:** NYPL Picture Collection. **243:** Bettmann Archive. **244:** Culver Pictures. **245:** (T) Collection of San Antonio Museum, San Antonio; (B) Nebraska State Historical Society. **248:** (L) Library of Congress; (R) George Eastman House Collection. **250:** Museum of American China Trade; Milton, Mass. **252:** Bettmann Archive. **253:** Southern Pacific Lines. **254:** NYPL Picture Collection. **255:** NYPL Picture Collection. **256:** Olivier Rebbot/Stock, Boston. **259:** (T) Peabody Museum, Salem, Mass.; (B) NYPL Picture Collection. **260:** NYPL Picture Collection. **261:** NYPL Picture Collection. **265:** Nebraska Historical Society, Butcher Collection. **266:** (L) Courtesy of William L. Katz, Union Pacific Railroad Museum; (R) NYPL Picture Collection. **269:** *Buffalo Hunter under Wolf Skin*, George A. Catlin, American Museum of Natural History. **271:** Bettmann Archive. **272:** *When Sioux and Blackfeet Meet*, Charles M. Russell, Gilcrease Museum. **273:** Granger Collection. **274:** Bettmann Archive. **275:** Adam Wolfit/Woodfin Camp. **276:** Michal Heron/McGraw-Hill. **277:** (T) Dennis Stock, Magnum; (B) Peter Dublin. **280:** USDA. **281:** USDA. **286–287:** Fred Ward/Black Star. **288:** Bettmann Archive. **290:** Bettmann Archive. **291:** Bettmann Archive. **292:** Bettmann Archive. **295:** New York Historical Society. **297:** University of California, Berkley. **298:** Bettmann Archive. **300:** UPI. **301:** (BL) NYPL; (BM) Bettmann Archive; (BR) Daniel Kramer. **303:** E. Thelma Flink/Photo Researchers. **304:** UPI. **306:** Brown Brothers. **307:** FDR Library. **310:** Bettmann Archive. **311:** U.S. Army. **312:** (TL) Bettmann Archive; (TR) UPI. **314:** Bettmann Archive. **315:** (BL) UPI; (BR) Culver Pictures. **316:** Bettmann Archive. **319:** George Silk/Time, Life Inc. **320:** Wide World. **321:** UPI. **322:** (TL) UPI; (TR) Wide World. **323:** (TL) Wide World; (TR) UPI. **325:** Henri Bureau/Sygma. **326:** UPI. **328:** UPI. **330:** NASA. **331:** Spinelli/Woodfin Camp. **333:** Jan Lukas/EPA. **335:** Brookhaven National Laboratory. **336:** National Park Service. **337:** Bettmann Archive. **338:** Erich Hartmann/Magnum. **342–343:** Dan McCoy/Rainbow. **344:** Clyde Smith/Peter Arnold, Inc. **345:** (L) Leonard Nadel/McGraw-Hill; (R) Owen Franken/Stock, Boston. **350:** National Film Board of Canada. **352:** George Hall/Woodfin Camp. **353:** Burt Glinn/Magnum. **354:** Albert Moldvay/Woodfin Camp. **356:** (L) Cary Wolinski/Stock, Boston; (R) Rene Burri/Magnum. **357:** Milton J. Heiberg/Photo Researchers. **358:** Michal Heron/McGraw-Hill. **359:** Michal Heron/McGraw-Hill. **362:** Wally McNamee/Woodfin Camp. **363:** (L) Michal Heron/McGraw-Hill; (R) John Launios/Black Star. **364:** Culver Pictures. **365:** (T) Peter Arnold; (BL) Daniel Brody/Stock, Boston; (BR) Olivier Rebbot/Stock, Boston. **366:** Ian Berry/Magnum. **367:** (T) Bjorn Bolstad/Peter Arnold, Inc.; (BL) Peter Arnold; (BR) Richard Avery/Stock, Boston. **369:** (L) Katrina Thomas/Photo Researchers; (R) James H. Karales/Peter Arnold, Inc. **370:** UPI. **371:** (TL) Nathan Benn/Woodfin Camp; (TR) John Lei/Stock, Boston; (B) Bill Anderson/Monkmeyer. **372:** (L) L. L. T. Rhodes/Taurus; (R) Christa Armstrong/Photo Researchers.